Families of Faith

AN INTRODUCTION
TO WORLD RELIGIONS
FOR CHRISTIANS

Paul Varo Martinson

Fortress Press

Minneapolis

To my mother, who would have much liked to have read this,
and to my wife, who constantly urged me to write
something people could understand

FAMILIES OF FAITH
An Introduction to World Religions for Christians

Cover photography © 1999 PhotoDisc, Inc. Used by permission.
Cover design by Marti Naughton
Book design by Beth Wright and Timothy W. Larson

Library of Congress Cataloging-in-Publication Data
Martinson, Paul Varo, 1934–
    Families of faith: an introduction to world religions for Christians / Paul Varo Martinson.
    p. cm.
Includes bibliographical references.
ISBN 0-8006-3222-2 (alk. paper)
1. Christianity and other religions. I. Title
BR127.M34 1999
291–dc21
                             99-2593
                             CIP

The paper used in this publication meets the minimum requirements of American National Standard for Information Sciences—Permanence of Paper for Printed Library Materials, ANSI Z329.48-1984.

Manufactured in the U.S.A.   AF 1-3222
03   02   01   00   2   3   4   5   6   7   8   9   10

Contents

PREFACE

⸺

This text has arisen from a variety of contexts. Some of it began to take shape in congregational presentations and lay classes, some of it in seminary classes, and some of it in my study and travels. It first became a serious project when Alice Peppler, attending a lay class, suggested that I develop my presentations into a manuscript. It has dithered along the way since then—until now.

My goal was to present information that would be useful in congregational contexts while embedding many theological implications within the text without the use of technical language or methodological sophistication. But, nonetheless, I hoped to make the material interesting for academic settings as well. Readers will have to decide if I have been successful.

Many persons are to be thanked. First of all, those who endured some of this in presentations are to be thanked for not objecting more loudly. A student or two has been referred to in the text, but since I have not received specific permission to use names, I leave such unnamed. A number of colleagues were helpful along the way: Duane Olson, with whom I taught several classes in tandem, patiently listened to parts of this. Some of his influences are present in the text. I also gained much from exchanges with Paul Sponheim. He looked at a major part of this manuscript early on and raised a number of important points. I have responded to a number of these; although, I am not sure I have done so adequately. Lois Malcolm graciously read a good portion of the manuscript amidst her own busy schedule. Her counsel is valued. Craig Moran also gave good counsel. He has had to endure this text more patiently than others since we have used it in various stages in our teaching together. Mary Knutson made some use of essay material I had written in one or another of her classes, and her appreciation of it encouraged me to use some of the material in this text. Many other colleagues have greatly influenced my thinking over the years. I express my gratitude to all of them. Also to be thanked are Ron Klug for suggesting the inclusion of the material on Judaism, and Timothy Larson for his careful editorial work.

I trust that this book will be helpful for Christian people who wish to think intelligently about their faith as it relates to that of others. I also hope that I have been honest and fair in the presentation of the various faiths. I have learned much from my study of them and through meetings and discussions with committed adherents of them.

PART I
THOSE OTHER RELIGIONS

✳ ✳ ✳

In this section we shall try to do two things. We will first try to find a way to organize the complex world of the many religions. Maybe we can begin to find our way around in what otherwise seems like sheer chaos. The first two chapters will help us do this. The second thing we shall do is to take a careful look at the kind of attitude we might want to have. This will help us take an honest look at the convictions of others and begin to think as Christians about our response to them. Chapter 3 tries to get us beyond a common but, I believe, very mistaken way to understand religious pluralism. Chapter 4 suggests a way for us as Christians to deal with the question of this pluralism.

THREE FAMILIES

Y<small>ES</small>, "what about those other religions?"

Have you ever asked that question? If you have, you are only one of a growing number of people who ask and wonder. The world was never a simple place in which to live, but it is now more complicated than ever. It is one thing to try to work out our relations with Catholics and Baptists and Presbyterians and Pentecostalists, not to mention Mormons and Jehovah's Witnesses. Some of us may also have grown up with Jewish friends. But now the whole scene has changed, and people of those far-off religions that we once thought had to be converted to Christianity are right in our midst and even attracting many of our daughters and sons. On top of this, New Age religions seem to pop up everywhere. Is all this bad, or is it good? Should we be happy or mad? Are people of other religions to be feared or befriended? Does it really matter what we believe as long as we lead a decent life and do our best to help others? After all, aren't religions, as we hear on television or read in magazines, just different glasses through which people of diverse cultures see God? Maybe there is even something we can learn from these other religions? We shall try to work through these and many other questions in this book.

I find it helpful to have a sketch of some of the world's major religions and worldviews in my mind. There are at least three major families of religions and worldviews. By religions and worldviews, by the way, I do not have some sophisticated definition in mind. I simply mean the way major groups of people or civilizations have continued to experience and understand their world so that it makes sense and gives meaning to their existence.

The three families I have in mind represent the three major civilizations that have shaped our world: the Western, the Indian, and the Chinese. All three have roots that go deep into history; all three developed written languages so that a long tradition of interpreting their worlds could develop; and all are the source of major worldviews that influence the world today. Most of the world's people have been shaped by one or the other of these three families. We can diagram these this way:

Semitic   Indic   Sinic

(GOD)   (SELF)   (WORLD)

The Semitic Family—God

The first family of religions I shall refer to as the Semitic family. This includes Jews, Christians, and Muslims. The second family of religions is the Indian. I shall call it the Indic family.[1] The third family, which I refer to as a world-view rather than a religion, is the Chinese. I shall call it the Sinic family.[2] What is the distinctive mark of each of these families?

In the Semitic family of religions—Judaism, Christianity, and Islam—if one wants to understand one's world and give meaning to one's life, it is necessary to speak of God. One might talk about many things in life, but unless one brings God into the picture, one has missed the biggest point about life. Without God there is no Judaism, Christianity, or Islam. Of course these three understand God in somewhat different ways, which is important, but what they all share deep down is a commitment to faith in God.

It is not hard to show this from the scriptures of these three. In Deuteronomy 6 we read:

> Hear, O Israel: The Lord is our God, the Lord alone. (6:4)

And it doesn't stop there. It goes on to say:

> You shall love the Lord your God with all your heart, and with all your soul, and with all your might. (6:5)

In other words, nothing is more important. If you miss God, you have missed what is most central to life. But it doesn't stop there—it goes on to say how this shapes one's behavior:

> Keep these words that I am commanding you today in your heart. Recite them to your children and talk about them when you are at home and when you are away, when you lie down and when you rise. Bind them as a sign on your hand, fix them as an emblem on your forehead, and write them on the doorposts of your house and on your gates. (6:6-9)

Is this still done today? Indeed it is. Many faithful Jews do precisely what these words instruct. We often see this in pictures from Jerusalem, or even from New York.

These words are important for us Christians as well. When someone asked Jesus what the great commandment was, he used just these words. A scribe approached Jesus and asked: "Which commandment is the first of all?" Jesus answered:

> The first is, "Hear, O Israel: the Lord our God, the Lord is one; and you shall love the Lord your God with all your heart, and with all your soul, and with all your mind, and with all your strength."[3]

Take this out of the Christian faith, and what is left? Anything? I doubt it. The most common prayer we use is equally clear: "Our Father, who art in Heaven, hallowed be thy name, thy kingdom come, thy will be done."

No less is this the case with Islam. Here the faith in the oneness of God reaches a white-hot pitch. The Muslim confession begins, "There is no God but God." The Qur'an hammers home this truth, that God is One:

> He is God;
> there is no god but He.
> He is the knower of the Unseen and the Visible;
> He is the All-merciful, the All-compassionate.
> He is God;
> there is no god but He.
> He is the king, the All-holy, the All-peaceable,
> the All-faithful, the All-preserver,
> the All-mighty, the All-compeller,
> the All-sublime.
> Glory be to God, above that they associate!
> He is God,
> the Creator, the Maker, the Shaper.
> To Him belong the Names Most Beautiful.
> All that is in the heavens and the earth magnifies Him;
> He is the All-mighty, the All-wise.[4]

Some years ago a scholar of Islam from Beijing, China, was visiting the Twin Cities. I called the local Islamic Center and asked if they would like him to come and share something about Islam in China. They were interested, so we arranged an evening. Before his presentation, I was talking with a young Muslim. He had a bright, excited look in his eyes, as though he had made a new discovery. Talking with me he eagerly and earnestly said, "You know, Islam has only one doctrine!" "Yes," I replied, "and what is that?" In measured words he said, "*God . . . is . . . one!*" It was as if the full impact of this had only recently occurred to him. Yes, God is One, and all of life belongs to God. How rich, how captivating is that truth when truly discovered.

This is what is at the heart of the Semitic family of religions. God is the big question, the big answer. The members of this family all share in this central conviction. Remove this and all that is left is a lifeless corpse.

The Indic Family—Self

Hinduism and Buddhism are the two most important examples of the Indian family of religions. Hinduism is like a collection of many religions rather than a single religion. But whether a collection or a single religion, it and Buddhism share a very important common characteristic. One may or may not speak about God—in Buddhism there is no God—but if one wants to understand life then it is necessary to ask about the nature of the self. If one fails to ask this question and find its answer, then one has missed that which is most important about life.

Of course, within Hinduism there are many traditions for which God is exceedingly important, even central. But even here, God is in the final analysis the highest instance of the self, the Universal Self, the Soul of the universe.

We in the West do not often ask the question about the self in the way that the Hindu or Buddhist does. If we ask about the self it is because we are troubled by a poor image of the self and need encouragement, or we are fearful or confused or anxious and want to find a happy self. We are very concerned about the self that we think we are, the self that feels, thinks, is self-aware, that hopes, wills, wants, that gives us our sense of identity—my-self.

Our concern seems to be about what we can call the empirical self. That is, the self that thinks, feels, knows, and of which we are constantly aware. For the Hindu and the Buddhist, this is a falsely constructed self, an illusion. The real truth about the self has nothing to do with our body, our emotions, our mind. It is a different, deeper, more important reality.

For the Hindu the self can only be discovered by peeling away all the outer layers that hide the real self. That real self, sometimes called the *atman*, is invisible and untouchable. It is beyond the experience of hope and fear. It is a quiet zone deep within of eternal bliss, a fragment so to say of the Eternal Self, sometimes called *Brahman*. The real self is not the self that can feel pain and loss. That is the outer, empirical self, which needs to be peeled away to discover the real self within which cannot experience either pain or loss. Eternally quiet, it is eternally blissful. The religious purpose of yoga, for instance, is to peel away the outer layers of the self and free this eternal self within.

Buddhism is very different and, perhaps, much more difficult for us to understand. Buddhism says that when one begins to peel away the outer layers one will find that the peeling continues, like with peeling an onion, and that when everything has been peeled away there is nothing left. There is no core. There is no inner, real self to be discovered. The only truth that matters is the truth of nonself, or *an-atman*.

How shall we understand this difficult teaching? Perhaps we could use the illustration of a cloud. We see a large thundercloud, let us say, floating across our summer sky. It seems like a powerful thing indeed. Perhaps it is dark and swirling. Maybe there is lightening and thunder. Perhaps it throws hail upon us. What is that cloud really? It is not really what it appears to be. Maybe in a short while the cloud will even disappear. What happened to it? Where did it go? Where did it come from? We then begin to realize that the cloud is only the result of many factors—moisture, air, temperature and so on—that converge in a particular way at a particular time. When these conditions change—the air becomes drier and the temperature is warmer and so on—so does the cloud. The cloud was nothing in itself. It was simply a temporary phenomenon that appeared because a certain set of conditions were in place. The same is true for tornadoes or hurricanes. The same is true for flowers and bees. The same is true, in fact, for everything, including human beings. There is no core to things. There is no substantial self, no permanent, independent, eternal self.

This, the Buddhist says, is a discovery that frees and liberates us from our endless lives of desire and selfishness. How foolish it is to be full of desire and gathering up for myself when in the end my self is only an impermanent and transitory phenomenon. Much better to realize that our identity is not really in the individual thing but in the entire network of things. Much better to realize that our finite selves are really interconnected with all things. This wisdom leads to compassion towards all things.

It is important to remember, then, that for the Indian family of religions it is not necessary to talk about God when one must talk of that which is most important. Indeed, to talk about God but to be mistaken about the nature of the self is in the end to miss the most important fact of our lives. It is the question concerning the nature of the self that is the most important. To miss this is to end up being mistaken about all else.

The Sinic Family—World

If "God" is the key for understanding the Semitic family of religions and "the nature of the self" is the key for the Indic religions, then it is "our relationship with the world" that is the key for the Sinic worldviews.

Here, you may notice, I use the term *worldview* rather than *religion*. Many scholars don't think Confucianism and some forms of Daoism (also spelled Taoism) should be called religions because they are more ethical and philosophical in character.[5] At the same time, however, they clearly have religious overtones. By this I mean that they are offering what they consider to be the most important thing possible. In the final analysis religion has to do with what is regarded as more important than anything else. At least, that is what I am concerned about in this book. As worldviews then, Confucianism and Daoism are offering ethical and philosophical ways to speak about what is most important.

But what are they concerned about? The Confucian is concerned about our relation with the social world. The Daoist is concerned about our relation with the natural world around us. It isn't whether or not one relates to God that is most important, or whether or not one has a particular understanding of the self that matters most, but how one lives in relation to the world.

The Confucian is concerned about the social world around us. There is a Chinese character that captures the heart of what Confucianism is about. It is the character *ren*, which is written this way:

仁

This character has two parts. The left part is written like this:

亻

When this stands as a character by itself it is written this way:

人

Grade school kids could probably guess what it means more quickly than we adults, since they tend to see things more simply and directly. It means "human being." It is just a stick figure. Put a head and arms on and you will see what I mean. The right-hand side is written thus:

二

A single stroke like this:

一

means one. A much more relaxed one, we might say, than our Western one that has to stand straight up. Two strokes simply means two. Three strokes: three. After that it becomes more complicated, four being written like this:

四

Ren is the character for "two" combined with the character for "human being." *Ren* literally means two people together. This character can be translated as "humanity," "benevolence," "love." It represents the highest value in Confucianism—the heart and mind that fosters genuine community.

There is a saying in the ancient *Analects* of Confucius that says that "a filial attitude is the root of *ren*."[6] We human beings all live within certain relationships—parent/child, husband/wife, brother/sister, friend/friend, ruler/ruled. All these relationships require certain kinds of behavior to be fulfilled. The parent/child relationship underlies all other relationships, for there is no human being who is not also a child. Many also become parents. But we are all children by birth. Therefore, the attitude of respect and honor that a child has for the nurturing mother or father is the basis for all other character development. The Confucian vision for humanity builds on this idea.

> Only if a parent is a person of character (that is, one who shows the characteristics of ren or humanity) can the family be established; only when the families are established can the nation be rightly governed; only when the nations are rightly governed can there by peace and equality under all of Heaven.[7]

That is the Confucian vision. It is one we share too. We envision the time when all nations will turn swords into plowshares. This attention to relationships, the Confucian says, is more important than anything else. Talk of God may have its place, but the one essential thing, whether you talk about God or not, is how one lives in relationship to others.

Daoist philosophers think all this is foolishness. The Daoists saw the Confucians creating all kinds of rituals, rules, and norms for social behavior—exalted Emily Posts one might say. The Confucians, they thought, were too busy trying to construct a world according to their own wishes. It would be much better, they felt, to let things follow their natural course.

In this vein, Zhuangzi, an early Daoist philosopher, was sitting outside his hut beating a drum and singing happy songs. A Confucian happened by and was flabbergasted. Zhuangzi's wife had died only the day before, and here he was singing as if nothing had happened. Being very persnickety about mourning rites, as were all Confucians in those days, he challenged Zhuangzi: "What are you doing singing like this when your wife died yesterday?" "Oh yes," Zhuangzi replied, "at first I felt a twinge of sorrow. But then I thought how she has simply entered into the great transformation."[8] And with that he went back to his drumming and singing.

If one were to ask Daoists what is the best tree in the world, they would give a very simple answer. We might quickly imagine the giant sequoia of California as a tree unparalleled in beauty and grandeur and worthy of our protection. Probably we would be right. But because they are so big and tall and straight, they are seen by loggers as a crop to be harvested, cut into boards, and sold. I have driven in northern California and seen the vast ranges of hillsides devastated and eroding because of clear-cutting and bull-dozing of once grand sequoia forests. The Daoist would understand this. The Daoist would say the best tree is the most useless tree. Consider an old gnarled tree, for instance, on the edge of a cliff. No one will disturb this tree. People will simply let it be and enjoy it for what it is. The useless is the best.

There is an ancient Daoist fable I like to call an "anti-creation" myth. It goes like this:

> The Emperor of the South was called Shu (impetuosity). The Emperor of the North was called Hu (carelessness). And the Emperor of the Center was called Hundun. Shu and Hu met together from time to time in Hundun's territory, and Hundun always treated them very generously. Shu and Hu, then, discussed how they could reciprocate Hundun's virtue saying: "People all have seven openings in order to see, hear, eat, and breathe. He alone doesn't have any [being a blob]. Let's try boring him some." Each day they bored one hole, and on the seventh day Hundun died.[9]

Hundun was a blob, a shapeless mass of primal matter. Perhaps some of you have eaten wantons. A wanton is a shapeless blob of dough with meat inside. Actually "wanton" is the Cantonese pronunciation of the Mandarin word *hundun*. It is the same character as in this myth, except it has a sign for food beside it. So you who have eaten wanton have eaten poor Hundun. When Shu and Hu tried to give him a face and make him like the rest of us, he died. It's much better then, argues the Daoist, to leave things the way they are, to follow the rhythms of nature itself.

The primary value for the Daoist is not *ren*, a social virtue, but *wuwei*, a letting be or, literally, nothing-doing, without artifice. The problem with the world is that everybody is trying to make everybody else into what they want them to be. Let us instead imitate nature. When rain falls, the water simply flows, following the contours of the earth. Never does it try climbing back up the hill to get a better view of things. So let us likewise conform to the contours of life. That is sufficient.

Reflection

We have briefly considered these three great religious patterns. Most of the world's people have been shaped by these seven religious commitments—Jewish, Christian, and Muslim; Hindu and Buddhist; Confucian and Daoist. How different they are! What shall we make of it? That is what this whole book is about. In the next chapter we will look at even more religions, to get a more complete view. Then we will be ready to try and do something with all of this and find where we as Christians fit into this vast mixture.

But let us first ponder briefly what we have discussed. It is interesting that these three commitments, coming from three different civilizations, should focus one on God, one on self, and one on world. None of us can be without all three of these in some form. Certainly that is the case for we who are Christians. We don't just talk about God. What we do is talk about everything, world and self included, in relation to God. To try to save oneself is to lose oneself. We are to die to self that we might live to God. Jesus said there was a second commandment: "You shall love your neighbor as yourself."[10] So all three are important for Christians, but God is the one who holds it all together.

What about the Buddhist who doesn't believe in God? Even here there is a concern for all three. The one who discovers the truth of the nonself discovers instead one's relation to all things, for all things are the condition for one's own passing existence. This "all things" includes, of course, the world and at least indicates, if not God, a reality that is infinitely great and ultimately good.

So also the Confucian. Actually, Confucius did in fact have a belief in Heaven, which is one Chinese term for God. Yet, he seldom talked about Heaven. It was a background for his experience of the world, not the foreground. When asked about what happens after death, Confucius replied: "Not yet knowing this life, why inquire about the afterlife?"[11] When asked if the spirits of the dead ancestors were present when filial sons sacrificed to them, he answered: "Sacrifice as if they are present."[12] Whether or not spirits were present wasn't the important thing. It wasn't worshipping spirits, but honoring the deceased that was important. When asked what caused him to persist in his teaching when few in his day cared about what he said, and some even tried to harm him, he replied: "Heaven has given rise to this virtue within me. What can Huan Tui [an enemy who sought him harm] do to me?"[13]

So it is with all of these religions and worldviews. All three elements are important in some way. They are, however, put together in different ways. Is there something in the Semitic way, and again in the Christian way of putting these together that has a particular importance? Is there revelation here in a unique and special sense? We will deal with this question at a later time.

2

And Then There Are More

Three Other Groupings

There are, of course, many more religions being practiced today than those represented by these great families. We can collect most of them together in three big groupings. The first I shall call indigenous traditions, the second I shall call popular religion and the third I shall call cults. They fit in with the world religions diagram this way:

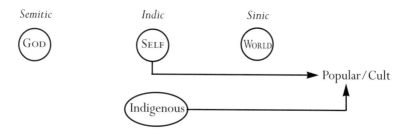

When I speak of indigenous traditions, I am thinking of all those local religious practices that have deep roots in the oral traditions of tribal communities around the world. One may think of the many tribal beliefs and practices in Africa, in Australia, in North and South America. One thinks too of the aboriginal peoples of Asia who over the centuries were not part of the three great families. The aboriginal peoples of Taiwan, for example, were driven into the mountains by the invading Chinese of an earlier century and were never absorbed into Chinese culture.

This has happened all over the world. In Europe, what is left of the indigenous traditions—Nordic, Celtic, Germanic, Gaelic, and so forth—has disappeared so far into the cultural background as to be almost forgotten, remaining perhaps only in literature or opera. Today some have a renewed interest in them, especially those involved in the New Age movement. Of the three groupings, we are mainly aware of the indigenous traditions, particularly those connected with American Indian cultures. These indigenous traditions have some common features I will identify below.

Another grouping is popular religion. What is special about this? First of all, it is not identical to either the indigenous traditions or the great families, though it might have a close relationship with either or both. Popular religion is not so much a clearly defined religion as a way of being religious, the way a religion is practiced. Two things at least are typical of popular religious practice. The first is that popular religious practice is eclectic or, if one prefers, parasitic like an orchid. That is, it depends on already existing religious sources.

I visited Brazil some years ago, where I observed a festival in honor of the Virgin Mary. Interestingly enough, before the Portuguese came to Brazil, there was a female deity associated with the ocean. Today, the concept of the Virgin Mary contains characteristics both from what was brought from Europe and from what the ocean deity from the original traditional religion meant. In the modern Brazilian festival, it is hard to tell how she is related to the mother Mary of the Bible.

A second feature of popular religion is that it is always concerned about the usefulness of religion. That is, does a religious belief or practice accomplish what I want it to accomplish? Does it comfort me? Does it provide the health and the wealth that I want? Does it protect me from dangers that threaten me? In other words, popular religion is a way of practicing religion so that it will be useful for the purposes I have in mind, purposes that can assure me of what I want in this life and sometimes also of my wants for the next life.

The third grouping is cults. This subject has become especially popular in recent times. Cults, like popular religion, are not so important because of what they believe or do, but because of how they believe or do. But I think it is helpful to distinguish between popular religion and cults. There are a number of reasons we might use the word *cult* to describe a religious movement. Among these reasons is, first, the fact that cults are highly focused. Cult followers might focus on a particular belief or practice, such as the belief that the world is coming to an end in the year 2000 or 2050. In a cult, everything is focused around a single belief, or perhaps around a practice that provides this focus. We have seen cults in our day that think drinking or eating something, a certain technique of meditation, or even violent action is absolutely important. This practice becomes a defining focus of the group. Again, it may be a charismatic leader. This person holds such a power over the followers that they will do anything the follower says to do, however crazy it might seem to the rest of us. One of the more infamous examples is

Jim Jones, who in 1978 ordered 911 of his followers to drink juice laced with cyanide. Or consider the mass suicide of Heaven's Gate believers in 1997, who believed their deaths would permit them to hitch a ride on a spacecraft lurking around the Hale-Bopp comet.

Second, along with possessing a particular focus, cults are also very intense. The emotions are intense; the will is intense. There is unquestioning commitment. Authority is very clearly defined. And third, because of the focus, there is a narrow range of interest in the world about one. In particular, the mind does not take into account anything that does not fit a prearranged scheme, or else it forces that to fit the scheme. A genuine dialogue on matters central to the faith is simply not possible. One must speak within a prearranged framework. Beyond this there is little interest or genuine curiosity. Again, fourth, because of the narrow focus, cults tend to be exclusive, drawing a very tight social circle around their own community. Some would want to include, fifth, recruitment practices (social pressure, isolation, dissembling, and so forth) and "brainwashing" into the definition of a cult. To be sure, some do this, but not all. I think these other four factors are sufficient when taken together to pinpoint cults and cultlike behavior. As we read our newspapers, or come into contact with groups that reflect these characteristics, we can make our own judgments about them.

It is clear that I am not speaking in a positive way about cults. I am suggesting that movements that reflect this collection of tendencies are, in a general way of speaking, not healthy. In my opinion, a cult is not necessarily a religion separate from others; it can also be a way of practicing one's beliefs, whatever religion one may adhere to. Christians, for instance, can hold to their Christian beliefs and practices in a cultlike manner. The checklist of factors I noted above may help to note where and when this becomes the case.

What is the difference between popular religion and cults? I would say popular religion is never a cult and a cult is never popular religion, even though a cult may be very popular and popular religion may use beliefs or practices from a cult. Perhaps the major difference is that popular religion has no intense focus; it is simply practicing religion in a way that serves one's personal or communal interests. Cults are highly focused commitments. Popular religion is concerned with "anything that works." Cults believe that "only this works." These are two extremes.

Indigenous Traditions

Indigenous traditions are largely local religious traditions that are practiced around the world. Terms that have often been used to refer to them are *primitive religions* (but today many people think this sounds too patronizing), *primal religions* (some think this is a better collective term), *animism* (religions that think everything—people, animals, plants, stones, mountains—has a life or soul), *tribal religions*, and so on. Indigenous is broad enough to include religious practices that are indigenous to a place and that are distinct in some important way from the three great families we have already talked about. Thus, something like Shinto in Japan or Shamanism in Korea would be included as an indigenous tradition.

There are some characteristics that I think are generally true of all indigenous traditions, however much they differ otherwise. The human being is seen as just one part of a larger cosmos that is full of life. The gods themselves are usually a part of this cosmos. Sometimes there is a high God who lies behind everything but is so exalted or remote that the best way to approach this deity is through many kinds of intermediaries. So there are many gods and spirits in the heavens, the sky, on the earth and beneath the earth. Besides spirits there are also things that can have magical power. These things might be so simple as a collection of grasses. They might also be much more elaborate fetishes (artifacts). Having been subjected to the proper ritual, they embody some kind of power. Finally, there are the ancestors who, in some cases, are the most important intermediary between God or some greater Spirit and the human world. All of these represent different kinds of powers that influence our world in different ways.

Several concerns seem to be uppermost for indigenous religions. They are concerned about matters of health, matters having to do with wealth and welfare, about fertility and progeny and how these relate to the natural world, the spirit world and the social world around us. Their concern is that all of these be in a happy and life-enhancing balance. They are concerned about the well-being of the whole, not just this need or one individual. To foster this life-enhancing relationship, there are many instructive myths and legends, many rituals, sacred places, objects, and times, and a wide range of spirit powers. Frankly, they share many of the same concerns that we have about our life here and now.

There is much that causes disruption in life. There are natural disasters, whether earthquakes, floods, drought, storms, volcanoes, or pests. There are illnesses that threaten our health and our lives. There are social disturbances from quarrels to wars that upset the proper rhythms of our lives. Through appropriate rituals the causes of all these things can be discerned and dealt with and their consequences weakened if not eliminated.

Along with all of this, there are also the various stages of life that mark important points for the individual and community. There is birth, initiation, marriage, death. There are seasonal festivals. All of these passages of life also need the protective and life-enhancing power that one or another ritual may provide. I like to speak of the rites and myths of the indigenous traditions as custodial in character. Ritual behavior and the retelling of myths by a priest or other ritual performer serve as custodians of our life together. They serve to keep all things in a proper relationship to each other and to the various kinds of powers that are present in the world about us. In a way our own rituals do something like this, don't they? In fact, even our Bible and the ancient beliefs and rituals of Israel were influenced and shaped by the indigenous traditions of times past.

A brief example of how an indigenous tradition works might be cited here. In some Native American traditions, like the Navajo, sand paintings have an important healing function. Today we can see sand paintings in shops and museums throughout the United States, which we might buy as beautiful works of art. These in fact are not real sand paintings, for when a sand painting has been used in a ritual it is destroyed, not preserved.

A sand painting is a diagram, often very complex, drawn in sand that has, in some cases, been spread out upon a floor in a ceremonial space. A ritual specialist guides the procedure, saying or singing certain things as the design takes shape. The content of the design and the colors used are provided by the myths that accompany the ceremony. There isn't room to present the details here.[1]

Such a ceremony might be used to bring healing to a sick person. The design represents a mythical world where everything is in its proper order and relationship, in other words a whole and complete world. When the design has been properly constructed, the sick person may be placed in the center of the design, with more words and songs accompanying ritual actions. The point is to place the imperfect into the midst of a perfect world, thereby fostering a healing process. The sick person enters into the stories told and the actions performed and the perfect world that has been drawn, or perhaps these realities enter into the sick person.

Through this ceremony, then, a disordered world experienced as sickness has been incorporated into a well-ordered world. The sand painting becomes a part of the life world of the sick person. It can no longer exist as a separate sand painting—for then it would fail to express the reuniting of disordered parts into a single whole. The painting is therefore destroyed. Sand painting and sick person have become one.

Might we not want to regard this as a beautiful parable of the wholeness and healing that we all seek? Do our Christian rituals in part perform similar functions?

Sometimes such myths provide the basis for the self-understanding of a whole society, as the ancient Shinto myths did for Japan earlier in this century. The myth described below, for example, provided the basis for the divinity of the emperor and the sacred character of Japanese soil and people.

Part of that myth goes like this. Out of the primordial chaos emerged a number of *kami*, or divine beings. At first three indistinct *kami* arose; nevertheless, they remained hidden from view, still shrouded in the depths of mystery. Numerous other *kami* emerged as though spontaneously. Eventually there emerged a more distinct pair, the original male and female. Izanagi, the male who invites, and Izanami, the female who invites, take up the task of giving birth to the drifting land. Much sexual symbolism is involved. They push a spear down into the chaotic mist, stirring the salty brine below. As they raise the spear, bits of matter congeal on its tip, and these drop off to form islands. A mating ritual follows, and they give production to innumerable other islands and produce gods—millions of them. The final deity to which Izanami gives birth, the Fire god, so sears her in childbirth that she dies.

Distressed by this loss, Izanagi follows her to the underworld. Warned not to look, he nevertheless does. In a rage Izanami, who had been seen in the revolting state of death and decay, chases after him to secure him also to the underworld. Fleeing for his life, he manages to escape, but just barely. After his escape he purifies himself from this contamination with death, and in the meantime from his soiled clothing and from his washing, innumerable other gods are formed. Among these is Amaterasu, a sun goddess, a moon god, and a rascally deity name Susa-no-o, a storm deity. These ascend to the celestial realm and more deities are produced.

Eventually the sun goddess sends her grandson, Ninigi, to the islands below, to the island of Kyushu. With him are the imperial insignia—a mirror, a sword, and a jewel, still the imperial insignia of Japan today. It is the great-grandson of this Ninigi, Jimmu, who eventually moves to the Yamato region of the main island of Honshu, conquers the other local deities, and founds a Japanese state (according to mythology) in 660 B.C.E. The Japanese imperial line is descended from his line. The religion associated with this mythology was later to be called Shinto.[2]

This is one of many myths associated with the diverse forms of Shinto in Japan. All express the idea of continuity between the divine and the earthly or human realms. They also express the desire to be separated from all forces that lead to death and decay. Shinto seeks through its rites to purify existence from these harmful aspects and join us in continuity with the productive life of the *kami*.

Childhood Cancer and Popular Religion—A Taiwan Case Study

We have already discussed what we mean by popular religion. It may help to have one example of popular religion before us. So I will give an extended report of one way I have discovered popular religion to work. It is based on research my wife did in Taiwan in 1980 and 1981 on childhood cancer and the response of the family. I participated in the study on the religious response.

This study was funded by the Taiwanese government and conducted together with the faculty from the two leading nursing schools in Taiwan.[3] Seventy-five families from throughout Taiwan were included in the study. This covered the greater part of children who were available in hospitals in Taiwan at the time and who were either just recently diagnosed (Group A), had experienced a relapse after an initial round of treatment (Group B), or had recently died (Group C). The large majority of families practiced what we defined as "folk" or "popular" religion. It is these practices that I will describe below.

Religious practice in Taiwan is shaped by several traditions. There are the influences from Confucianism, Daoism, Buddhism, and indigenous religion, as well as now also from Christianity. Interacting with all of these is the popular religion. There are also a number of newly arisen religions, which some may consider cults. At the time of our study, the vast majority of the population engaged often or occasionally in what we termed "folk religious practice."

Bai-bai, meaning simply "paying respects," is the term used to describe the basic practices. Typically, people would pay their respects to a wide assortment of deities and spirits and resort to a vast array of practitioners of one religious ritual or another. In the home there would be an altar upon which one or more deities, usually more, would be honored, together with the customary ancestral tablets. These would be honored with a daily ritual of incense burning and perhaps the offering of simple gifts of food and drink. On festival occasions one or more nearby temples might be visited. At times when family or work affairs needed some higher guidance, a visit would be made to a ritual specialist, perhaps a fortune-teller. There was often little sense of belonging to a particular religious tradition.

It was typical of the families engaged in this popular religion that with the onset of illness, or with the progressive deterioration of the health of the child, ordinary religious activity would intensify. In some cases this was no more than more earnest or frequent worship. This might be confined to the home but often included worship at a nearby temple as well. A prayer of petition to the deity concerning the ill child would probably also accompany the act of worship (*bai-bai*), which was little more than bowing with the ritual waving of incense before the altar. In many cases this seemed to be all that happened. For those who wanted more, there was an endless array of possible temples, ritual specialists, and religious observances.

The religious actions described in the study formed a religious system of its own—a popular religious system.[4] First, we noticed that in most cases the religious act was an individual act, even though several in the family might sometimes act together. Second, there was little thought given to the meaning of the religious activity itself. The overriding concern was for what was called *ling*, efficacy. That is, did the action work as expected? Was the child healed? A third thing we noticed was that the relation of the worshipers to the deity was a tit-for-tat relationship. It was like the relationship between a store clerk and a customer. The god was expected to provide the goods needed and paid for. If the god didn't, then the supplicant would often seek another deity in another temple. Fourth, this whole system of popular religion as it showed itself in the lives of those who had children with cancer took on a free-enterprise market idiom. The basic principle determining religious action can be expressed as simply as this: "Whenever we heard that a god was efficacious, there we went to worship." So, when some gods had gotten a reputation, however deserved and however short-lived, that they could produce results for their petitioners, their fame would spread by word of mouth. One would shop around for the deity that best met one's specific needs.

Finally, this popular religious activity became a paramedical system, as the god gave diagnoses as well as prescription and treatment for the disease. In this study, it became apparent that under the pressure of devastating childhood illness, the popular religious activity developed and expanded in a way consistent with the above five characteristics.

In our analysis of the data, we noted five kinds of expectations that the families had from their religious practice. Some hoped for physical healing of the child by the performance of religious acts; some hoped for at least some information about the destiny of the child—will it live or die. These were what I call objective expectations, because one could prove whether they had been realized or not. In our study, in no case was there proof of physical healing by religious means, though many tried. There were, however, some cases in which the fortune of the child had been rightly predicted.

Most hoped for some emotional support through their religious activities. Some sought for some way to make sense out of a world in which their child died of cancer. Some sought for moral direction—what is the proper way to act in this situation? These expectations I refer to as subjective, because only the person who has these expectations can tell whether they have been met or not. As it was in the study, some felt one or more of these expectations had been met, others felt not.

It might be helpful to illustrate some of these. In the popular religion, healing and fortune telling were very common expectations. In one case, for instance, a mother would frequent the local temple, a Daoist-oriented temple with popular deities, and seek the help of the local ritual specialist there. He would provide her with charms, which were pieces of paper on which special magical characters had been written. Having burned these, she put the ashes in the bath water or, as some did, mixed it with the child's drinking water. This was intended for the cure of the child. Nevertheless, whenever she inquired from the god at the temple about the fortune of her child, the god told her the child would die. Thus, she lost interest in the temple and went elsewhere, where the gods provided a more desirable prediction. As it turned out, however, her daughter did die. Commenting on this, the mother mentioned how much stronger her belief was in the god she used to go to, because this god had told the truth even if it couldn't heal.

A more tragic case involved a family who came from southern Taiwan. They brought their child up north to Taipei because the only hospitals sophisticated enough to treat cancer were located there. When the doctor gave the diagnosis—a curable Wilms tumor—the father insisted on conferring with his own father, a particularly ardent follower of folk religious practice. The grandfather refused surgery since, following an old Confucian tradition, one ought not cut into one's body. The mother was beside herself but could do nothing. So the child was taken back down south without treatment. Meanwhile the grandfather visited every temple in his and the neighboring counties and treated the child with herbal medicines. But all to no avail.

Finally the boy's situation became so desperate that they had to seek help from a local hospital. The local hospital said they must send the child to Taipei immediately. But still the grandfather was unwilling. The father then went north to Taipei to seek the help of a fortune-telling friend. This person read the birth signs (hour, day, month, year) of the child and saw a sign of blood in the reading, a sign of something bad to come. The fortune-teller advised him to bring the child immediately up north. But still the grandfather resisted. Once more he sought information from the gods. Finally, one god said, "Out of trouble good will come." From this he decided it was all right to send the child up north for treatment, even if it meant surgery because, as he interpreted the cryptic prediction, out of the trouble caused by surgery (that violates the supposed Confucian injunction against surgery), healing would come. They immediately brought the child up north, but unfortunately it was too late for treatment. The child died.

The adherents of these traditions believe that the various causes for the illness of the children can be discerned. It may have been due to a past disturbance to the child's emotional equilibrium (caused by the tearing down of a building next door, for instance), it might be indiscretion at a funeral (for instance, children running around in the room in the presence of the body lying in state), it might be due to some cosmic imbalance of the *yin* and *yang*, or it might be due to a deceased uncle who had died as a little boy and was now in this way demanding ancestral worship (though the spirits of dead children are not normally included in the ancestral cult). Many other causes were identified. People often resorted to *tong-ji,* or spirit mediums. In one such case, the spirit medium informed the family that the child was the incarnation of a certain god. This god had decided to reconnoiter upon earth for a five-year visit to see how things were. To do so, he entered the world by way of a regular birth. The child's illness was this god's means of leaving the body to return to his divine abode. However, the earnest prayers of the parents had detained the god longer than expected. But now, they were informed, the god was definitely scheduled to go. In this way, presumably, death was accepted as necessary, the status of the child was exalted, and the parents saw some rationale that helped make sense, small though it might be, of the suffering of their child.

I have mentioned the subjective expectations of the parents. For some it was simply emotional stability that they sought through religious means. Thus, they would report, "I am more at peace," or "My mind has something to rely on," or "I don't think there is such a thing as a religion that can bring physical healing, but religious faith is meant to lead us to seek good and to find peace of mind," or again, "Of course it gave emotional support and comfort to pray for the god's protection. I feel that we simply went everywhere to find a way out, and didn't fail to give our son the opportunity for treatment, so that I am free of all regret." In some cases religious activity was an encouragement to do good deeds. Within the context of popular religion this would normally be to gain merit.

What we did not discern in the popular religious activity was some sense of a larger purpose and meaning to life, something greater than the solving of immediate problems and needs. For this one would have to turn to the few Buddhist and Christian participants in the study. For the Buddhist families, for instance, they would see this tragedy within the larger truth that all existence is painful and as one more reminder to strive for enlightenment whereby one would see the emptiness of all self-seeking efforts.

3

ALL RELIGIONS ARE THE SAME—RIGHT?

The title of this chapter is one of the most common things that is said to me when people hear that I teach about world religions. We read about religions in our magazines and have many programs on television telling us about this religion and that. Isn't it interesting how different they all appear to be? Even so, perhaps they all really teach us the same thing? Isn't this an illustration of how rich and diverse our cultures truly are? Isn't it terrible that missionaries go and destroy these wonderful cultures? Even though this idea that all religions have the same goal comes so easily off of our lips, some very hard and important questions need to be raised. How do we respond? Shall we agree? Disagree? Be noncommittal?

Why Do We Say This?

Why do statements like "All religions teach the same thing" or "All religions lead to the same end" roll off our tongues so easily? No doubt there are many reasons people make statements like this. Perhaps some people say this because they have a generous spirit. We don't want to pass judgment on other people and act as if we are right and everybody else wrong. Charity, after all, is a Christian virtue. Perhaps some say this because they have never thought much about religion and feel they have to say something that sounds wise. And so, without knowing much about any religion, and more or less indifferent to all of them, they say something that shows their wisdom on such an arcane and remote subject. Perhaps some people say this because they have thought long and hard on the subject and really believe this to be true. As a matter of fact, many books by learned theologians can be bought in our bookstores that use hundreds of pages to say this. Perhaps we need to try to understand what some of them are saying. Perhaps some people say this because they believe that religion is a deeply private affair, not something that one talks about in public, and certainly something that one shouldn't argue about. Truth is always personal, they say. Truth is always what is true for me. That doesn't mean it has to be true for somebody else.

Just like some people like steak and others prefer vegetables, so we each have our ways of being religious. And that is just fine. Let everybody and every culture enjoy what they like best and then let us get down to really important things—like raising a family, earning money, being a good citizen.

Some people who think about these things suggest that this way of thinking fits our cultural style today. Consider, for instance, the democratic form of government in the United States. In order to have democracy, we need to allow different points of view to exist. Everybody is allowed to have his or her own say. We are conditioned by our political culture to accept this kind of pluralism. Others suggest that our culture is shaped by a pattern of thinking that befits a market economy. That is to say, the market drives the economy. It is not somebody sitting up in Washington, for instance, who decides that we should all eat corn flakes for breakfast. Not at all. We go to the supermarket and, even though we may be confused by the innumerable brands of dry cereal, we still make our choices and eat them for breakfast. Perhaps this consumer mentality conditions us to think of religion in the same way. We like what we like, and nobody should tell us what we ought to like. If you don't like a certain kind of cereal, for instance, should you be made to eat it?

Others will push even further, and suggest that our scientific worldview has made us find it easy to separate facts and values. That is to say, we all know what facts are. They are public. Say a grade school kid looks through a microscope and sees E. coli bacteria swimming around in the drop of swamp water. That's a fact. And so we don't drink swamp water. We pipe purified water under our streets, or we dig a well deep enough to get clean water. But even so we might get fooled. A new fact is discovered—that lead is poisonous—so we have to change our water pipes. We all know what facts are. They can be demonstrated, proven. But values? Who can prove that this picture is pretty and that is ugly? Sometimes we worry about what our children might see on the television or at the movies. The material available on the World Wide Web may worry us even more. There is hardly any value that people have held that isn't depicted on these media. But values are not facts. We can't prove that this value is good and that bad. One person's smut is another person's entertainment. And so, if we try to censor what we think is smut, then someone else will try to protect the smut in the name of free speech. Values are something that we should be free to choose. They are not demonstrable, public facts. And so, that is the way we see religion too. Religion doesn't have to do with facts, but with values. So let us keep values to our private lives, and live with the facts in our public life.

And so we often say, "Religions are all the same." They are different ways of finding our values. The reasons some have offered for thinking this way— democratic pluralism, market economy, the split between fact and value— may have something to them. But still I don't think they carry the discussion forward far enough. For one thing, in our democratic society, unlike in totalitarian societies that tell people how to think, we are always making public arguments. Now as I write, our nation is gearing up for another election. Each candidate thinks his or her view of things is right, and they quarrel and argue about it on the television right before our eyes. I haven't yet heard them say that "our policies are the same in the end after all." Have you? If they did, which one would you vote for, or would you even bother to vote? So I am not sure that our democratic culture is enough of a reason for people to think that all religions are the same after all.

Neither do I think a market economy explains enough. Befuddled as we are by supermarkets offering endless choices, we still end up with arguments about things. Some don't like easy access to guns. Others dislike Barbie dolls. Sometimes toys turn out to be dangerous and we take them off the market. The Food and Drug Administration imposes an approval process to protect us from useless or dangerous drugs. Food packages are required to have an honest description of their contents. So even with our supermarket mentality we know choices aren't endless. There are limits. We know it's not anything goes.

Nor do I think a scientific worldview with its fact/value split is a good enough reason. Even here we have our arguments about what should be sold and what should not be sold. Take cigarettes, for instance. Many people enjoy them and want the freedom to be able to smoke. Other people think smoking is bad, they don't like to breathe other people's smoke, and they are angry about advertisements that target our children. The truth is, fact and values get all mixed up together. Fact one, smokers have a greater incidence of cancer. Fact two, many heavy smokers live long and happy lives— like George Burns, puffing on his cigars up to the end of his very long life. Maybe you could smoke and live to one hundred too. These facts only tell us that there is a matter of risk involved. But isn't there risk in everything we do? Car driving is very risky. Maybe we should junk all our cars. Why not? Many lives would be saved. Some people value the pleasure derived from smoking; others value a life lived with less risk of cancer. When we look at it from the point of risk, which is more important, facts or values?

So I don't think the way we have been conditioned by democratic values, by a market economy, or by the split between fact and value gives all the

answers. Of course, they may give part of the answer. A main reason I look
for a better answer is that I have heard people from many cultures say that all
religions are the same. I have heard people in China say the same thing, for
instance, even though when I heard such things being said, China was totalitarian and undemocratic. In India this has been said for centuries, long
before modern science appeared on the scene promoting a fact/value split.
I conclude that there must be deeper reasons for so many people saying this.[1]

A Habit of Mind

I wonder if it isn't due to a habit of our minds. Our minds are different from
that of dogs and cows. For example, when animals see things—trees,
fences, grass, people, barns—they react to them according to their needs at
the time. A cow sees grass and goes and eats it, perhaps even knocking a
fence down in the process. A dog sees another dog and wants to go and sniff
it. We humans also see and respond to things according to our needs. We do
it all the time. But human minds often do something else as well. We may
wonder, for instance, what holds it all together. The many trees, fences,
grass, people, and barns we see are all part of one world. If there are many,
there must also be one. Many without one leaves things unconnected. One
without many is unknowable and doesn't exist. Somehow our minds need
both one and many. It is this habit I refer to. Ultimately, I believe, it is
because our minds are wired in this way that we think this way about religions too. And so we see many religions and immediately think that they
must all be manifestations of one single thing. That's the simplest, but not
necessarily the best, way to exercise this habit of the mind.

Philosophy is the intellectual enterprise that specializes in this way of
thinking. Maybe that is one reason philosophers seem so profound. Better
than the ordinary run of human beings, they seem to have an uncanny ability to see how many things are connected to one thing. Of course, even
though this is a common philosophical project, it doesn't mean that every
philosopher is right simply because he or she sees the one in the many in a
particular way. Some ancient philosophers saw the one that held everything
else together in fire, or air, or numbers, or Idea, or something else. Modern
philosophers see it often in more complicated and sophisticated ways. But
they are all concerned to reduce the many in some way to the one. Sometimes science, too, begins to sound like philosophy. For instance, some scientists are trying to find that "golden grail" of a unified theory that will
explain everything in the world in one fell swoop. Let us wish them luck.

Can this help us when we begin to talk about religions? I think so. To put it simplistically, each of the great world religions is a particular unified theory of the one truth that is more important than any other truth, the one reality that holds all things together. So religions are the same in that they are all concerned with what is more important than anything else. But, as we've discussed in the first two chapters, they are different in what they affirm is most important. So, when Christians believe God is more important for us than anything else, that is hardly the same conviction that Buddhists have. They believe the world is held together, so to speak, by itself—by what some call the Buddha nature.

This is why it strikes me as premature to claim that because religions are all concerned with what is most important they therefore all amount to the same thing. Our habit of mind, which likes to see the one in the many as quickly as possible, leads us astray. It would be much better to ask what the religions actually teach and believe, what is it they take to be *most important*, and what connects everything to everything else. Does the "most important" have any content? Or is it just an empty idea? In fact, the religions each in their own way say, "No, it is not an empty idea, because this is what it is like." Only consistent agnostics think it is an empty idea; naturally, they don't think *their* idea that religions are empty of ultimately different content is empty. Even atheists, who are more honest, have some idea of what they think is most important, sure as they are that it is not God.

Reasons Some Give

Those who insist that the many religions are in the end one use many kinds of argument. Try as I might, it seems to me that all the arguments really are different variations of a single theme: all religions are partial ways of knowing a truth that cannot be fully known.

Sometimes this is talked about from the perspective of the observer. For instance, many different paths lead to the top of Mt. Fuji. Some paths are more direct, some more roundabout, some steeper and some more gentle slopes, but all eventually lead to the same goal, the top of the mountain.

Or consider the ancient story of the blind men and the elephant. A king wanted to have some fun, so he had some blind men brought in to tell him what an elephant was. None of the men had ever seen one. The king had an elephant placed in front of the blind men and asked them to describe it. One grasped a leg and said it was like a tree, another grasped the tail and said it was like a rope, and so on. The joke, of course, was on the blind men, who had only a partial, and so terribly funny, perspective on a greater reality, the elephant.[2] There are more modern versions of this as well, some having quite a scientific flair to them, but all have to do with the perspective of the observer.

Sometimes religion is talked about in terms of its function. Here there is a concern to identify what we might say is the inside of a religion and distinguish it from the outside of a religion. The inside is what a religion is truly concerned about, so it may be said; the outside may be useful for a while if it can lead to the real thing, the inner meaning of a religion. Once this happens the outside of a religion ceases to have any more importance except as a nice decoration or comfortable habit or a healthy way to channel our mental and physical energies.

A philosopher of religion like John Hick, who has written a great deal on the subject, believes that all religions are true insofar as they point to a "Real" that transcends them all. We can't really say what that Real is, but the great religions all point to it. This is their value. And whenever a religion serves to point in this direction and transform us from self-centeredness to Reality-centeredness, then a religion is true. Any religion can be true in this way. This approach pays special attention to the object of religion and the influence it has on us.

Another student of religions, Wilfred Cantwell Smith, also an author of many influential books, is more interested in the subject of religion, that is, the inner mind and heart of the believer. For him, faith is at the heart of all religions. Whether the content of that faith is Jesus, or the Qur'an, or Buddha, or Krishna, or whatever, is not so important. What really matters is that there is faith, an attitude of devotion, trust, sincerity, and the like. Again, any religion worth being called a religion is true in this way.

Yet another student of religions, Paul Knitter, whose book *No Other Name?* has been very widely read and who continues to write extensively, looks at it a bit differently. He is not so much interested in the object of religion (the Real), or in the subjective side of religion (feeling and faith), but in the behavior that religion leads to. Only when a religion leads to liberating behavior, especially justice for the poor and the oppressed, is it truly serving its purpose. Again, almost any religion, almost any belief, can contribute to this. Belief in Jesus, of course, has through the ages been very important for many in serving this purpose. But so also has belief in other deities and truths. What really matters is whether or not that behavioral purpose has been served.[3]

All of these perspectives see religions as a partial truth that serves an end that is greater than them all. These writers—Hick, Smith, and Knitter—call themselves pluralists. By this they mean that there are plural ways to the one truth. The one thing important for us to do, they say, is to find which of these ways best suits us and then believe and live that way to the best of our ability.

Problems with the Reasons

Frankly, I cannot with integrity agree with the pluralist conclusions. Why? First, all of these arguments are made in a way that places these individuals outside of any particular religious tradition, as they operate from a position of knowledge superior to any particular religious commitment. I could not do that. These philosophers are like the king in the story of the blind men and the elephant. Only the king knows the higher truth—that the thing the blind men are perceiving in their limited ways—is actually an elephant. Or, these philosophers are the only ones who can see the whole mountain and thus know that all paths lead to the top. But I think that anyone who claims to know what all religions are really about, despite what religious believers themselves might say they are about, knows too much. Such a person is claiming to know what believers intend better than the believers themselves do. In other words, each of these persons takes, so to speak, a "God's eye view." In fact, no one can see things from that perspective, and I consider claiming such a perspective to be intellectually dishonest. We are only earthbound, even those who make claims to such higher knowledge. We are all living in a history and a context. No one stands on higher ground here, not Muslim, Buddhist, or Christian, much less someone who claims to know more about these religions than the followers of the religions them-selves claim to know.

Second, all of these views make a distinction between the intention or content or inside of a religion and what is considered to be its outer form of beliefs and practices. I cannot accept the idea that the intention is what matters and that the form is secondary. The claim is essentially that all religions intend to get to the top of the mountain, but the path taken, what is believed and done, is secondary. Of course one needs to take some path, but one could just as well jump from one path to the other and still get to the same place. What one believes, then, doesn't really matter after all. Pluralists might compare religion to a tube. What is important is that the tube lets the water pass through. The tube itself is merely a channel, a passageway. Thus, we should not get too excited about Jesus or the Qur'an or Krishna, since they are only the channels for something much more wonderful than these beliefs themselves. The religions are the outer form. The Real to which they point, or the faith that they instill, or the behavior that they incite is what really counts. This is their real content. But I can't accept this dualism of real content and utilitarian form.

Third, all of these views assume something about the religions that I think is simply false. They assume that all religions seek the same goal, the same salvation, the same end. If one listens to what the religions themselves say is the goal and end they seek, I don't see how one can make such an assumption. If we want to find what end a religion seeks, then let us listen to that religion and learn from it. What does the Buddhist really want? Let us listen to the Buddhist. What does the Jewish believer really want, or the Muslim, or Hindu, or Shintoist, or New Age practitioner? Let us listen to them. It is very possible that the many religions seek many different forms of salvation. Let them define their own salvation. No Buddhist that I know wants her or his faith to serve a Christian end—an unending relationship with God. The Buddhist really does want what the Buddhist calls nirvana. Let us take that with all seriousness. The aim of a particular religion and the pattern of life it commends are inseparable.[4] One can disagree with another and yet take the other seriously. But to separate practice from belief, that is, to separate what a believer regards to be inseparable, is in fact to belittle the religious commitment itself.

An illustration from a different field may be helpful here. The United States' system of government is enshrined in the Constitution. Citizens of the United States know there are many other governments in the world besides theirs. Do they, therefore, say that the goal of all governments is the same? It is, in a sense. They all seek justice of some kind. But that only tells us something very general about government and is really not very helpful. We want to know, what justice? The understanding of justice in Nazi Germany meant that genocide was permitted. Communism had its own idea of justice and within that understanding of justice, freedom of religion and freedom of the press, among other things, were not permitted. The U.S. democratic government evolved from what used to be a society of kings and subjects and before that a feudal society. In each case, the understanding of justice was quite different. Do we therefore say that all in the end accomplish the same thing? They all do accomplish some form of justice, but the justice they accomplish is quite different. In talking of religions, one could simply substitute the word *salvation* for *justice* to get the point. The only way to identify justice is to live from within a particular commitment. Surely we would acknowledge that no idea of justice existing today is yet adequate. Therefore we can learn from other cultures and other societies and their understanding of justice. But we would just as surely not say that no idea of justice is more adequate than another. We would hardly say that all ideas of justice are just different paths leading to the same mountaintop of a just world—for example, slavery leads to the same goal of justice as does freedom, or rule by decree achieves the same end as rule by law and democratic process. That would be sheer nonsense. To say this would be to say something we don't really believe. And the moment we distinguish between better and lesser justice, we take a position from within one or another understanding and commitment to justice. It is no different with religions.

Let's set aside this image of one mountain with many paths. The world that I live in is a widely varied landscape. When I visit the West Coast, I marvel at the majestic, lonely Cascade Mountains—Rainier, St. Helens who blew her top, Jefferson, Shasta, and the others. All are part of a landscape. When driving or hiking I realize how important roads and paths are. They lead different places. That's the real world. Let's not be simplistic and reduce the many to one too quickly. Let's recognize the landscape within which we in fact live.

All religions are the same—right? Wrong. Let us listen to the religions and not to our abstract theories. Even more important, we might each ask, "In what do I finally believe?" What would that be if you were to write it in one sentence? If you're a Christian, do you say that Jesus Christ is more important to you than anything else? Or might there be something you feel is even more ultimate to which you are committed?

4

What Can We Expect When We All Differ?

Be Attentive to That Which Is Common

No doubt it is a matter of ordinary wisdom to say that we cannot have a good relationship with someone else unless we have something in common. I remember as a child seeing advertisements for carnivals and circuses that had some abnormal human beings on display—a dwarf, someone with six fingers and toes, Siamese twins, or whatever. Of course these "freaks" that were put on display were still human beings. But we tended to forget what they shared in common with the rest of us and only paid attention to what was strange, abnormal, or different. So they became objects like animals in a zoo. We were inattentive to that which was common. Today we don't think of freaks; rather, we think of people challenged in one way or another. That has the merit of reminding us of that which, even though different, we share in common.

The Christian has many very good reasons for being attentive to that which is common when we consider other religions and people of other commitments. Were we not to recognize this we might end up thinking that everyone who was different from us was odd, unworthy of our interest, dangerous, or someone to take advantage of. When we discover something of great worth shared in common, then we begin to relate to others as people, neighbors, and even friends.

What are some of the good reasons a Christian has to pay attention to that which is common? We believe in one God who alone created the world. We thus all have a common origin. We come from the same earth and return finally to the same earth. It was into Adam, who represents all of us, that God breathed the breath of life. We share something profoundly common in the very roots of our existence. We share a common world, we share a common humanity, we also live from a common divine source. Indeed, we are all created in God's image.[1] This image has not been lost, though it has been distorted by our human failure before God. But not only has God created us, God also reveals something of God's self to all people. All of creation is a sign pointing to God. Nature even speaks:

The heavens are telling the glory of God;
  and the firmament proclaims his handiwork.
Day to day pours forth speech,
  and night to night declares knowledge.
There is no speech, nor are there words;
  their voice is not heard;
Yet their voice goes out through all the earth,
  and their words to the end of the world.[2]

This is quite a remarkable passage, isn't it? Nature doesn't speak and yet it speaks for all to hear! Paul too talks about this in Romans 1, as do many other places in the Bible.

But not just nature gets into the act. Throughout history God has revealed God's self among the nations. At points the Old Testament even hints that Exodus and Covenant are signs of the way God works with all people. "O People of Israel," God says, "Did I not bring Israel up from the land of Egypt, and the Philistines from Caphtor and the Arameans from Kir?"[3] Isaiah even envisions the day when Israel and its enemies will be joint witnesses to God's covenant. "On that day Israel will be the third with Egypt and Assyria . . . whom the LORD of hosts has blessed, saying, 'Blessed be Egypt my people, and Assyria the work of my hands, and Israel my heritage'" (19:24-25).

It is not strange, therefore, that we repeatedly see the people of the nations portrayed in a very positive light. As starters one thinks of Melchizedek of Salem,[4] Baalam from the region of the Euphrates,[5] Naaman of Syria.[6] Even Cyrus, if unknowingly, becomes a servant of God.[7] And Malachi contains those unexpected and cryptic words, which report that the religious cults of the nations do more honor to God than the cult of the Israelites: "For from the rising of the sun to its setting my name is great among the nations, and in every place incense is offered to my name, and a pure offering; for my name is great among the nations, says the LORD of hosts."[8]

Not only do we have a common share in God's creation as well as God's revelation, we also all have a continuing share in God's ongoing presence in the world through the Spirit. The Spirit is the power of God that hovered over the original chaos.[9] The Spirit gives wisdom in all kinds of skills and arts.[10] The Spirit is the power of God that searches the very mind of God.[11] The Spirit is that presence of God that articulates the longing for freedom of the cosmos itself.[12] This Spirit is like the wind, which blows hither and thither and cannot be pinned down.[13] But whatever it does, it gives life to all things[14] and brings transformation into life.[15] Thus, the Spirit is at work everywhere in the world, and the same Spirit that animates the church, giving to it its life, whether that life be expressed in community,[16] in prayer,[17] in confession,[18] in proclamation,[19] or discernment.[20]

Since we believe these things, Christians have every reason to be interested in the world, including most certainly, interest in other religions. And we should not imagine that areas which we share in common with other religions are trivial. Let me share an experience.

Experiencing something deeply in common with the Muslims happened to me in a rather profound way some years ago. I had been asked by the local Muslim community to participate in a dialogue with a Muslim apologist. On the night of Good Friday that year, someone else was to meet this controversialist in a discussion about the Trinity and the Unity of God. I was not able to attend that evening, but I was scheduled to appear the next day, on Saturday before Easter Sunday. An urgent telephone call I received late on Friday night from a deeply concerned Christian indicated that not all had gone well for the Christian side. He wanted to come and tell me how to prevent a second disaster on Saturday. He wanted to show me how to make some knockdown arguments that would shut the mouths of the Muslims. I was chagrined but had to oblige his visit. At noon the next day some four hundred or more people, mostly Muslims and a few Christians, gathered in the Great Hall of the student union at the nearby university. We had about three hours together.

I was asked first to present for thirty minutes what I had to say on the Christian understanding of the Bible and the Qur'an. Badawi, the Muslim controversialist, then gave his understanding of the same topic. I then responded to him and he responded to me. At that point the floor was opened to the audience to pose questions. A long line immediately formed at the microphone on the floor.

Up to this point I thought things had gone quite well. We had genuinely exchanged views. I was not therefore ready for the first question, though I probably should have been. A young man, by his dress I judged he was perhaps from Nigeria, simply shouted out the challenge: "Why are Christians so violent?"

I did the best I could, making a few brief comments about the Christian teaching about love and the Christian failure to live up to that call. I referred to some of the primary historical instances of that Christian failure, ranging from crusades to Palestine. And then I concluded with a measured comment to this effect: "Yes, we Christians have much for which to repent. But I think both Christians and Muslims have much for which to repent." After a pause, I said "That is why we both need a God of mercy!" I was stunned by a hushed "Ahhhh" that went through the whole crowd. "Yes," that hush seemed to say, "that is why we both need a God of mercy."

The hush was thunderous and startled me into awareness of how much and how deeply we as Christians and Muslims do indeed share. Insights of this kind do not come often in one's life, but when they do come they permanently shape the assumptions from which one proceeds from then on. That evening, at the gracious invitation of our Muslim hosts, my wife and I spent several hours at the Muslim center and joined with them as they broke the fast of Ramadan, participated in their mosque supper, and sat in attendance as they queried Badawi about matters that concerned them in their faith and life.

What we share, then, with people of other religions can be very precious indeed. What is held in common, may of course be quite different with each different religious community. But let us be attentive to that which we have in common.

Be Alert to That Which Is Different

If what we hold in common with our neighbor of another religion makes a relationship possible, it is what is different that makes it significant. For example, people do not give their lives for what we all agree on or find we have in common. People give their lives because of that which is different. Difference is fraught with significance.

Every religion is unique. Who would argue against that? So also is the Christian faith unique. Of course, to say something is unique isn't the same as saying it is the best or most true. That is a different question we will talk about in a later chapter.

What, then, is unique to the Christian faith? What does the Christian witness contain that all other religions lack? The answer is obvious—any child should be able to answer it. What makes the Christian religion unique is the story of Jesus. The Christian community, alone of all the religious communities, grounds its life on the life, death, and resurrection of Jesus. Take that out and what is left of Christianity? Obviously, nothing. It is that story that makes the Christian faith unique.

But no story interprets itself. This story too needs interpretation. In fact to tell a story is at the same time to give it an interpretation. The earliest story we have, the witness of the early apostles, is already an interpretation.

They witnessed to Jesus from their perspective and experience. The story might be very different if we heard it from a Roman officer who assisted with the crucifixion or from a Sadducee who brought charges against Jesus. The Christian faith is founded upon this earliest telling of the story by the apostles. So it tells the story of Jesus in a certain way, with certain emphases, with particular insights. That is to say, they told it from the perspective of faith in Jesus. That is the way we hear the story, and it is the way we continue to tell it.

But as we continue to tell the story, we continue to interpret it in ever new and fresh ways. That is what Christian tradition is about, the collection of these fresh ways of telling and experiencing the story. Out of this collection and over time doctrines and confessions arose. Some Christians have told and even today tell the story in a way that other Christians find is not in keeping with the way the early apostles told the story. In other words, the story as they tell it is not biblical, not in agreement with the New Testament. And so the main body of Christians will not accept that way of telling it. Again, some Christians emphasize one part of the story, some emphasize another. This helps account for the very many different traditions within the Christian faith. Although we may each have a different emphasis, it still fits with the story as told in the Bible, and so Christians as a whole accept it as a faithful telling.

But what has guided the Christian community through the ages as it has told and retold, interpreted and reinterpreted the story of Jesus? The theologian George Lindbeck is one who has studied this question. He suggests that three guiding principles led the church as it interpreted the gospel story. These principles, he believes, were at work in the forming of the first major confessions in the fourth and fifth centuries. At that time there were many arguments about how Christians should understand Jesus. Some said one thing, some another. In response to these questions, the unity of Jesus with God was clearly affirmed, and so the basis was laid for the doctrine of the trinity. The Nicene Creed that most Christians confess publicly in worship is one result of these conflicts. What principles guided Christians in making their confession at that time? Lindbeck suggests three.

First, there is the monotheistic principle. That is to say, there is only one God, the God of Abraham, Isaac, Jacob and Jesus. Today we would also say the God of Sarah, Rebecca, Rachael, Elizabeth and Mary. Second, there is the principle of historical specificity. What does this mean? It means that the stories of Jesus are not make-believe tales, like the fairy tales we tell our children. These stories refer to a real human being who was born, lived, died and arose in a particular time and place. Third, there is the principle of Christological maximalism. That is to say, without violating the first two rules, one ascribes to Jesus as much honor and dignity as one can.[21]

Now I agree with these. But at the same time I am still puzzled. I don't think these three go quite far enough to explain why the church ended up making the confessions that it did.

Islam is a case in point. Islam too honors its prophet, Muhammad. And it too gives Muhammad all the honor it can without violating the principles of monotheism and real history. But Islam will not speak of Muhammad as an incarnation of God or speak of Muhammad as equal to the Father in dignity. That would be to them idolatry and violation of the unity and sovereignty of God. This is what they think Christians have done with Jesus and the doctrine of the trinity. God's honor has been violated by making something less than God equal with God. Lindbeck's principles don't help us answer why Christians from earliest times gave Jesus the honor that is alone proper for God,[22] let alone speaking of Jesus as the incarnation of God.[23] Why did early Christians do this?

I think something else very important guided the early Christians in their understanding of Jesus. It had to do with what they understood about God. God was not only high and mighty and majestic, but sovereign of heaven and earth, as if God were a bigger and better version of some earthly king or ruler. God's freedom, power, and sovereignty included the freedom to be bound to another, the freedom to condescend, the freedom to become vulnerable to that which was not God, the freedom to become weak, in short, to love. God is one who makes promises. To make a promise is to bind oneself to that promise. One cannot violate a promise and still be faithful. Making promises and becoming vulnerable are marks of love. And because of love God could and did suffer. We will have much more to say about this later. But right here it is important to note that this character of God is a necessary reason for why Christians ended up talking about Jesus the way they did both in the Bible and in later tradition.

Take away this difference from the way Christians speak about God, and one brings to an end what is unique about Christians. It is important to be alert to difference, not least this difference! But it is also important to be alert to what is unique and different about other religions. This we will consider in part 2.

Open to Change

If we are attentive to that which is common between us and people of other religious commitments, we can find many good reasons for becoming friends. If we are alert to the differences, then we will both know who we are and take the other seriously for who they are. These are necessary and important. But when we talk about being open to change, isn't that like starting to question our own faith? Not at all. It is, rather, to take both ourselves and the neighbor seriously.

We all know what it is like to talk with someone who has a closed mind. One might as well change the subject and talk about the wind and the rain instead. Having an open mind is not in contradiction to having conviction. In fact, it is the one who is uncertain about one's convictions that must close the mind either by substituting assertiveness for conviction or by denying the validity of any convictions that extend beyond a person's private world. Faith in fact is the perfect coming together of conviction and openness. Faith enables one to risk all, since one has a confidence that reaches even deeper than the risk. This confidence is in the faithfulness of God, who will not let go of one who has discovered in Jesus the very heart of God.

Later we will also talk about what it means to be a witness and what it means to dialogue. A witness always wants to make a convincing and persuasive witness of what one has seen, heard, and believed. This is so for us, and it is also so for the other. If we expect others to listen to our witness and heed it when and where it is persuasive, then others can rightfully expect that we too will listen and heed whatever in their witness is persuasive and compelling.

With these things in mind, I would like to talk about big and little conversions. In a big conversion, a Christian becomes a Jew, or a Buddhist becomes a Muslim, or a Hindu becomes a Christian, or a Jew becomes a Buddhist. In these situations the difference has become so clear, and the persuasiveness of what differs from one's present conviction so overwhelming, that one undergoes a change of the very foundation for one's life.

We all know that these changes do come about. This risk is always there for those who honestly meet one another and bear faithful witness. But much more common, and always to be expected, is what I call little conversions, the kind of changes that come about in ordinary life. We meet a person with a conviction different from ours in some way. In the process of sharing and being neighbor to each other, we each influence the other. Perhaps one comes to appreciate one's neighbor in a new way and has a better understanding of his or her conviction. Perhaps one sees one's own faith in a new light. Perhaps new ways of looking at things and new vistas and new possibilities open up. All of these happen in a way that sustains and nourishes the faith with which one began. It is a deeper entrance into one's own faith. It is an enrichment that ultimately is beneficial both to oneself as well as to how one deals with others.

I have experienced many such little conversions. I will share one of these. In the 1960s, while working in Hong Kong, I attended lectures at a graduate program in Chinese studies at what was then called New Asia College. It was led by several leading Chinese Confucian scholars. While I was there I heard that the mother of T'ang Chun-yi, one of the professor's whose lectures I was attending, had died back in China. Because of the "bamboo curtain" between China and the British colony, travel between the two countries was very restricted, and T'ang was unable to return for her funeral. Instead, he arranged for a memorial service at a small temple in Hong Kong. I decided to attend.

About fifty students and professors gathered at the temple for the event. Some Buddhist monks were chanting sutras to one side. As a good filial son, T'ang was honoring his mother's devotion to Buddhism. T'ang himself was up in front dressed in sackcloth. At front and center was a flower wreath, his mother's picture, and incense. Everyone was quietly waiting for the arrival of Ch'ien Mu, a noted historian, who was to perform the ritual. Ch'ien Mu stood less than five feet tall as I recall, yet he cut an impressive figure dressed, as he always was, in his blue Confucian scholar's gown. After some time his arrival was announced. The group opened up to let Ch'ien Mu through, who strode forward with grave steps to stand before the memorial shrine. Ch'ien bowed deeply, and the whole group bowed with him. Standing in the back, I remained standing upright, perhaps only slightly nodding my head. It was absolutely quiet. A second time he bowed, and all with him. A third time they bowed together. Stubbornly, I remained upright. Then, he slowly turned and walked out whence he had come. The ritual was over. At that point I resolved that I would never let this happen to me again. Was I worried about idolatry? Whatever the reason, it had made me unable to share in the grief of a filial son as he honored his mother for whom he was unable to perform the deeds expected of a filial son. I had closed myself off from sharing that grief.

I believe this little conversion I underwent was the result of the Spirit's work. Doubtless the Spirit of God was present that day. I believe it spoke to me. Is it the Spirit that calls a filial son to grief? Is it the Spirit that draws friends and colleagues to share in the mourning? Is it the Spirit that invites us to honor one another, not least those who have recently died? Might the Spirit even have had something to do with the chanting of the Buddhist monks, who were doubtless chanting sutras that sought to extend mercy to the undeserving? I believe that these things reflect the universal dimension of the Spirit's activity. In contrast, I was so constrained by my concern for the specific tie with the Word who is Jesus Christ that I shut myself off from the universal work of the Spirit.

We need to be open to such little conversions all along through life. Luther made much of our need to return daily to our baptism. In baptism we are buried with Christ, dying to ourselves. I died to myself, a little, in the back of that room in the temple in Hong Kong and came to understand the Spirit of God in a new way.

Where Are We Now?

In this first part of the book we have talked about three religious families. We also talked about indigenous and popular religion, as well as mentioning cults, suggesting how they also had distinctive traits. With this general intro- duction to the broad field of religion, we then wondered if, after all, they might be accomplishing the same thing, even if doing so in different ways. We suggested several reasons why this way of looking at things is neither intellectually honest nor dealing with the religions in a serious way. What in effect that way of looking at things does is cut the feet of the religions to fit the shoe of someone's theory about them. No honest religion or person of religious integrity is ready to let that happen. The purpose of this discussion was to help us take the religions seriously for what they understand them- selves to be.

In this chapter we have completed what we wanted to do in this first part. This chapter has been concerned to help us sort out how we begin to think about and respond to other religious commitments. We have sug- gested a threefold attitude, one which is attentive to the common, alert to difference, and open to change. All three of these attitudes need to be pre- sent. Simply being attentive to the common ends up either making others look like us or making others fit some universal scheme. To just be alert to difference may cause one to dismiss the other as irrelevant or result in a very narrow understanding of the other, even leading to misinterpretation, quarreling, or trying to assert one's own superiority. Simply being open to change obviously will lead nowhere. Only with conviction can there be a real openness to change, because genuine change goes in some direction, not hither and thither.

If we were to connect these three concerns with our Christian confession, it might help us see why they are so important. To attend to what is common is to affirm the first article of the Creed, "I believe in God the Father Almighty, creator of heaven and earth." It is based in our faith in God, the source of all. To be alert to the difference is to affirm the second article of the Creed, "I believe in Jesus Christ, his only Son, our Lord. . . ." If the story of Jesus Christ is not at the heart of our response to other religious commitments, then we are not responding as Christians. To be open to change is to affirm the third article of the Creed, "I believe in the Holy Spirit." Note how in Luther's explanation to this article the Spirit is the one that "calls, gathers, enlightens and sanctifies," and that our faith is not our own, for "I believe that . . . I cannot believe . . . but the Holy Spirit . . . is the one who moves me."[24]

Of course, God, Word, and Spirit are involved in all three of these, but always in distinctive ways. In God's creating work, the Spirit moves over the chaos as God speaks. In God's redeeming work, the Father through the Spirit sends the Son. In God's work of summation, the Spirit gathers all things up into faith in Jesus Christ, who returns all things to God. It is a full circle, and we are embraced in God's love from start to finish.

With some sense of the map of the world religions, or at least a main part of it, we are ready to listen to what the followers of some of these religions actually believe, and, it is to be hoped, not impose our own theories upon them. Only then can we prepare our response as Christian people.

PART II
MEETING OUR NEIGHBORS

✳ ✳ ✳

It is likely that you have met people with religious convictions very different from your own. It is almost impossible to live in our world today and
not experience this. Maybe you know a Muslim, or a Buddhist, or a Hindu,
or a Confucian, or a person of New Age convictions. Perhaps a marriage in
the family has made this issue very real and personal. Or maybe you have
children or grandchildren who have taken an interest in these things.

Some years ago I taught a seminary class in which we studied some of the
things that we discuss in this book. One student shared something very
interesting with me in one of the papers she wrote for the class. She said
that as children she and her younger sister had been very close. But when
they went to college her sister took an interest in Buddhism, eventually
becoming a Buddhist. The result was that for some years they had not had a
conversation. It was very painful for her. After having read and discussed
Buddhism, however, she gained the courage to call her sister and renew
their contact. She said they had a good conversation, the first for some
years. Her newly gained knowledge about the beliefs of her sister made
them not seem so strange and fearsome. I imagine their conversation has
continued since that time.

This is what I hope the following chapters will help to happen. We need
not be afraid of our neighbors who hold other beliefs. They are a part of
God's world; they may well be God's gift to us. Let us get to know them and
the convictions that they hold dear. Only when we take a real interest in
them and their concerns will it be possible for us to share with them and
they with us what is most important to us in our different ways. Maybe in
this way we can all grow together. Maybe in this way we can begin to share
in a more wholesome way the same world that we believe God has given to
us all. When we meet our neighbors in their deepest convictions, we have
really begun to meet them.

5

Meeting Our Buddhist Neighbor

I Take Refuge

Some years ago, as I mentioned earlier, my wife did a research project in Taiwan on childhood cancer and the response of the Chinese family to this trauma. Most families showed a mixture of religious practices coming from Confucian, Buddhist, Daoist, and local traditions. To follow through on the Buddhist practices, one thing I did was visit monasteries and nunneries, as well as temples with which the particular family had been associated. A question I would ask of the abbot or other leading monk or nun was, "How does one become a Buddhist?" "It is something like with you Christians," as one put it, "You too have a rite of entry—baptism." He then described this Buddhist rite of entry. A person will come to a temple and in the presence of a monk recite these words: "I take refuge in the Buddha; I take refuge in the Dharma; I take refuge in the Samgha. I will resort to no other refuge over and above these." Normally one will also then take the five preliminary precepts: to abstain from (1) taking life, (2) stealing, (3) immoral sexual behavior, (4) lying, and (5) indulging in intoxicants.

This triple refuge, or threefold jewel, is universal to Buddhism. What does this taking of refuge mean? To take refuge, of course, means to find a place of safety from harm and danger. It means to be secure, in the protection of a power that works only for my welfare and the welfare of others. As jewels are precious and indestructible, so also is this power.

What then do the terms *Buddha, Dharma,* and *Samgha* mean? Buddha means "the enlightened one." It is a title of the historical person Gautama, who lived in the fifth century B.C.E. in what is today Nepal and northeast India and who gained an enlightenment that qualified him to receive the title of Buddha. It is something similar to giving the title of Messiah, "the anointed one," or Christ, to the historical person Jesus. One who wishes to be truly Buddhist takes refuge in this enlightened one. Dharma means "the teaching." As Christians we too have our dharma. One example is the Apostle's Creed we confess regularly on Sundays. The Buddhist too has a teaching to which one is committed and in which one may find refuge. Samgha means "the community," referring especially to the monks and nuns who have taken vows of poverty and chastity. Used broadly it can also include the lay followers who have taken the triple refuge and who follow the basic precepts. In the Apostle's Creed we confess, "I believe in the holy catholic church." That is something similar to the Buddhist taking refuge in the Samgha. In this triple refuge, the Buddhist finds a safe and secure existence.

What is the danger from which one seeks protection? What sort of a refuge is the Buddha, the Dharma, and the Samgha? These are the questions that will concern us in this chapter. A brief look at the Buddha's life will begin our answer.

The bare bones of the story of Gautama, who was to become the Buddha, can be given very quickly. He was born of royal parentage around 566 B.C.E., growing up in well-to-do circumstances. He renounced a happy life as he went in search of a solution to the problem of suffering. After many years of searching he finally awakened to the truth, becoming the Buddha. A life of teaching and discipleship in the middle reaches of the Ganges River basin followed. He died at about the age of eighty around 486 B.C.E.[1]

In the Buddhist telling, the historical core of the story of the Buddha is clothed in many elaborate myths and legends. These are important for later developments in Buddhism. In these tellings, the Buddha had had many previous lives during which he was a human being who set out on a path to enlightenment, becoming eventually an *arhat* or enlightened monk, and then a *bodhisattva*, that is, an enlightened being that has compassion for the suffering world. It was only in his final historical life that he attained complete Buddhahood.

He was not the first to become Buddha, of course. There were numerous Buddhas of previous ages, but it was his destiny to become the Buddha of our age. Over the course of these lives, through countless trials and tribulations, he gradually developed the moral and spiritual traits necessary for his future Buddhahood. Before his final birth he awaited in a heavenly realm, usually called Tushita heaven, for the proper circumstances of his birth to occur. From this heaven he could survey the whole of the four-continent world and select the best time and place for rebirth. It is Queen Maya that is selected to bear him in her womb and give him birth. In her immaculate conception of the Buddha she sees the apparition of an elephant entering her womb. He is fittingly born in a miraculous way from her side as she is standing. An earthquake accompanies the birth, and cleansing waters stream from heaven to wash the newborn baby. His birth is a cosmic surprise, as it were, for the birth of a Buddha-to-be is a rare event indeed. The infant immediately walks and talks, and his body bears all the marks of a great person. In one version the infant takes seven steps and says: "I have been born for awakening and for the well-being of the world: this is my last birth."[2]

He grows up in royal opulence, masters the arts and sports of the day, marries, and has a son. He gradually develops a revulsion towards this life of luxury, triggered by his four important encounters—with an old man, a sick man, a corpse being borne to the cremation grounds, and a holy sage. He renounces worldly life and sets out on the quest for the solution to suffering. Many teachers and methods are tried with no success.

Seated under a tree he resolves not to arise until he has awakened to the truth. This he does, after seeing into his numerous past lives and having had a vision of the endless and frightening rounds of existence of all living beings. When he has broken through into the truth about suffering he is severely tempted by Mara, the evil one, and his hosts. The Buddha calls heaven and earth to witness to the truth of his awakening. A tremendous earthquake and showers of flowers bear witness. Mara is defeated. Thus, his perfect enlightenment, like his conception, birth, and renunciation, is marked by cosmic wonders.

Having become the Buddha he seeks out former friends and in the Deer Park sets in motion the wheel of *dharma* (teaching). This first sermon presents the Four Noble Truths. The rest of his life is spent teaching others what he had discovered in becoming a Buddha. Large numbers of disciples gather around him as he journeys from place to place addressing all who will hear, including kings and persons of wealth and power. Living a mendicant life he forms his closest followers into a monastic order, the *Samgha*. And so, the triple jewel of Buddha, Dharma, and Samgha has been established.

These things having been done during a space of some forty-five years, he enters into complete and final Nirvana. His death, the Great Decease, is also accompanied by marvelous events in which not only humans but gods do him homage. His body is cremated and the remains of the cremation are distributed among his followers. These relics—bits of bone and ash—were eventually placed into small caskets and inserted into mounds called *stupas*. These became the centers of the community's ritual life, especially for the lay followers. Meanwhile, his monkish followers form their own monastic community. The rest is history.

The Samgha and the History of Buddhism

Beginning some five centuries before Christ, Buddhism was to become the world's first great missionary religion. According to traditional accounts of the Buddha's life and teaching, he gives these instructions to about sixty of his early followers to spread the teaching:

> O monks, I am liberated from all human and divine bondage and you too are liberated. So start on your way and go forth for the good and the happiness of many in compassion towards the world, for the benefit, for the good, and for the happiness of gods and men. Do not go two by two on the same road. Preach the Law which is charitable in its begin-ning, in its middle, and in its end; preach its spirit and its letter. . . . There are those who by nature are not blinded by passion; but if they do not hear the Law preached they will be lost—those will become converted to the Law. As for me, I shall go to Urubilva, the town of the army's chief, in order to preach the Law.[3]

After the death of the Buddha, the Buddhist community continued in two basic forms. One was the monastic community, which eventually developed a standard governing monastic life consisting of some 227 rules. For nuns there were more. It was within the monastic community that the teachings of the Buddha were also preserved and elaborated. Eventually this led to the formation of a body of scriptures called the Three Baskets. These scriptures were divided into the *sutras* or supposed sermons of the Buddha, the *vinaya* or rules and regulations governing the monastic life, and the *abhidharma* or interpretations by leading Buddhist thinkers of the teachings of the Buddha.

Over time a great variety of teachings developed, all purporting to come from the Buddha, leading to many different schools of thought within Bud-dhism. The single most important division that entered into the Buddhist monastic community was that between the Mahayana, that is the followers of the Great Vehicle, and the Hinayana, or those who were followers of the so-called Lesser Vehicle. Actually, the group today that represents this latter community call themselves the Theravada, or the Tradition of the Elders. They consider themselves to be the earlier and more original form of Bud-dhism. The word *vehicle* indicates that taking refuge in the teaching of this community serves as a raft (vehicle) that conveys one across the vast ocean of suffering to the farther shore of nirvanic bliss. An important difference between these two Buddhist communities is that the latter places great emphasis upon the monastic community and the importance of the monas-tic life for attaining full enlightenment. The former, the Mahayana, however, is based on the fundamental teaching that all beings possess the Buddha nature so that enlightenment is a possibility for all, lay and monastic alike. Therefore, it is the "great vehicle."

The second direction taken by Buddhism was in the form of the lay community. In the earliest times these lay communities tended to emphasize a devotional life centered on the stupas, which contained the relics of the Buddha. They, of course, always remained in close relationship with the monastic community, which in fact depended upon the lay community for its material support. At the same time the lay community depended for its spiritual welfare upon the monastic community. Monks and nuns would foster their devotional life and give them instruction. Eventually elaborate rituals served the lay community at times of death and mourning, in times of danger, whether from the human or the spirit world, and at times of celebration.

During the first centuries after the Buddha, Buddhism gradually spread throughout India. The most significant person in the dissemination of Buddhism was the famous king Asoka (reigned from ca. 270 to 232 B.C.E.), who played a role for Buddhism much like Constantine (reigned from C.E. 306 to 337) played in the history of Christianity. Asoka was a devout lay follower of Buddhism and sought, after he had brutally united all of India before becoming a Buddhist himself, to rule according to the lay Buddhist precepts of morality. He has since been revered as the model for devout Buddhist rulers. It was also during his reign that missionary ventures were begun, bringing Buddhism to lands beyond India, including areas to the northwest of India and to what is now known as Sri Lanka. Thus, by the end of its first five hundred years, Buddhism had spread throughout India and into some neighboring regions.

During the next one thousand years, Buddhism spread to become the main religion throughout Asia. Beginning in the first century after Christ, it began to spread into Central Asia and China. From there it moved to Korea around the fourth century and then to Japan in the fifth and sixth. It thus became the single most important religious influence throughout East Asia. Around the fourth century it began to spread into Nepal, and by the seventh the conversion of Tibet began. All of these became Mahayana Buddhist countries. Meanwhile, from the third century on it moved, often together with Hinduism, to the countries of Southeast Asia. Eventually these were to become the Theravada Buddhist countries of Sri Lanka, Myanmar (Burma), Thailand, Laos, and Cambodia. Vietnam, however, was largely influenced by the Buddhism coming from China.

In the twentieth century, Buddhism has begun to spread further, so that today there are numerous forms of Buddhism practiced in Europe and North America. One can quite safely guess that in the United States alone more forms of Buddhism are practiced than in any other single country in the world. Most important of these are Theravada forms of meditation, Pure Land devotional Buddhism and other sectarian forms from East Asia, Zen of various kinds, and the several varieties of Tibetan or tantric Buddhism.

Basic Buddhism

We referred to the first turning of the wheel above. In this supposedly first sermon, the Buddha declared the Four Noble Truths. The first is the truth of existence. This truth is that all existence is ultimately sorrowful and unsatisfactory. Everything bears the indelible mark of impermanence. Thus, the experience of the greatest joy is just the beginning of another sorrow. So the birth of a healthy child, an occasion of joy, is also the first day leading to that child's death. Marriage is a time of celebration, but it also guarantees that there will be a separation some day, for sickness and death will inevitably have their say. And so it goes with all things in life. Some may call this a pessimistic view of life, but it is, at least, an honest view.

The second truth is that there is a reason why life is experienced as sorrowful. This reason does not lie in life itself but within us. Ignorance and desire are the culprits. Ignorance is the intellectual side of the problem. This ignorance can be a practical sort of thing—we are aware of impermanence but simply ignore this fact of life. It can also be theoretical—we delude ourselves into thinking that there is something permanent. Desire is the feeling side of the problem. No matter what, we always put our own interests, or what we think are our own interests, first. We fear death and so desire life. In fact, the strategy we use to overcome this fear and to satisfy this desire is to cling to something—anything—that we feel can satisfy our wants. We cling to things that bring joy; we develop attachments to things and people around us; we strive for some sense of permanence, for something that doesn't just pass away. For many people this means they cling to the idea of an eternal self or soul, or even the idea of God. This is the reason that life is experienced as sorrowful. We cling to what is impermanent as though it were permanent. Such clinging is a clear recipe for failure.

The third truth is the truth of cessation. The first truth describes the real condition of our life as it is, impermanent, and the second truth diagnoses the problem. The third truth provides the remedy. This remedy is the truth of nonself. That is to say, there is nothing permanent, not even an inner self to which we can cling. All beings bear the mark of impermanence and nonself. If we realize this in a full and deep sense, then we will not experience life as suffering—we will, rather, experience life as it is—receiving what comes with equanimity, not demanding what cannot be, and living in a way that brings benefit, especially the benefit of awareness and enlightenment, to all beings.

The fourth truth follows from this. It is the Noble Eightfold Path. By following this pathway one can gain the needed enlightenment. It is a pathway that combines right moral behavior with the right kinds of meditation practices and the right kinds of knowing.

The third truth is the keystone to all Buddhist thought and practice. One way the truth of nonself is described in the earliest texts is to say that the human person is a composite of five factors. One of these is material energy itself; the other four are different kinds of mental activity. The person results from the joining together of these several factors. There is no "personhood" above or behind these factors. The person is not essentially different from, say, a car. We know there are assembly plants in which cars come to be. But a car is nothing more than an assemblage of factors—frame, wheels, motor, seats, and so on. There is no such thing as "carhood" over and above this assemblage. To be sure, the car is a single functioning unit, but no more. Take it apart and it ceases to be a car. The human person is not essentially different. The only significant difference is that a car is only an assemblage of material factors whereas a human person is an assemblage of both material and mental factors. But it is an assemblage nonetheless.

We each have our own distinctiveness. As a functioning unit of material and mental factors, we each show the uniqueness of the assemblage that makes us individually what we for a short time are. Realize this, and one is on the way to a nonclinging existence that takes life as it is, others as they are, without self-centeredness, and without trying to make the world fit what we might selfishly wish it to be.

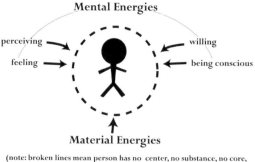

(note: broken lines mean person has no center, no substance, no core, but is a temporary collection of energies)

This is the heart of the dharma. It is to this that the Buddha awakened. It is to this awakening that Buddhism invites us to awaken. Can we?

Ways of Being Buddhist

There are many ways of being Buddhist, and we can only touch on some here. But common to all forms of Buddhism is the Triple Refuge. All Buddhists revere the Buddha as the first in our world to awaken to the Truth. There are, of course, countless other worlds past, present, and future with their own Buddhas. All Buddhists acknowledge the Samgha in some form, whether in its monastic or lay form. All hold to some common teachings.

The Buddhism of Works

Nevertheless, Buddhism is not quite that simple. I will identify three different ways of being Buddhist. All these ways accept the above basic teachings. These ways of being Buddhist are not equivalent to an institution or denomination, but rather they are orientations and practices that might be important to different Buddhist people. It is more like saying that there are liberal and conservative Christians than like saying there are Lutheran, Presbyterian, Catholic, and Pentecostal Christians.

The three ways of being Buddhist I will describe as the way of *karma* Buddhism, or the Buddhism of works; the way of *karuna* Buddhism, or the Buddhism of compassion; the way of *prajna* Buddhism, or the Buddhism of insight. The following diagram may help illustrate it.

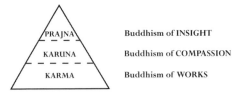

This diagram is in the shape of a triangle. This is intended. The wide base rightly suggests that the majority of Buddhists are karma Buddhists. The apex is narrow, rightly suggesting that those practicing the way of the Buddhism of insight are an elite minority. The broken lines between each of the three sections rightly suggests that there are no clear boundaries but that one or more of these ways of being Buddhist can, though often may not, be present to some degree in the life of any individual Buddhist.

What then is a karma Buddhist? Here it is necessary to pay attention to the way traditional Buddhism views the world in which we live. In fact, the Buddha shared with other Indian communities, religious and secular, the

same assumptions about our world. It is a view common to all Indian traditions. Life is envisioned as a circle or wheel, thus:

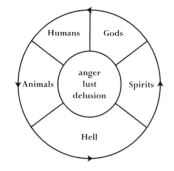

(note: anger, lust and delusion penetrates all spheres, thus the arrows)

The circle or wheel can be labeled *samsara*. This word means passage. The
point is that all of life is a continual passage from one moment to the next,
from one life to the next, without ceasing. It has always been so and will
always be so. There are different realms of humans, gods, animals, spirits,
and demons. All of life continually passes through these different realms.

What is it that keeps this cycle spinning? It is karma. This word means
"action" or "work." It refers above all to action resulting from an intention.
It is moral action and always bears consequences. In Galatians Paul writes
that "God is not mocked, for you reap whatever you sow."[4] If one removes
the word *God*, then we have exactly what the teaching about karma is saying. It is like a seed that is planted, which then sprouts under the proper
conditions and bears fruit. It is this moral power or energy in the cosmos
that keeps the wheel of life spinning. What I do in this life will bring consequences for a subsequent life, on and on and on for all eternity.

The notion of *moksha* or "liberation" completes this view of things. This
endless cycle of lives driven by karma is seen as dreary, indeed ultimately
fearsome. How does one get out of this ironclad rule of karma? Is there no
escape? Can one be freed from endless retribution? Of course, the power of
this question lies in the fact that everyone seems to do the things that create
too much negative energy. How can I escape the consequences of my own,
not to speak of other people's, negative actions? The various Indian religious
traditions offer different ways to achieve this liberation. Buddhism, as we
have seen, has its own unique insight.

But the karma Buddhist does not aspire to the heights of Buddhist
insight. The accumulation of unfavorable karma is so great that such an
achievement is impossible, certainly in this life. The hope is, rather, that by

living a modestly moral life here and now one can attain a rebirth in a better circumstance that provides even better conditions for moral practice, perhaps even for meditation and insight. Of course, the alternative is to be born in a less desirable realm—in hell under perpetual torture, for instance. Or, perhaps, one might even be reborn in heaven as a god. But even this is impermanent, and when a god's (or even God's) time is up the karma the deity has built up across the eons will take effect, for good or for ill.

This is the worldview within which the karma Buddhist lives. A couple of examples will show its influence in life. In the Taiwan study referred to earlier, one father deeply mourned the loss of his young daughter, whom he dearly loved, to cancer. He wondered why such a tragedy should occur to them at this time. He wondered out loud: "We have had no major problems in our family. Everyone is doing well. There have been no untimely deaths. My wife has difficulties from time to time, but they don't amount to anything. Why should this evil suddenly appear? Could it be that there is a hidden cause?" That everything had been going well for them was a sign they had good karma. Why should evil karma suddenly show up? The hidden cause he suspects would be the effects of karma from a previous existence, which until now had been hidden and which happened to suddenly ripen at this time and bring about the sad death of their daughter.

Here's another example. My wife and I went to a nunnery in the mountains near Taipei to visit the spot where the cremated remains of a girl had been placed. Here on the death anniversary day and at other times, rites designed to benefit the deceased would be performed. As we talked with the few nuns there, evidently not too well educated in their teachings, we asked how they would minister to and comfort parents who came there and had experienced such a sorrow. It was a question that they had not apparently pondered. A younger nun joined the group. When she understood the question being discussed, her eyes brightened and she said, "Taozhai!"

Taozhai means to reclaim a debt. That is to say, because of a past misdeed by one or both parents, doubtless something done to this girl in a previous existence, she had been reborn as their daughter so as to get back at them. The joy of a birth of a young child was followed by the pain of the loss of that child. It may seem unusual to us, but this was a common explanation for this kind of tragedy, and it brought a measure of comfort to the parents. Though they still loved the child and placed no blame against it, the idea that the child's death had set something right helped to make some sense out of an essentially inexplicable sorrow.

Of course, we should realize that there are also karma Christians. My
wife once worked with a child dying of cancer in Minnesota many years
ago. The parents asked their pastor, a Lutheran, the inevitable question:
"Why our child?" The pastor's response as reported by the parents was to
quote Exodus 20:5: "For I the LORD your God am a jealous God, punish-
ing children for the iniquity of parents, to the third and the fourth generation of those who reject me." This is the biblical doctrine of karma.

There is a measure of hope within this worldview. The hope is that by
behavior in this life one will gain a more advantageous birth in the next, and
the next, and that eventually one will have the chance to gain the necessary
enlightenment. Indeed, there is the hope of a coming Buddha, Maitreya
Buddha, who is the Buddha of the future. All who are reborn in that Buddha's
age will have the chance for final liberation.

The Buddhism of Compassion

We now shift to what I call compassion Buddhism. I will note two forms of
it, though there are actually many varieties. The first emphasizes the way in
which everything is part of one interdependent whole. I will call it a monistic form of Buddhism, that is, a Buddhism that stresses how everything is
ultimately linked into one. The second emphasizes the special promise that
a certain Buddha makes. This Buddha creates a distinct realm of joy and bliss
into which believers can be reborn. Because this Buddha is almost like a
god, I will call this a theistic form of Buddhism. Both of these emphasize
compassion.

To illustrate the monistic form, I will use a story from a Mahayana scripture called the *Vimalakirti-nirdessa*. It is a long passage so we will focus on
one of the main threads here. This scripture tells about a certain lay disciple
of the Buddha by the name of Vimalakirti. Let's call him Vim for short. Now
on this particular occasion it so happens that Vim has been sick for some
time. Yet, even though he is the Buddha's most accomplished lay disciple, as
fully accomplished as any of the monk disciples, no one has gone to pay a
sick call on him. As they were gathered together the Buddha wonders out
loud if it might not be good if someone would pay a sick call on Vim. No one
volunteers. The Buddha then points to one disciple and asks if he would be
willing to pay a visit.

"No way," the monk replies. "Why," the Buddha asks. "Well," this monk
replies, "I was once out in the woods sitting on a stump meditating. Along
comes Vim, and sees me. 'Hey!' he asks, 'what are you doing?' 'Meditating,'

I replied. At this Vim let out a big guffaw and said, 'Is that what you call meditating, sitting on a stump in the woods all day doing nothing? Why, true meditation is what one does in the marketplace amid the hustle and bustle of life. In the midst of all this one maintains one's equilibrium and equanimity and does what is appropriate for each moment. That is true meditation.'" The monk continues, "That was not the only time. Every time I meet him he humiliates me by his wisdom. I don't want to visit him."

And so the Buddha called upon others, each of whom had his own tale of woe. Finally the wisest of Buddha's disciples says with a shrug, "Okay, I suppose I can go."

The whole group follows as he pays a sick call on Vim. As Manjusri, the wise monk, approached, Vim looked up from his sickbed and said, "I see that with the air of non-coming you come; I see that with the air of non-seeing you see." Now you can imagine the conversation that went on between these two enlightened disciples, one monk, one lay. The upshot of the whole visit, however, turned out to be quite simple. Vim was sick, though he was not really sick, because he really was sick. What does this mean? Vim used the example of a parent and a child. Whenever a child becomes sick, the parent too becomes sick, and does not get well until the child gets well. So too with Vim. He was sick not with his own illness but with the illness of the world. His identification with the pain and sorrow of all things was so deep that not until all creatures achieved liberation would he become well. Such was his illness.

For the other kind of compassion Buddhism, I shall turn to Pure Land teachings. Around the time of Christ there arose a body of texts associated with a Buddha called Amitabha. This Buddha, like the historical Gautama, had a similar career. He began as an aspirant to become a Buddha. But this aspirant, or bodhisattva, began his career by the making of some forty-eight vows. They were vows, or promises we might say, that made his attainment of enlightenment conditional upon the liberation of all creatures. And so he made vows to this effect: "May I not attain enlightenment unless by my attaining enlightenment all creatures who simply call upon my name will also attain enlightenment." According to these scriptures, this aspirant did obtain enlightenment and became the Amitabha Buddha who has created his own Pure Land as his unique sphere of operation. All now who call upon him in faith can be reborn into that Pure Land of joy and bliss.

In China this school of thought gained tremendous popularity, eventually becoming the Buddhism practiced by the majority of lay Buddhists in

China. Over time a distinction was made between what was called self-power and other-power Buddhism. The Buddhism in which one gains enlightenment through the diligent practice of meditation was called the way of self-power. The Pure Land Buddhism in which one depended upon the mercy of another, the Amitabha Buddha, was called the way of other-power.

This form of Buddhism later received its greatest development in Japan with a follower named Shinran (1173–1262). Shinran was almost unique in the intensity with which he saw the human problem of karma. He recognized that he was totally devoid of any power to achieve enlightenment through meditation. Not only that, he couldn't even call upon the Amida (the Japanese pronunciation of Amitabha) Buddha with proper faith. Indeed, he didn't even *want* freedom from his desires and lusts. What hope was there for such a one? His insight was in many ways like Luther's insight into human unwillingness and inability to abandon sin.

This experience enabled Shinran to break through to a new level of understanding. He discovered that the promise of the Amida Buddha was in fact precisely for such as him, who were hopelessly bound in karma or, as we would say, in sin. As he himself put it, "If the good person can be saved, how much more the evil person" (*Tannisho* 22–23). That is to say, if as the Zen Buddhist claims, one can through meditation attain enlightenment, how much more is it true that a hopeless case such as he can attain liberation, for the power of the Amida Buddha is sure and his promise certain. Not even faith is a means to this liberation. It is simply the grateful response to a promise and mercy already given to the needy. It is not without reason that Shinran is frequently compared to Luther.

It would be hard for a Christian not to have some empathy for this kind of compassion Buddhism. While the similarities are truly striking, there are also some important differences. But these cannot occupy us at this point. Perhaps it is sufficient for us to realize that among Buddhist people there are deep, deep currents of the most profound compassion.

The Buddhism of Insight
Here we are at the heart of what Buddhism is really all about. In its truest sense Buddhism is much more than morality, and it is something deeper even than compassion. It involves a whole new way of seeing and experiencing the world. Buddhism aims to transform our consciousness at its very roots.

At the heart of the Buddhist view of things is the revolutionary doctrine of nonself, the Third Truth. Throughout the centuries those who want to be true to the basic instincts of Buddhism have always gone back to this doctrine. To explore this a bit further, let us imagine that we are in a Buddhist catechism class.

Recall the basic Buddhist teaching. We all experience life as sorrowful because we seek something permanent in what is only impermanent. This habit needs to be broken. Instead of believing there is a permanent self, we need to discover the truth that there is no permanent self. This is the beginning of all wisdom.

But, you ask, isn't there a "me" that feels and thinks and acts? Yes, indeed. But that me is only a temporary me. This me is the result of many prior conditions. When these conditions disappear so also will the me that you talk about. It is like the seed planted by a farmer. The seed has its own stream of inheritance. The farmer places it in the soil, which has its own composition; and the sun shines and the rains fall, each contributing to the seed's development. All these factors—sunshine, rain, soil—influence how the seed will grow. So it is with you. Your parents provided the genetic material in your conception, bringing two genetic histories together. Your mother's womb provided an environment of warmth and nutrition. All of these factors were dependent on time and space: just these particular parents, just this particular sperm and ovum, just these particular environmental factors. But one day the conditions that make possible your living and breathing, thinking and acting, will pass, and so will this me that you so earnestly cling to. Even in the Bible it says "you are a mist that appears for a little while and then vanishes."[5]

In fact, the mist or cloud we spoke of earlier is a very good image of what we are talking about. On a summer day you suddenly see a large thundercloud appear in the sky. Where did it come from? Perhaps there is lightning and thunder, rain and hail, strong winds. But then, after a while, as the cloud moves across the sky it gradually disappears into thin air. What has happened to it? At one moment it seemed so real, so real that it was even frightening. But now it is gone. We know that it arose from a certain set of conditions—temperature, moisture, pressure—and that when the conditions changed it disappeared.

Is there then nothing that is permanent? Buddhists have given somewhat different answers to this. Let us mention only three. In the very early texts it seems that the Buddha or his early followers believed that nirvana itself referred to a permanent state of bliss and quietude, devoid of any specific content to which you could give names—like box, or house, or person, or

God, or even mental activity. It was just bliss. It was contrasted to the world
of appearance, which is full of things and energies. It was nirvana in which
all passion and striving of samsara has been extinguished.

> There is, monks, an unborn, an unbecome, an unmade, an uncom-
> pounded; if, monks, there were not this unborn, unbecome, unmade,
> uncompounded, there would not here be an escape from the born, the
> become, the made, the compounded. But because there is an unborn,
> an unbecome, an unmade, an uncompounded, therefore there is an
> escape from the born, the become, the made, the compounded.[6]

One should not imagine that the Buddha, in speaking of an unborn and
unmade, means that this unmade is a thing like the objects of our daily
world. Much less is it God who made this world. He is talking about a state
of consciousness that is simply quiet and unmoving, about which nothing in
particular can be said. This state is in contrast to our worldly consciousness
so full as it is of anxiety, effort, planning, and bustle. If there were not such
a state to contrast with the worries of this life, then there would be no
escape from trouble and fear.

This then is one way the Buddha's teaching was understood. There are
two contrasting states of consciousness. In the worldly one there is a me, a
conscious subject, full of striving and worry. In the nirvanic state there is no
longer a me, just a simple awareness belonging to no one in particular that
remains uninvolved in the hurry and scurry of life.

There are two ways to imagine what it means that there is ultimately no
self, no final me. One way would be to think of it in the same way we think
of time. Time is an unending series of moments. I sit and watch the digital
clock as one second after another comes and goes. So it is with time, though
the moments or instants are much more minute—just a billionth of a second, let us say.

Or consider a motion picture. As we watch, perhaps we laugh, cry, react
in fright, become anxious about what will or will not happen—but we
know all along that these images are an illusion. It is silly because we know
that nothing is really happening on the screen. It just looks that way. It is
only a series of still pictures displayed in rapid succession across the screen.
Anyone who mistakes a film for reality is a fool, right? And so it is with life.
Events pass by in a series of instantaneous moments. We end up superim-
posing upon this series a continuity or a self that is not really there. It is one
moment after another, nothing more. We can depict the worldly and
insightful views of life this way:

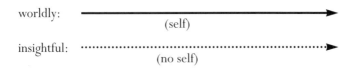

worldly:
(self)

insightful:
(no self)

Or we might think in spatial rather than temporal terms. I remember that as a child in Hartford, Connecticut, I once sledded down a hill and bumped into a tree. The tree seemed quite solid. But at school, under a microscope, I discovered that wood is full of pores and other hollow spaces. It's not solid at all. Scientists, using more powerful methods of observation, have shown that there is even more empty space at the molecular, atomic and subatomic scale. It turns out that the tree I ran into with my sled is almost nothing but space and energy. The Buddhist sees the self disappear something like that. There is no solid core to a self, no real me to hold on to.

One final example. Today we can experience a technology called virtual technology. Computer programmers can design programs to turn the pixels in our computer monitors on and off in patterns that create the stunningly realistic illusion of depth and motion. (As soon as the electricity is cut off we discover how unreal it is.) In a recent *Time* magazine I read about a new teen idol in Japan—a pretty, long-legged, micro-skirted sixteen-year-old singer named Kyoko Date.[7] She is becoming the rage of the country. She looks like a real human being to me. Yet she is nothing but a pattern of ever-changing pixels. She is no more real than these patterns of change. That is to say, she is as real as the electrical energy that generates her. She is merely virtual reality. So it is with the self. There is no solid core that fills us. We are empty. We are virtual. We are nothing more than changing patterns of matter and energy.

Are these factors real, like tiny atoms? Some thought so. But now Buddhists more or less agree that they are not real in themselves. In Zen Buddhism, for instance, everything is seen to be empty. This does not mean it is nothing, or no-thing. It just means it is empty of its own, independent existence. The bigger the emptiness, the greater the fullness. A thimble has a small emptiness, a tea cup more, a lake bed yet more, the ocean more still, space a virtually infinite emptiness. That is why it can contain so much. So too we are empty of self. There is no solid core that fills us. We are empty. We are virtual. We are no more than the sum of all the conditions, all the energies that account for our present existence.

Indeed, our emptiness is so vast that each of us contains the whole of the universe. That is our identity, not a measly little self. To attempt to make a self independent of these conditions is foolish. Rather, if we truly know who we are we will then be open and transparent to the entire world, indeed, open to the infinite, for the conditions that account for my existence here and now, this moment, are infinite. Everything is absolutely interdependent. In the end nirvana and samsara are not two separate realities but one reality seen differently—with insight or with ignorance.

My head always spins a little when I try to think through these things. The Buddhist, of course, thinks it is better to just meditate and experience through quiet contemplation the impermanence and emptiness of all things. Then one doesn't need an explanation because one has already experienced it.

The Practical Key

However abstract these ideas may seem to be, we should not imagine that Buddhism is essentially a head trip. Buddhism is above all a way, a practice, an experience, not a set of doctrines. To remind ourselves of this we should take note again of the Fourth Truth, the Eightfold Path.

We earlier indicated there are three aspects to it. There are moral practices, there are meditation practices, and there is insight itself. Insight cannot be separated from the first two. One cannot, for instance, be in a drunken rage and at the same time have insight. The two are like oil and water. Neither will one gain insight simply from reading books, however well written. The practice of meditation is integral to the attainment of insight. Of course, one can engage in moral living and never attain insight, and one can engage in endless meditation and also not attain insight. Attention to the basic teaching, the dharma, is also important. Thus, all aspects of the path hold tightly together.

What kind of persons can we expect Buddhists to be? If we take note of the three ways of being Buddhist discussed above, we can get some idea. One whose Buddhism is a Buddhism of works (karma) will not be very different from what I have called karma Christians. These are Christians who believe that living an upright life is important, who care for their families and neighborhood, and do kind deeds as occasion permits. While they really believe it is important to do good things, they also hope that they will be rewarded, or at least assured, of eternal life because of this.

Karma Buddhists think and live much the same way, though they hope for a better rebirth instead of eternal life. Of course, karma Christianity misses what the gospel is about. So also karma Buddhism misses the truth of nonself. But both will produce good, decent people, the kind we would like to have as neighbors.

Those who practice a Buddhism of compassion will show even nobler qualities. They will show an empathy in life for all suffering beings, not just human beings. They will care for all kinds of life forms; they will be vegetarians; they will exercise compassion to those in need of it. They will be the kind of people that will put to shame many who call themselves Christians.

And what about one who has attained insight? There might be different kinds. Some might as monks withdraw from the world, secluding themselves from the affairs of life. Others, because they believe that through insight one discovers the interconnectedness of all things, will have a sense of engagement with the world, seeking to bring benefit to others. They will be much like the Buddhists of compassion. Some, however, such as some practitioners of Zen or Tibetan tantra, may feel they have gone beyond the need to follow rules and regulations and stress instead spontaneity and freedom. Thus, Zen monks are often married, something that would never happen in Theravada Buddhism, and can drink beer and eat meat as much as any of the rest of us. Some might do even more astonishing things. You would probably find them very interesting characters. At the same time, all who reach the insight Buddhism speaks of, because they have trained long in meditation, will demonstrate the attentiveness, calm, and deference that such training instills.

Thus, insight, which is something that takes place in my consciousness, expresses itself in the practical area of morally wholesome living and the practice of meditation. With this in mind we shall say a few things about meditation first and then something about what is called today "engaged Buddhism."

Meditation

I am not practiced in meditation. What I say draws from what those who do practice meditation have to say about it. The whole subject itself is enormously complex, and it would not serve our purpose here to discuss it at length. Essentially, two kinds of meditation are widely practiced.[8] One form of meditation concentrates on some object, like a spot on the floor or a *mandala* (a symmetrical design or drawing of Buddhas and other figures).

It can lead to different results. One result could be that one becomes in effect unconscious for a period of time. One's breathing and other physiological functions slow down. It is like a catatonic state. One can enter it for a designated period of time and then at the right moment pop out of it. (This kind of meditation, however, is more closely related to the practices of Hindu yogis.) The practice of concentration can also lead to powerful mental gymnastics. In the case of Tibetan tantra, one can create any images one wants, which are as clear or clearer to the mind than actual things as seen with the eyes. So one can visualize a Buddha, or a demon, or whatever, and then mentally manipulate that image—like a computer can manipulate an image it creates—and ultimately identify one's own self with that image, so the two become one. In this way one gains complete control of the Buddha and so becomes as the Buddha oneself.

The more specifically Buddhist style of meditation, however, is rather different. Instead of concentration upon one thing, it is the practice of awareness, especially the awareness of the impermanence of all things. One of the less delightful ways of practicing this awareness is to contemplate a corpse, becoming aware of its previous relation to a living body and what now transpires with it as it begins to rot and the worms eat it. This is considered a worthwhile meditation subject especially for those who tend to lead an overly indulgent life.[9] Any candidates for this meditation?

The more common practice is to mix elements of both kinds of meditation together. Thus, in Zen one takes a position—preferably the full lotus position—and then concentrates one's attention upon one's breathing. What happens? One soon finds that whenever one becomes quiet the mind starts manufacturing all kinds of ideas: what time is it? what is that noise? did I remember to . . . ? and so on and so on. But in meditation one learns not to cling to these ideas or anxieties. One just lets them pass on their way, like unexpected guests who drop by to say hello and then pass on. One simply takes note of how impermanent these mental activities are. Eventually, when the mind finds nobody is noticing it, like a naughty child who is ignored, it will begin to quiet down. Then one begins to become aware of the breathing in and the breathing out in new and deeper ways. One becomes intimately aware of what is happening with the body. One becomes at the same time more clearly aware of everything about one. One senses how everything is changing and impermanent—mind, body, world. So concentration combined with insight leads also to expansion of awareness.

An anecdote illustrates the difference between concentration and insight. Some years ago, scientists decided to use an electroencephalograph machine to measure the brain activity of a meditating Hindu yogi, a Zen monk, and a Trappist priest. First in the experiment was the yogi, who promptly went into a trance. The scientists made noises and other disturbances, but the yogi was unperturbed and the EEG needles remained steady. Then it was the Zen monk's turn. He entered into meditation, and again the scientists made noises and disturbances. Here there was an immediate response. The needle moved up quickly, but immediately back down. Normally, as I understand it, the needle will go up and then gradually go down as one's attention to the disturbing event passes. In this case, the quick movement of the needle in the Zen monk's case agreed with Buddhist claims of awareness without attachment. As for the Trappist monk, the fellow got all tangled up in the wires as he was pacing around doing his devotions.[10]

It is through this practice of meditation that one becomes aware of the incessant activity of life and its continual change and impermanence. One gradually becomes attuned to the interdependence and emptiness (lacking a solid unchanging core) that characterizes all things. One's moral life will then comport with this truth.

Engaged Buddhism

A criticism that Christians have often made is that Buddhism too often tends to lead to a passive attitude to life—just let things be—rather than to an attitude focused on changing things for the better. It is not only Christians who have made this criticism. When Buddhism came to China this was also a main criticism that Confucianism made, including the criticism that it encouraged sons and daughters to leave their families for life in a monastery, thus neglecting their parents, or spouses and children if they had them.

There is something to these criticisms. But Buddhism has also throughout history contributed to social welfare projects. We mentioned king Asoka earlier, who is perhaps the single most important historical example. Today, however, many Buddhists, for a variety of reasons, have become socially active in what is being called "engaged Buddhism." I will conclude this chapter with a word about this phenomenon.

The socially activist Buddhism we see today, especially in Asia, is something new and unprecedented in Buddhist history. It is a response to the troubles that Buddhist peoples have suffered because of colonialism, foreign invasion, civil wars, westernization, various kinds of indigenous oppression,

injustice, poverty, and discrimination.[11] In addition, they have been influenced by the emphasis upon social responsibility so evident in Christianity,[12]
which has shaped so much of the Western ethos in this regard.

These Buddhist movements are taking place throughout Asia: Tibet,
Japan, Taiwan, India, Sri Lanka, Thailand, Myanmar, and elsewhere. All of
these movements draw upon something central to the Buddhist commitment, and relate that commitment to major problems that face their societies. Perhaps the most important teaching they draw upon is that of the
interdependence of all things, combined with selflessness and compassion.
The Dalai Lama is only the most prominent figure in this area, having been
a recipient of the Nobel Peace Award. Here we will limit our comments to
another important figure, Thich Nhat Hanh.

Nhat Hanh might be a new name to many. Yet he is well known in some
circles and has written more than sixty books, big and small, over half of
which have been translated into English.

Born in Vietnam in 1926, he was educated in both Theravada and Zen
Buddhism, though himself essentially Zen.[13] From early on he had a
reforming spirit. In 1950 he founded the Ung Quang Temple in Saigon, and
in 1956 a new monastic community. Active outside the monastery, he
taught in a high school and edited a Buddhist magazine. It was during the
Vietnam war that he began to come into prominence outside his country. In
1961 he studied religion at Princeton and in 1963 lectured on contemporary Buddhism at Columbia University. At the urging of Tri Quang, one of
the radical leaders of the Buddhists in Vietnam, he returned in 1964. He
entered into a host of activities, helping to set up the Van Hanh Buddhist
University, founding the School of Youth for Social Service, edited the official publication of the United Buddhist Church, and wrote poems and
books. He was critical of both the North and South Vietnamese regimes, as
well as the U.S.-perpetrated violence.

In 1965 he founded his own Tiep Hien Order, which combined meditation and social action. In 1966 he lectured overseas in nineteen countries on
behalf of the Fellowship of Reconciliation. He met with world leaders,
including some from the United States—members of the Senate and House,
Secretary of Defense Robert McNamara, Martin Luther King Jr.—and
appeared on television. King nominated him for a Nobel Peace Prize, which,
however, he has not received. In 1966 he put forward a "Five Point Proposal
to End the War." Because of his activism, he was advised not to return to
Vietnam by his fellow Buddhists, and because of the unsympathetic attitude

of the Communist regime to Buddhism after the U.S. withdrawal, he has remained overseas, mainly in France. In 1969 he headed the Vietnamese Buddhist Peace Delegation in its effort to influence the Paris Peace Talks.

He is now devoted not to criticism but to reconstruction and reconciliation. For some years he withdrew from public activity, focusing upon meditation and gardening in rural France. In 1976 and 1977 he was active in help for Vietnamese boat people. Based in Plum Village in southern France, he continues to work on behalf of political prisoners, refugees, the poor, and the needs of the Vietnamese people. He continues to speak and write widely.

His central idea is that of inter-being. All things inter-are. Nothing is its own. There is ultimately no self and no other; there is not absolute good or evil. All things are interwoven and ultimately one. His work against the war in Vietnam was directed towards relieving the suffering of the people. If all things inter-are, then someone else's suffering is equivalent to my suffering; somebody else's evil deed is equivalent to my evil deed. In fact, both sufferer and perpetrator are victims of their circumstances, of their karma.

In a short book entitled *Peace Is Every Step*,[14] these ideas are expressed in a very practical way. He writes of flowers and garbage. How beautiful and pure the one and how smelly the other. But we know that it is because there is garbage there can be flowers, and flowers turn into garbage. Each depends on the other. He then ponders young prostitutes in Manila. He realizes that they don't want to be prostitutes, but he sees that they are somehow forced into that life. But then he goes on to say:

> The girl in Manila is that way because of the way we are. Looking into the life of that young prostitute, we see the lives of all the "non-prostitutes." And looking at the non-prostitutes and the way we live our lives, we see the prostitute. Each thing helps to create the other.
>
> This is true, because the affluent society and the deprived society inter-are. The wealth of one society is made of the poverty of the other. "This is like this, because that is like that." Wealth is made of non-wealth elements, and poverty is made of non-poverty elements . . . . The truth is that everything contains everything else.

He then concludes:

> Only by seeing with the eyes of interbeing can that young girl be freed from her suffering. Only then will she understand that she is bearing the burden of the whole world. What else can we offer her? Looking deeply into ourselves, we see her, and we will share her pain and the pain of the whole world. Then we can begin to be of real help.

A poem by Nhat Hanh vividly expresses these basic ideas:

Please Call Me by My True Names

Do not say that I'll depart tomorrow
    because even today I still arrive.
Look deeply: I arrive in every second
    to be a bud on a spring branch,
    to be a tiny bird, with wings still fragile,
    learning to sing in my new nest,
    to be a caterpillar in the heart of flower,
    to be a jewel hiding itself in a stone.
I am the frog swimming happily in the
    clear water of a pond,
and I am also the grass-snake who
    approaching in silence,
    feeds itself on the frog.
I am the twelve year old girl, refugee
    on a small boat,
who throws herself into the ocean after
    being raped by a sea pirate,
and I am the pirate, my heart not yet capable
    of seeing and loving.
My joy is like spring, so warm it makes
    flowers bloom in all walks of life.
My pain is like a river of tears, so full it
    fills up the four oceans.
Please call me by my true names,
    so I can hear all my cries and my laughs at once,
    so I can see that my joy and pain are one.
Please call me by my true names,
    so I can wake up,
    and so the door of my heart can be left open,
    the door of compassion.[15]

6

Meeting Our Muslim Neighbor

It is not possible to live in our world today and not know that Islam is a powerful presence. Islam and Christianity are the two most widely spread faiths. Like Christians, they number over one billion people, about one-fifth of the world's population. Twenty-five countries are almost 100 percent Muslim. Forty-two nations have a Muslim majority. Seventy-seven countries have at least 100,000 Muslims. Not only have Muslims and Christians had a tumultuous history together for many centuries, even today Western nations and Islam are trying to figure out how to come to terms with each other. Often in our newspapers and on our televisions Islam appears associated with some sensational event. At the same time, Islam is gaining an increasing presence in the West, not least North America. After Christianity it will soon be the second largest religion in the United States, even though at present it is still only about 2 percent of the population.

One way to think about Islam is to make use of some concentric circles. I will do that here. Each circle indicates one major aspect of Islam. When all the circles are put together one then sees how Islam is a single dynamic whole even though it is filled with so much diversity.

Islam, the Religion of *Tawhid*

Tawhid means unity, oneness. God is One. That is the central creed of Islam. Muslims are brothers and sisters of Jews and Christians, who all believe in one God. But of the three, Islam is the most single-minded and insistent on this one point.

We can begin our diagram, then, with a small circle, the innermost of the cluster of circles we will use. We shall label it Allah.

The central confession that Muslims make is simple and clear. "There is no god but God." Or perhaps we could better say "There is no god but THE GOD." That is what the Muslim means by Allah.

One can get a glimpse of the awe and humility that the Muslim senses before God in this beautiful psalm from the Qur'an, sometimes referred to as the "Throne Verse":

> God
> there is no god but He,
> the Living, the Everlasting
> Slumber seizes Him not, neither sleep!
> to Him belongs
> All that is in the heavens and the earth.
> Who is there that shall intercede with Him
> save by His leave?
> He knows what lies before them
> And what is after them.
> And they comprehend not anything of His knowledge.[1]

It would not be hard for Christians to take this as their own prayer, would it?

That God is One refers both to number and quality. There is only One God, period. Moreover, this God is unlike anything else, singular. This profound sense of God's singularity rings through every pore of the pious Muslim. The Qur'an reads:

> Say: "He is God, One,
> God, the Everlasting Refuge,
> who has not begotten, and has not been begotten,
> and equal to Him is not any one."[2]

This is what they celebrate in the mosque, as they bow in prayer before God. If we were to miss this point, then we would never understand the first thing about Islam.

This One God is not static and far off, but present and powerful. This power is made concrete in creation and judgment. As creator, God is the sovereign over all things. All belongs to God, everything without exception. And nothing escapes God's control. On the lips of every Muslim are the words, *Allahu Akbar!* "God is greater." This is said because:

> To God belongs all that is in the heavens and the earth. Whether you publish what is in your hearts or hide it, God shall make reckoning with you for it. He will forgive whom He will, and chastise whom He will; God is powerful over everything.[3]

The worst sin is that of *shirk*. This means to associate anything with God. Such association would split God's unity. God's sovereignty is not to be compromised. To believe in any other god is *shirk*. To try to control God in some way by my own reason or strength is *shirk*. To disbelieve God's revelation and make it of no account is *shirk*. God and God's power is at the heart of all that is, of all that happens. Few words are spoken more frequently by Muslims than *in sha'Allah!* ("if God wills"), whether in commenting on the progress of daily affairs or in bidding farewell. The devout Muslim is always conscious of God's powerful presence.

And Muhammad Is His Prophet

The second circle we shall label Muhammad.

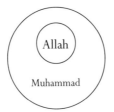

If the first half of the Muslim confession testifies to God's Oneness and sovereignty, the second half brings that sovereignty into history: " . . . and Muhammad is his Prophet."[4] To confess these two things is sufficient to make one a Muslim.

Not only is God a God of power. God is also the most merciful. In fact, "the Gracious, the Merciful" is the most common way the Qur'an refers to God. This God has given to us all good things—nature with its water, earth, camels and goats, trees and dates, sun, moon, and stars. "Do you not remember?" the Qur'an repeatedly asks. How wonderful to be reminded of these gifts of God. And He has given family and home, friends and healthy bodies, and strength to do and understand things. God's bounty is great. Above all God has sent prophets and revealed His wonderful will. No wonder we must praise God as most gracious and merciful.

The epitome of God's revelation was given through Muhammad—the Qur'an. Not only is Muhammad the messenger, the vehicle, of God's climaxing revelation, he is also the true model of response to God's revelation. In the figure of Muhammad, heaven and earth, so to speak, come together.

There is the tradition of Muhammad's call. It happened around 610, when Muhammad was about forty years of age. He was a pious man, and from time to time visited a cave on Mt. Hira near to Mecca for prayer and meditation. He was there on one occasion when the angel Gabriel gave the command to "Recite!" One tradition has it that at first Muhammad, taken aback by the experience—was it a hallucination?—did not respond. It came a second and third time, ever more forceful. Finally, it came with such force that Muhammad feared for his life and submitted to the demand, and recited. The traditional first recitation, on what later was to be called "The Night of Power," were these words:

> Recite: In the Name of thy Lord who created, created man of a blood-clot;
> Recite: And thy Lord is the Most Generous,
> Who taught by the pen,
> taught man that he knew not.[5]

In this incident we have two of the most important words in Islam. The one word is *recite*, which is the word for Qur'an. The Qur'an is a reading or a recitation. The Qur'an is the direct speech of God. It is not Muhammad's words, nor his own thoughts about God, but God's own words spoken into and through Muhammad. Nothing of Muhammad's personality went into the words. From beginning to end the Qur'an is God's speech. Muhammad only recited.

The second word is *submission*. This is what Islam means, to surrender, to submit. It comes from a root *slm,* which means both peace and surrender. In other words, in surrendering to God is peace. We might notice that Muhammad was much like Moses in the face of the burning bush. He too hesitated to accept God's call—in Moses' case, to deliver the people of Israel from Egyptian rule.

While not the first prophet, Muhammad was the last, the seal of the prophets. Adam, Noah, Abraham, Lot, Ishmael, Isaac, Jacob, Joseph, Moses, Aaron, David, Solomon, Job, Jonah, Elijah, Elisha, Zechariah, John the Baptist, and Jesus were among the prophets who came before Muhammad. Prophets were sent to communities of people, summoning them to heed God's guidance and, in some cases, to give them holy books. Thus, Moses gave the Torah, David the Psalms, Jesus the Gospel, and Muhammad the Qur'an.

Initially, Muhammad took up his task as prophet with fear and reluctance. Only through the encouragement of his first wife, Khadija, who became the first believer, did his courage return. He then began to preach further revelations to the people of Mecca. At that time Mecca was an important commercial center and the people were believers in many gods. Muhammad called them to believe in the One God and to practice justice in their business and social dealings. Muhammad himself had grown up as an orphan and from his own experience was acquainted with the plight of the needy. He warned them of a day of judgment should they not heed.

Most rejected his message. Both he and his followers faced considerable personal risk if they stayed in Mecca so Muhammad made arrangements for them to depart for Medina, some one hundred miles north of Mecca, in 622, for the *hijra*, or emigration. Here the Muslim community became formally established. A couple of years later the Meccans, annoyed that Muhammad and his community raided their camel trains, especially during the month when according to Arab custom all warfare was to cease, came to the attack. Facing overwhelming odds, the small Muslim band of some three hundred soldiers defeated the Meccans. This battle of Badr was a decisive turning point. In the following years, more revelations were given to shape the life of the fledgling Muslim community; more battles were fought, some successfully; the Arab tribes were united; and eventually the Meccans had no more heart to resist Muhammad. He and his followers made their first pilgrimage to the Kaaba in the vicinity of Mecca in 629, and in 630 Mecca itself came under Muslim rule.

In 632 Muhammad made his final pilgrimage to Mecca. He spent ten days there with his family, and the activities he engaged in during those days set the pattern for the pilgrimage up to the present. Traditionally the following words from the Qur'an were revealed at this time: "Today I have perfected your religion for you, and I have completed My blessing upon you, and I have approved ISLAM for your religion."[6] And with that the name for the religion was established.[7]

About two months after his return to Medina, Muhammad took ill and died with his head in the lap of his favorite wife, the fifteen year old A'isha. Umar, one of the Muslim leaders, declared to the people that Muhammad was not dead but would return and threatened anyone who claimed he was dead. But Abu Bakr, perhaps the closest friend and associate of Muhammad, went to the tent to see for himself. Seeing he was dead, he went out and declared: "O men, if anyone worships Muhammad, Muhammad is dead; if anyone worships God, God is alive, immortal." The people listened to Bakr, and believed him; even Umar said: "By God, when I heard Abu Bakr recite these words, I was dumbfounded so that my legs would not bear me and I fell to the ground knowing that the apostle was indeed dead."[8]

After the death of Muhammad the spread of Islam was explosive. In little more than a decade (by 644), Egypt, Palestine, Syria, Mesopotamia, and

Persia (the great Sassanian Empire) had been conquered. Even the Byzantium Empire was defeated, though it continued in weakened form. From there Islam spread like wildfire both to the west and to the east. In 711 Muslim armies entered what is Spain today. By 715 they had conquered Kashgar in far central Asia. By 732 it was on the borders of what is today France. About the same time it was on the borders of China far to the east, with Muslim troops invited into China to help quell a rebellion there. No other religious community has ever experienced such wide dissemination so suddenly.

The *Ummah*

The third circle we label the *ummah*.

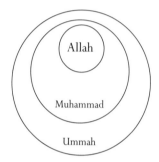

The *ummah* refers to the community. Those who believe in God as proclaimed by Muhammad, who are surrendered to God (Muslims), make up a single people or community. We shall briefly touch on the outer marks of this community, the sources of faith and the forms that the community takes.

The Life of Servitude to God

To become a Muslim is to surrender one's will to God's will and henceforth to live a life of service, even servitude (*ibadat*), to God. The public marks of this servitude are five. The first is the confession (*shahada*) itself, that "There is no god but The God, and Muhammad is his prophet." This confession is Islam. To make this confession is to take upon oneself this servitude. We have already indicated how this confession speaks first of God's oneness and then of God's revelation in history. Now we see that it creates a single people out of all nations of the world. Before such a God there is only equality, not superior or lower status.

This equality is dramatically demonstrated in the second "pillar" of Islam, *salat,* or prayer. Five times a day Muslims are called to prayer, and the devout heed that invitation. Devout Muslims observe these prayer periods.

The first is between dawn and sunrise, the second is just after midday, the third is in the middle of the afternoon, and the fourth after sunset. The fifth comes before bedtime.

All who have been in countries with many Muslims have heard the haunting call to prayer. Properly it should be done by a *muzzein* or person assigned that responsibility, one who has a good singing voice. It can then be most beautiful as the call reverberates through the town. "Allah is most great!" the muzzein intones, and then repeats it three more times, once to each of the four directions. He then continues: "I bear witness that there is no god but Allah!" once repeated. Then the second half of the confession follows: "I bear witness that Muhammad is the messenger of Allah," again repeated once. Then the invitation itself: "Come to prayer! Come to prayer!" This call to prayer is referred to as *dawah* and is the term Muslims use to speak of Muslim missions. He then continues: "Come to salvation! Come to salvation! There is no god but Allah!"

Muslims do not tend to be bashful about their faith as are many Christians. For them it is something of which to be proud. It is thus not uncommon to see Muslims partake in prayer in the most public, and seemingly unlikely, of places. I have seen them, for instance, engaging in prayer in crowded airports. The invitation to prayer is even whispered into the ears of a newborn baby so that these words become the first words it hears. The act of prayer itself involves several different bodily positions, involving the hands, standing erect, kneeling, and prostration. The act of prayer is preceded by a ritual washing of face and arms in a prescribed manner.

The third mark of submission is fasting. This is done during the month of Ramadan. Since the Muslims follow a lunar calendar, making the months shorter than those in the solar calendar, Ramadan slowly moves its way around the year as we know it. During this time Muslims do not eat or drink during the day. If strict rules are followed, one will not even swallow saliva, which would seem to be an almost impossible prescription to follow. Nights, however, are the time to enjoy life, eating and drinking heartily. This month is made holy because it was during this month that the revelation was first given to Muhammad.

Zakat (almsgiving) is also a sign of surrender to God. This giving is meant for charity, for the needy. The amount to be given is a certain percentage of any income over and above what is needed for the basic necessities of life. For example, if the income is in the form of cash, the expected donation should amount to 2.5 percent; if the assets are land and the like, then a donation of 10 percent of what is produced is expected.[9]

Some years ago I was invited to a meeting at the local Islamic Center. The question came up as to how the funds accrued from the almsgiving should be used. Could it be used, for instance, to develop the facilities and services at the Center or of the mosque? The visiting Muslim scholar responded that it was best to use it for charity, rather than for their own needs.

The final mark is the *hajj* (pilgrimage) to Mecca. Every devout Muslim hopes to be able to make the pilgrimage at least once in a lifetime. It takes place about a month after Ramadan. At the present time, one or more million people will converge on Mecca at the same time. No non-Muslims are permitted in Mecca or its vicinity at any time. It is believed that the Kaaba was built by Abraham and Ishmael. In it is a black stone, a meteorite presumably, but according to one legend brought from heaven to earth by Adam.[10] It is lodged in the northeast corner of the courtyard. The first major ritual of the pilgrimage is walking around this site in a counterclockwise direction seven times. The lucky ones will be able to get close enough to touch or kiss the stone. For seven days there is a series of rituals undertaken in the area that connects in particular with the life of Abraham, Hagar, and Ishmael. On the final day there is the most important Muslim festival, the *Id-al-Adha*. At this time animals are sacrificed to recall Abraham's offering of his son and the deliverance provided for by a sheep caught in the thickets. Muslims all over the world will join the festival, sacrificing a cow or sheep.

The pilgrimage is a profoundly moving event. I recall a conversation some years ago with some Muslim friends who were visiting us in our home. One of the women, a psychologist who worked with children, had a beautiful silk scarf on her head. A question was asked if wearing the scarf had any special meaning for her. Indeed it did. She said that she had decided to wear this because of the pilgrimage she made to Mecca a couple of years before. This was, she said, the deepest religious experience of her life. While there the sense of worshiping the One God with people from all over the world was simply overwhelming. She made a determination then and there to show some public mark of her gratitude to God. The wearing of this scarf was this sign. She did not consult with her husband or children. It was her own religious act. As it turned out, the children were a bit upset, because it helped to set them off from other people in America and made them feel conspicuous. But this was something they needed to grow into. Her feminist friends also took exception to her wearing this sign of what to them was subservience to men. She said that in fact for her it was a sign of her independence and a sign to others that she was Muslim and expected to be treated with dignity as a woman. Doubtless for untold millions of Muslims the pilgrimage has had an equally life-changing impact.

Sources of Faith

The sources of Islam are twofold. The first, of course, is the Qur'an itself. The Qur'an is the supreme miracle. It is the very speech of God, merely recited by Muhammad. Muslims believe that the very cadence and lilt of the language itself in the Qur'an is incomparable and the evidence of inspiration.

At first the people of Mecca did not receive Muhammad's message kindly. "They say: This is but a forgery which he himself has concocted and certain other people have helped him in this." The Qur'an, of course, refutes this, saying that "these people speak unjustly and lie."[11] It speaks further of the manner of revelation:

> It belongs not to any mortal that
> God should speak to him, except
> by revelation, or from behind a veil,
> or that He should send a messenger
> and he reveal whatsoever He will,
> by His leave; surely He is All-high, All-wise.
> Even so We have revealed to thee a
> Spirit of Our bidding. Thou knewest
> not what the Book was, nor belief;
> but We made it a light, whereby We
> guide whom We will of Our servants. And thou,
> surely thou shalt guide unto a straight path.[12]

Whether God spoke audibly to Muhammad, or whether he sensed something in his inner spirit, or whether it came through Gabriel as an intermediary does not much matter. What matters is that it came, and in a miraculous way.

The Qur'an itself is composed of 114 chapters or *suras* beginning, except for the first chapter, from the longest to the shortest. Its most important use is not what we think of when we engage in Bible study. Rather, it is the act of reciting the Qur'an that is its most important and praiseworthy use. In content it reads very differently from the Bible, since there is very little narrative. There are hymns of praise, there are reminders to heed God's goodness, there are warnings, teachings, laws, and regulations for life. There are many allusions to biblical or other stories. Overall it conveys a sense of God's rule and God's majesty.

The Qur'an is essentially guidance, showing to humans what God's will for life is. Because of this, it soon became necessary to supplement the guidance given by the Qur'an. As Islam spread in a sudden burst into the world scene, it became necessary to figure out what God's will was in entirely new circumstances. Since all of life is to be guided by God's will, down to the smallest details of one's life, including toilet training, and since the Qur'an could not address, much less anticipate, all these matters, it soon became the practice to inquire from those who knew Muhammad what his daily practices were. And so a rich body of tradition developed in various collections called *hadith*. These were collections of brief accounts of what Muhammad did in the various circumstances of his life. This indirect guidance from God through Muhammad's life then supplemented the guidance given directly by God in the Qur'an.

In addition, a large body of law that interprets both the Qur'an and the hadith has developed. Drawing upon the basis of the traditions concerning Muhammad, Muslim scholars drew analogies from their present day to make them apply. In such and such a situation Muhammad did such and such. Today the situation is such and such and so we can guess from what Muhammad did then that he would probably do such and such today. Through this process of interpretation and application, supported by a consensus of the community, voluminous traditions developed. In the first centuries private interpretation was also utilized. However, by the eleventh century it was decided that no further private interpretation was permitted. From that time on the practice has been to repeat and imitate the already fixed traditions. For most of the Islamic world this is the way it is today.

This has helped to create a problem for Islam to be able to respond to and change in the modern world. If the only guidance we have for life is already fixed, then how can we adjust to the new situations of today? It has become a deeply troubling question for Islam. What shall be done about different political practices such as democracy? How shall we understand the relation between men and women in our day? Is male dominance a given? Is monogamy preferred to polygamy? What shall we do about economic practices, like interest on loans, something condemned in the traditions? What about the severe punishments the traditions require for thieves—like chopping off the hand? And the questions go on and on.

The Qur'an is the primary revelation. However, it has already been interpreted by the traditions, and so the Qur'an is, so to speak, encased in or held hostage to the traditions. There are a small number of contemporary scholars who, in a sense, want to get back to the Qur'an itself, without dependence upon the traditions, something like Luther sought to do in his day. This, however, has created many troubling questions about interpretation. It will take a long time yet for these issues to be worked out in a way that serves Islam well at the same time as Islam modifies itself to meet a modern world.

Forms of Community

Islam is, of course, very complex. There are as many ways of being Muslim as there are of being Christian. But a few words here can be of some help.

The most important division in Islam is between the Sunni and the Shi'a. The Sunni Muslims are often called the Orthodox Muslims. The word *sunna* itself means custom, or customary practice. These make up about 85 percent of the Muslim world. The Shi'a, which is a word that means "partisan" or "follower" (referring to their preference for Ali to succeed Muhammad), make up roughly the rest. Iran, of course, is the most important Shi'a nation, being almost wholly Shi'a.

This division goes back to the beginnings of Islam. When Muhammad died, there was of course discussion as to who should succeed Muhammad as leader of the Muslim community. As it turned out, the majority wanted Abu Bakr, whose daughter, Amish, had been married to the prophet when she was only six years old. He thus became the first caliph or successor to Muhammad. The Shi'a however, never accepted this arrangement. They believed that Muhammad had designated his own successor, and this successor was to be a member of his family. The person they had in mind was Ali, who was both the cousin of Muhammad and his son-in-law because he had married Fatima, Muhammad's daughter. It is not surprising to find that rivalry between the women, especially between A'isha his favorite wife and Fatima his favorite daughter, reflected the division within the early community.

There are other differences between the two groups besides simply the question of succession. They also had different ideas about how to make decisions. The Sunni group wanted to proceed by consensus of the group, or of the leading persons of the group, while the Shi'a wanted the leader himself to make decisions for the group. The Shi'a had a more charismatic idea of leadership. Thus, even in matters having to do with the interpretation of the Qur'an, the Shi'a believed that the leader had a special inspiration from God to make right interpretations. The Sunni, instead, would not accept an interpretation unless it received consensus. The Shi'a also developed a complicated notion of a coming Mahdi. According to the majority of the Shi'a, for instance, the twelfth successor of Muhammad, whom they called Imam, not Caliph, disappeared as a small child into the heavens. There he awaits someday to return, when he will come to bring justice and peace upon earth. Finally, there is a great sensitivity to suffering among the Shi'a. Being in the minority, they suffered greatly from the majority Sunni, with most of their Imams dying violently at the hands of the Sunni. In particular they remember the brutal death of Husain, their third Imam, who was also a grandson of Muhammad. In a dispute leading to military action, Husain and his followers and family were surrounded by followers of the Sunni group at Karbala in present day Iraq and ruthlessly slaughtered. Since that time, the Shi'a have yearly remembered the passion of Husain. This often is reenacted by the very pious who will beat themselves to the point of drawing blood, thus experiencing that passion in a sympathetic way. Though the fundamental beliefs of the Shi'a and Sunni are very similar, these factors give the two groups characteristic differences.

The first four caliphs accepted by the Sunnis were Abu Bakr (632–634), Umar (643–644), Uthman (644–656), and Ali (656–661). Only Abu Bakr died a natural death. Nevertheless, for all the strife of these early days, these four have been historically considered the "rightly-guided" caliphs.

Subsequent Muslim history is characterized by its rapid expansion. We have already noted its explosive growth after the death of Muhammad. In 680 the Ummayad Dynasty was established. This was located in Damascus and unified most of Islam. During this time Arab language and customs were spread throughout the empire. The rulers themselves acted more like potentates then real caliphs and were generally not known for their piety. In 750 the Abbasid Dynasty was founded, located in Baghdad. This led to the golden age of Islam. But in 1258 Baghdad was conquered by a Mongol invasion. By this time Islam had already begun to split up into different states. There was the Islam of Spain (ending in 1492), North African Islam or the Berbers (750–1269), the Fatimads of Egypt (901–1174), and the Seljuks and Ayyubids of Turkey and the Middle East (1055–1243). As it happened, the Mongols themselves soon chose Islam as their faith, and as a result, much of Central Asia eventually became Muslim.

The defeat of Baghdad was followed by the rise of several centers of Muslim power. Most important of these were the Mamluks of Egypt and Syria (1250–1517), the Safavids who were Shi'a in Persia (1501–1722), the Ottomans of Turkey (1326–1924), and the Mughals of India (1526–1857) with roots going back to 1210. In 1517 the Ottomans commenced to unify most of the Middle East under their rule. The threat that the Crusaders and their successors posed to Islam during the eleventh to thirteenth centuries was repaid back to the West by the threat that the Ottomans posed to Europe during the time of Luther and thereafter. In 1453 they captured Constantinople and brought a final end to that city as a Christian center. In 1529 they laid siege to Vienna. The threat remained until their defeat near Vienna in 1683. From this point on they were in decline. After the collapse of Baghdad, the now-nominal office of caliph, a symbol of Muslim unity, was located in Cairo, and then it was transferred to Istanbul (formerly Constantinople) in 1517. This symbol of unity, for a now irreversibly fragmented Muslim world, was abolished in 1924.

Throughout this time Islam continued to spread. Beyond central Asia it moved into China; beyond India it moved into Malaysia and Indonesia; and beyond Egypt and North Africa it moved south into extensive parts of Africa. With the rise of Western colonialism, especially in the nineteenth century, 90 percent or more of the Muslim world was subjected to Western colonial rule. With the breakup of colonialism during the middle of the twentieth century, Islam entered into its present situation. One issue that has dominated relations between Islam and the West since colonialism is the establishment of Israel, with the support of the Western powers, on May 14, 1948. We still await its final resolution. Meanwhile, Islam has continued its spread and growth. This now includes both Europe and North America, where it is fast becoming, if it is not already, the second largest religion followed by the people.

Despite the linguistic, political, cultural, and practical divisions in the Muslim world, there remains a sense of a single community. This is fostered above all by the centrality of the Qur'an as an Arabic revelation, the marks of servitude to God of which we have already spoken, and perhaps most of all the increasingly important pilgrimage to Mecca.

Dar Al-Islam

The next three circles we will label as Dar al-Islam, Dar al-Sulk, and Dar al-Harb.

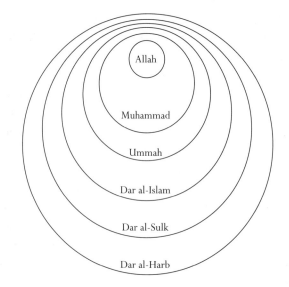

Dar here means "abode". *Dar al-Islam* refers to the Muslim world insofar as both state and religion are Muslim and means the *Abode of Islam*. Such places as Iran and Saudi Arabia would be such abodes. *Dar al-Sulk* is the *Abode of Contract* and refers to that portion of the world that is not Muslim but has good relations with Islam. Here one can include the relations between an atheist nation such as Cuba and a Muslim state such as Libya or the relationship between the United States and Saudi Arabia particularly during the Gulf War. Finally there is the *Dar al-Harb,* which means the *Abode of Warfare.* This of course refers to states and peoples with whom the Muslim world has a hostile relationship. The relations between the United States and Iran would be an example.

From the beginning, Islam has not only been a religion, but a political power as well. Muhammad in his own person, much like a Moses of old, combined both religious authority, which was his because he was the recipient of revelations, and political authority. This was also the case for the first four, rightly guided caliphs. Subsequent Muslim rulers tended to be much more secular, and political authority became their primary interest. As a result, religious authority gravitated increasingly toward to the Ulama, the interpreters of the Qur'an and the Hadith, who decided on matters of religious law as it governed the life of the people in their daily conduct as well as matters involving inheritance. In Iran this separation has taken a form in which the ayatollah, the acknowledged religious leader, does not rule in the political realm directly, but legitimizes the political ruler and the political program. In Turkey the opposite extreme happened, when the position of caliph was abolished by secular rulers in 1924, and a Muslim nation was declared a secular state. Here the political rulers define the boundaries within which religion must operate.

Dar al-Islam refers to those situations in which the political authority is in some way subservient to the religious authority. In principle, this is the goal of all Islam. In practice it is much more diverse than this. For instance, in North America, some Muslims hope and work for the day when America will become not only populated by Muslims, but a Muslim state as well. Obviously, this is a long-term goal. Most, however, accept the principle of the separation of church and state as a necessary and desirable political solution in a pluralist setting. In other words, the principle of the Abode of Contract is applied. That is, Muslims can live in harmony with their non-Muslims neighbors since there is no necessary enmity between and among the communities. It is only where hostility becomes the chief characteristic of the relationship that the principles of the Abode of Warfare come into play.

The Unifying Energy—*Taqwa* and *Jihad*

Through these several circles, and emanating from the center, we can draw two intertwining lines. The one line we will call *taqwa*. This refers to piety, in the sense of being devout and devoted. One Muslim writer calls this "perhaps the most important single term in the Qur'an."[13]

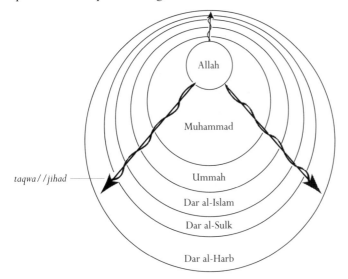

Central to the meaning of *taqwa* are two concepts. First, God has laid upon human beings the responsibility to act according to God's guidance. Humans cannot shirk their duty to act as God directs. Second, the judgment upon this action or behavior that decides upon its rightness and correctness does not lie in the mind or heart of the one who acts, but outside of the person. The final determination lies in God. This double situation creates a deep sense of "conscience," of accountability, of submission to the will and disposal of one's person to God. The whole point of the Qur'an is not to tell us what God is like but to tell us what God wants. Therefore, piety is not to know what God is like but to do what God wills. *Taqwa* is the deep interior realization of this, which then governs all of one's life and action. I think of Jesus' words to his disciples to "watch and pray"—so that one enter not into temptation and so that one is ready when the Lord returns—as precisely the call for taqwa.

The second term is *jihad*. Typically we think of it as "holy war." This is not entirely wrong, but neither is it completely correct. *Jihad* means to struggle or strive in the way of God. It is to seek to triumph over all that obstructs God's will.

Such a struggle encompasses the whole of one's life. Islam often talks about the "greater" and the "lesser" *jihad*. The greater *jihad* is the effort or struggle to bring one's inner life into conformity with the will of God, so that all one's thoughts, desires, and actions serve God's will. It is the desire for purity of heart, for the willing of one thing only—God's will. Thus, one must overcome one's weaknesses, of whatever kind they might be. This greater *jihad* applies to personal life. The lesser *jihad* is the overt form of warfare, overcoming obstacles to God's will that can only be addressed with military action.

To get a full picture of Islam, one might envision these two attitudes intertwining as they reach out from the center to the periphery of the diagram. There is a deep feeling in the heart of the individual and within the Muslim community itself that because God is One and because the world is one and created by God that the whole of reality rightfully belongs to God. It is to realize this divine lordship that is more important to the Muslim than anything else.

This commitment begins in the personal life, as we have indicated. It reaches into home and family. These too must become spheres where God's will is not only talked about but actually done. This reaches further yet into the neighborhood and community. The Muslim is under obligation to seek for the betterment of society, that society too might reflect God's goodness. Obviously this includes the economic life of the community. It reaches just as surely into the realm of politics and the state. If any authority needs to be subject to the divine will, it is the political authority, which has more power than any other authority to influence human life for good or for ill. Finally, where God's will is overtly obstructed, it may lead to a situation in which violent action is required.

Thus, all of life is to be brought into subjection to God. Humans were created as God's representative upon earth. Humans have been charged with the responsibility to fulfill this representative role.

> It is this mission—the attempt to create a moral social order on earth—which the Qur'an . . . describes as the 'Trust': We [i.e., God, Allah] offered the trust to the heavens and the earth and the mountains, but they refused to carry it and were afraid of it; and man carried it.[14]

Somewhat humorously the Qur'an both commends and chastises humans for having accepted this trust. They are commended for having taken up this awesome responsibility, which not even heaven and earth dared take up. But, humans have not yet fulfilled this trust, and in this "surely he is sinful, very foolish." As elsewhere the Qur'an says, "No indeed! Man has not accomplished His bidding."[15]

I remember some years ago when I witnessed the sincerity of these concerns. My wife and I had been invited to join the Muslims in our city to break the fast of Ramadan—though, of course, we had not been fasting as they had. It was broken with a glass of apricot juice and two huge dates. This was followed by a mosque potluck, where some four hundred had gathered. I joined my wife in line, until I realized I was the only male in the line. I quickly made my switch, though in the other line there was an occasional woman. Perhaps these women were not yet Muslim but there by virtue of marriage.

After our meal those interested were invited to ask questions of the visiting scholar guest. The rules of the conversation stipulated that questions would be written down and handed in for the guest to read and respond to. This was the way the first two questions proceeded. Issues raised were: "How can we instill Islamic values in our children?" "How do we determine the time to begin Ramadan?" This latter question led to a half-hour response. The complications in determining the exact time when to begin the month of fasting astounded me. Even international committees were involved. At issue was the first sighting of the new moon. It was discussed at such length, I gathered, because this community was a bit out of sync with most of the rest of the Muslim world.

This completed, a young man rushed forward demanding to ask his questions orally. He was granted permission and literally shouted out: "Is it *sunna* [proper] to mix sexes as we do here? Is it *sunna* to clap hands at meetings [as many had earlier in the afternoon]? Is it *sunna* for women not to wear head scarves [most women at the mosque supper did not]?" It was clear he was quite agitated about these issues.

The guest responded calmly and gently to the questions. Yes, it is good not to be careless about the mixing of the sexes. Yet, many of the women who come to our mosque are not yet Muslim. It is important that we be a hospitable community. We don't want to follow strict rules and make people feel uncomfortable. Moreover, there are different understandings among Muslims as to what is permissible and what is not. So we cannot be rigid about such matters. As for the wearing of head scarves, there is no point in wearing a head scarf if the reason for doing so does not come from within. We do not want to force people to conform. But when it comes from within, then it is a conviction. That is what we want.

The young man sat down, and the next question, submitted this time in writing, was whether the *zakat* (alms) could be used for the needs of the mosque or had to be used for the needy. The answer was: "It is much better to use *zakat* for the needy." Further questions were asked about an Islamic school for the children, about dating problems, about community aid in marriage, about birth control, about whether it is proper to take Christians and Jews for friends, and about how to help Muslims understand Islam more deeply. As to whether it is proper to take Christians as friends, I recall reading a guidebook for parents which said that it was preferable to make friends with devout Christian families since these homes shared values that were much closer to the Muslim values than homes where there was no religious practice. The guest's answers were consistent with this view.

There was one question that particularly drew my interest. It was the question about bank loans for the purchase of houses. A strict Muslim will not borrow money at interest. I was reminded of this later because of a conversation I was to have with Muslims from this community. Some years earlier they were contemplating purchasing some property, but it cost several hundreds of thousands of dollars. They didn't have the money. How were they to pay? They visited a bank and were given forms to fill out. When they informed the loan officer that they could not borrow money at interest, that of course was the end of the conversation.

They asked their lawyer what to do. He finally offered to see if he could find some among his friends who would be willing to make the money available without interest. Some days later he contacted them to say that he had some friends who would be willing to do so. The only difficulty was that they were all Jews. Would that be a problem for them? Their answer was, "No." And so, the Jewish community helped the Muslim community purchase property for their center and mosque.

Here we see the concerns of real Islam. A concern that shows genuine *taqwa*—watchfulness about behavior to make sure that it reflects the will of God and a concern, moreover, that shows *jihad*—attempting to overcome obstacles that hinder the full doing of God's will.

Concluding Comments

In this brief introduction we have missed a great deal of the richness and diversity of Islam. We have not talked about the important Sufi, or mystical, movement in Islam with its many brotherhoods. These have been decisive for the spread of Islam and are important for understanding many of the contemporary movements in Islam. We have not discussed the modern movements of Islam at all, whether reform or "fundamentalist" orientations. We have, however, attempted to give a fair representation of some of the more important themes that will help us understand the mainstream of Islam as it comes from the past and shapes the present.

It should be quite evident that the Muslim and the Christian share an obvious kinship. Such kinship seems more remote with respect to Buddhism, Hinduism, and Confucianism. These latter start with such a different worldview that it makes it more difficult to get into their way of seeing and experiencing things. Yet, these too are beginning to shape our patterns of thought in the West. In a unique way, Islam presents us with the challenge to live well with our neighbor, even when that neighbor, with whom we share so much in common, has a very different religious commitment. Such friendship is particularly difficult to come by in the light of the long history of enmity that has existed between Christian and Muslim, an enmity that is still played out before us on our television screens and sometimes even in our streets.

7

Meeting Our Chinese Neighbor— As a Confucian

W e face special problems in discussing the religions of China. It is easy enough to talk about popular religion in China, as we did in an earlier chapter. Buddhism, which has no God, still looks like what we think a religion should look like—rituals, worship, and so on. This is true also of certain Daoist religious movements which do have a God and gods—many of them. But Confucianism and the kind of Daoism we will be talking about later don't seem to fit so easily. This is one reason I like to use the term worldview for them.

In India religion is everywhere. You can't miss it. The person who has always been held in the highest esteem is the guru, a religious teacher or leader. In China the one who has always been held in highest esteem is the scholar-official. He is supposed to be a person of high virtue and of public responsibility. It is more a civic or political than religious role. In many ways, Confucianism looks more like what we call humanism than religion. Part of the problem is our own way of defining things. Let us simply accept that in China, besides what is obviously religion, there is also a long history of deeply set convictions that regard our human behavior as the most important thing to pay attention to. That is why in the first chapter we said that in the Sinic family our relationship with the world, not God, is of first importance.

Another problem with Confucianism is that there is nothing called "Confucianism" in the Chinese language. What we call Confucianism, as though Confucius were the founder of a religion or a school of philosophy, is usually referred to as "the teachings of the scholars" (ju-jia). What we call Confucianism is thus a deeply rooted tradition of wisdom, ethics, and philosophy in which Confucius did play a particularly original and creative role.

Heaven's Burden: A Boring Life?

We will begin with Confucius (552?–479 B.C.E.). I recall some years ago visiting his hometown, Qufu—almost no more than a village—in Shandong province. We stayed in the Confucian family halls and visited his nearby grave site. It was a quiet and uneventful visit, not unlike what we know of his life, which was, frankly, not very exciting.

He was born at a time when the emperor of the Zhou dynasty (1122–249 B.C.E.) was very weak, just a figurehead, and the many local rulers and nobles were vying for power. He was born in the small state of Lu. We know little about much of his life, though there are some legends. It may be that he was the direct descendent of the nobility of the long-defunct Shang dynasty (ca. 1766–1122 B.C.E.), but he grew up in relatively humble circumstances. If he had held public office, to which he always aspired, it was probably as nothing more than a police commissioner in his home state for about one year. He was fifty at the time. Some traditions say he was fired from his job. It was after this that the career for which he is known began. He gathered a body of students around him and in some ten years traveled to many states, peddling his teachings and seeking employment. Neither his advice nor his services were sought by the rulers. He lived to about seventy years of age, spending his last years in revising various ritual and other texts while continuing to teach his disciples.[1]

Confucius saw himself in quite modest terms. The Buddha, according to tradition, proclaimed his insight. Confucius did not do so. For one thing, he considered himself merely someone who handed things from one generation to the next, not someone who created new ideas. "I am a transmitter, not an innovator; I believe in antiquity and love the ancients."[2] On another occasion he remarks: "How dare I rank myself with sages . . . ?" His disciples thought he was one. He goes on: "I prefer to say of myself, that I strive without cease and teach others without weariness." That sounds rather ordinary, doesn't it? But the disciples saw something deeper. They responded: "This is just what we, your disciples, have been unable to learn."[3] Perhaps such persistence and steady purpose is a rare thing after all.

Sometimes quite uneventful lives can have tremendous impact. This was the case with Confucius, whose teaching profoundly influenced the history of China. What was it in his teaching that could do this? It was not that his teaching was highly organized or complex or stunning like that of the Buddha. It seemed much more straightforward; almost ad hoc, just a collection of more or less pithy statements in response to one situation or another. It seemed very ordinary after all.

The Outside of Confucius' Teaching

We can sum it up by saying that there is an inside and an outside to the teaching of Confucius. The outside had to do with the roles people played in society and the behavior that was appropriate to those roles. For instance, the ruler of a state had, among other things, the obligation to keep his people safe from outside threat. For this purpose he would need, say, some chariots. But only a certain number of chariots—say, one hundred—would be proper for someone in his position. It would be improper to have five hundred or a thousand, for that was only appropriate for the emperor would, even if he was only a figurehead. So also a noble might have, let us say, twenty chariots. To have one hundred would be improper and would indicate that he wanted to become ruler himself. Of course, in Confucius' day, everyone wanted to be emperor, so everyone was trying to have as many chariots and other weapons as they possibly could. Power was the name of the game, and social order was collapsing.

Thus, Confucius advocated the "rectification of names"[4]; that is, let conduct and deportment (the rites or *li*) fit one's position and role (signified by one's title or name) in life. This applied at all levels. In somewhat later Confucian teaching these roles or relationships were standardized as five: ruler-ruled, father-son, husband-wife, elder and younger brother, friend and friend.[5] It is interesting to notice that in this listing the most hierarchical one comes first (ruler-ruled), the most egalitarian comes last (friend-friend), and the three in between are all family relationships. These of course are all only broad categories, and they would in reality be spelled out in much more detail. Among the ruled, for example, there are many roles: high officials, low-level officials, common citizens, and so on.

It is also interesting to note that these are all paired relationships. There is no place for just individuals. Everybody is located in a relationship; located, in fact, in many relationships, and often in all of these relationships. Aren't we all children? Some of us also have brothers and or sisters; some of us are married and have children of our own; some of us have work and professions, and so on. Thus one can never act simply as an individual, for the person who corresponds to you in a particular relationship will always be affected. In other words, life is radically social; it is not for loners. Thus, a parent can never be seen apart from one's relationship with the child. So also, a child can never be seen apart from one's relationship with the parent. Over time the relationship between parent and child will change. When the child is an infant it is one way; when the child is a married adult it is another way; when the parent is aged and frail it is another way. So it is with all the other relationships as well.

We also notice that the traditional listing almost ignores women entirely, except where being a spouse is involved. Is patriarchy a necessary part of Confucianism? Some want to say yes. But there are good reasons for saying that is not the case.

For my own purposes I have developed a way to envision this Confucian model and apply it to our contemporary world. Projecting the three familial relationships I draw a circle called "kinship society." Projecting the friend-friend relationship I draw a circle called "civil society." Projecting the ruler-ruled relationship I draw a circle called "political society." These three circles always intersect in our lives in very complicated and often tension-filled ways. The main values of the kinship circle are those of nurture and intimacy. The main values of the civil circle are those of benefit, whether in earning a living or in finding relaxation and enjoyment. We all, after all, want equal access to benefits. That's what all our single issue politics are about. The main value of the political circle is justice, however it may be defined. Society is always wrestling with the proper relationship among these three. This may be a modern reading of Confucius, but I find it helpful.

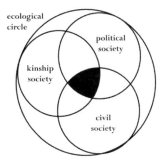

If one wanted to take Daoism into account, which has also influenced Confucianism considerably, I would add a fourth circle, embracing all the social circles and label it "nature" or the "ecological circle."

In chapter 1 we cited a quote from a later text called the *Great Learning* (*Daxue*).[6] It is a beautiful vision of what our world could look like—if only . . . ! Only if one is a person of character will the family be established; only if the families are well established will the nation be rightly governed;

and only if the nations are rightly governed will peace and equality under all of Heaven come about. It is this vision of peace that the doctrine of the rectification of names, properly relating role and behavior, is meant to serve. How far we are from it! Chaotic personal lives, abuse in the home, political intrigue and oppression seem to be the order of much of the day. Confucius sought to reorder the collapsing relationships of his day as everything seemed to be giving way to the quest for power and influence.

The Inside of Confucius' Teaching

In chapter 1 we also briefly touched on the inner solution offered by Confucianism.[7] You may recall our discussion about the character *ren*, meaning humanity, benevolence, or love. An enormous change that Confucius brought to the way the people of ancient China thought was to transform what before was a public virtue into a personal virtue. In *The Analects* Confucius speaks constantly of the *junzi*, or person of noble birth. Nobility had hitherto been something that one had by right of birth. It automatically belonged to one, and it could never be taken away however one behaved. One was born into a noble family and that was that. When Confucius speaks of the *junzi*, however, he speaks not of a person of noble birth but rather of noble virtue. The word took on another meaning. No longer simply "nobleman," *junzi* came to mean a person of excelling virtue or, we might say, integrity. This integrity is grounded deeply within one's own heart and mind, within one's sense of humanity. It expresses itself in all kinds of ways, always depending upon the circumstances. But however it expresses itself, it will always be a human-centered posture of heart and mind.

It will be worth citing some of the ways in which Confucius speaks of the inclusive virtue of *ren*. Here is how he speaks of *ren* as reciprocity and neighborliness: "To regard every one as a very important guest, to manage the people as one would assist at a sacrifice, not to do to others what you would not have them do to you."[8] This puts the golden rule in negative form. Or again:

> The Master said: "Shen! My teaching contains one all-pervading principle." "Yes," replied Zengzi. When the Master had left the room the disciples asked: "What did he mean?" Zengzi replied: "Our Master's teaching is conscientiousness (zhong) and altruism (shu), and nothing else."[9]

Zhong can also mean loyalty. *Shu* is the same as "reciprocity," which was described as "the negative golden rule" above. Confucius further says that one should "be able from one's own self to draw a parallel for the treatment of others."[10] That is, treat others as you would be treated—hardly any different from the positive golden rule.

For Confucius this posture of heart and mind begins from early childhood upbringing. Central to this is the notion of filial sons and daughters. *The Analects* go so far as to say that "filial love and brotherly kindness are the root of humanity."[11] This has close connection with the ancestral rites that we will touch on below.

At the beginning we said that Confucius was unassuming and that he did not lay claim to "sagehood" but only to effort and practice. He gives us perhaps the shortest moral autobiography in history, and it begins with the idea of learning as the practice of following the good example set by others including, of course, the ancients.

> At fifteen I set my heart on learning [by moral practice].
> At thirty I became firm.
> At forty I had no more doubts.
> At fifty I understood Heaven's Will.
> At sixty my ears were attuned [to this Will].
> At seventy I could follow my heart's desires, without overstepping the line.[12]

Notice that he claims to have understood Heaven's Will at age fifty. Does this have anything to do with the fact that it was at this age that he was retired (or fired?) as police commissioner and from then on held no further public office despite his desire for such? At one point he mourns aloud: "Is it perhaps only Heaven that recognizes me?"[13] That is to say, to recognize someone is to know that person's talent and to use it. "When others do not recognize one," he says, "yet one does not become resentful, is that not the mark of a person of virtue?"[14] It was through the experience of the sorrow of disinterest that he understood the destiny Heaven had assigned to him.

The Buddha, as you may recall, placed great stress upon the sorrowful conditions of human existence. Confucius did not. Despite failure he had a much more positive outlook and rather than retreat from life found failure the invitation to enter even more into life. Because of this he became known as one "who knew he would fail, yet persisted."[15] But Confucius also knew the limits of life. He recognized the physical limits of life, especially sickness and death. When one person he respected much was dying of a loathsome disease, he stood by the window and sighed, "Such a man, and such a death! Such a man and such a death!" His favorite disciple, Yan Yuan, died as a young man and never had the chance to realize his full potential. This was his greatest sorrow in life.[16] He also knew the moral limits of life. He recognized that he was always on the way to perfection, never there. He also knew human nature. Moral failure was not a matter of inability; it was ultimately a failure of will and desire.[17] And he also knew limits of a social and historical kind. We have talked about the competition for power in his day as well as the unwillingness of leaders to make use of persons of moral integrity.

This is where the importance of the idea of Heaven comes in. There was, for Confucius, a deep sense that his destiny was in the hands of Heaven (we would say God). Heaven had summoned him to be the clapper that sounded the bell of moral teaching.[18] When on one occasion his life was threatened he had no fear, for what could his enemies do to him unless they had been given leave by Heaven? There was a clearly personal dimension to his understanding of Heaven. This was lost in later Confucian tradition.

The Continuing Tradition

Overview

Confucianism is, of course, much more than Confucius. It has had a long history and many creative and devoted followers. The story of Confucianism ranges from the infamous book burning of Emperor Qin of the late third century B.C.E.[19] to the anti-Confucius campaign of the mid-1970s—but try as she might, China can't rid herself of Confucianism. Confucianism has soaked itself into the Chinese spirit and always seems to reassert itself. The successor dynasty to the Qin, the Han (206 B.C.E.–C.E. 220) began the process of making Confucianism the state orthodoxy. This orthodoxy persisted throughout much of Chinese history up to the beginning of this century when the Qing dynasty collapsed in C.E. 1911.

Confucianism was useful to the state for several reasons. By stressing personal virtue rather than birthright, as Confucianism did, the rulers were no longer so hamstrung by aristocrats and nobles, who had until that time held their position in society simply because of their bloodline. An enormously significant education system was developed through which even the lowliest peasant could rise to the highest official position—all depended on one's intelligence or virtue. Thus, rulers could find good talent and not be obligated to a noble class. Confucianism laid stress upon proper behavior fitting one's role at all levels of society. This provided internal glue for society, reaching from peasant family to imperial court. Confucianism honored the great leaders and court rituals of the past. This enhanced the dignity of the current ruler. They understood themselves, in line with the Confucian emphasis, as keepers of the Heavenly Mandate to rule. Associated with this was the ancient imperial cult of sacrifice to Heaven once a year on the bare altar open to Heaven, the emperor serving as a mediator between Heaven and Earth. Of similar importance was the Confucian sanction of the ancient ancestral cult that served the need for imperial continuity and became, as well, the moral basis for all of society. For these and other reasons, Confucianism was found useful as a state ideology, however much or little the emperors actually acted out the virtues of which Confucius so earnestly spoke.

There are four important periods in the development of Confucian thought. The first period was marked by the impressive teachings of such thinkers as Mencius and Xunzi during the third and fourth centuries B.C.E.[20] They were the first to give a well-ordered, systematic statement of the teachings going back to Confucius. The second period began when Confucianism started to be accepted as state orthodoxy in the Han dynasty (beginning in 209 B.C.E.). Key features of Chinese thinking were linked with Confucian thought, such as *yin* and *yang* and the correlation of every conceivable phenomenon in the world with ethical and ritual categories and lists. The third period was the fundamental rethinking of Confucian ideas, beginning in the twelfth century, which was triggered by the entry and growth of Buddhism in China. Buddhism asked all kinds of sophisticated questions about the nature of reality, something Confucianism had never done. So it was forced to become a philosophically sophisticated system of thought. Finally, today, especially in the last half of this century, Confucianism has responded to the impact of Christianity and the West. Some attribute the unparalleled economic explosion in East Asia in part to the Confucian ethos. Others want to show how Confucianism is something that has universal significance and is not just a Chinese or East Asian product. They call this the Third Era of Confucianism.[21]

Natural Feelings: Good or Bad?
Human nature is central to a Confucian understanding of the world. But what sort of human nature? This question concerned Mencius and Xunzi. They disagreed on the answer. What sort of people are we really? Confucius had placed much emphasis upon striving for true virtue. In *The Analects* we read: "The Master said: 'By nature people are close, by custom they are far apart.'"[22] This seems to suggest that we are all more or less capable of the good, but in actual practice we see both the good and the bad. Are we then all basically good, or are at least some instinctively bad?

For Mencius the answer was obvious. Of course we can all do the good. We need only consider our natural feelings as they are aroused by somebody else's need. Thus, when someone sees a child about to tumble into a well, the natural impulse is to reach out and rescue the child from the fall. Even someone who is a thief or worse would do that. We have other kinds of natural impulses as well, all of which become the fountainhead of virtue. So the feeling of empathy leads to humanity (*ren*), a sense of shame and dislike produces uprightness, an innate sense of modesty yields proper behavior, an instinctive sense of right and wrong expresses itself in wisdom. It is like a prairie fire. Just light a match to a dry prairie, and soon it will turn into a raging fire. So it is with the virtues, nurture these little beginnings and it will quickly overflow such that nothing can stop it. Human failure arises from stifling these little beginnings rather than letting them blossom forth.

Xunzi was more of a hard realist. All the talk about good impulses may sound fine, but in fact life isn't like that. The reason we act contrary to virtue is that we are driven by our own instincts, drives, or innate energies. These are largely emotions—fear, joy, anger, desire—and they are naturally uncontrolled. These are our true natural feelings. They willy-nilly express themselves and, unless we watch guard over them, they can lead us astray. Thus for Xunzi, education, training in virtue, and the inculcation of proper manners were required before virtue could be practiced. For both Mencius and Xunzi the doing of good was possible, but the one thought it was the product of our unsullied original nature, the other a product of a second nature that is cultivated. In my opinion, much of Confucian history has spoken like Mencius but acted like Xunzi.

This is only one snippet of their thought. Both had immense influence in later developments. One thing that should at least be mentioned is that Mencius, for instance, also contained the seeds of democratic and egalitarian convictions. For him it is the people that are to be valued over the ruler.[23] Moreover, when a ruler fails to govern in a way that benefits the people, rebellion is justified, for Heaven's Mandate has been removed from that ruler. This is an ancient pre-Confucian theme in China. One hears echoes of this too with Mao's call to Cultural Revolution in 1966—"to rebel is justified!" The danger is that without proper structures and safeguards (consider for instance constitutional government), democracy is not possible and egalitarianism quickly becomes demagoguery. Proper order and the necessary structures are matters that Xunzi worried about.

Extending Knowledge
Why do we send our children to school? Is it not to extend their knowledge? But what does extending knowledge mean? Does it mean to know

more information? Does it mean to become clever at using things like computers? Does it mean to know what is worthwhile and what isn't? I wonder if our education does not worry more about the first two than the last.

Confucians were also concerned about these matters. In the third period this was one of the central issues they worried about. In a key Confucian text, there is the admonition to "extend knowledge." What did that mean? For some, it meant that if you study the world about you very, very carefully, you will discover the guiding principle of every single thing. One will find out what makes a table a table, a tree a tree, and so on. They were not trying to be scientific, though it could contribute to a scientific attitude. They were more concerned about the principle in a thing that gave it a particular value. So what would you say is the guiding principle of a table or a tree? Maybe it is quite easy to decide on the main value of a table—it fosters community as people sit around it to eat, for instance. That principle is at work in Chinese feasts, unlike in the Western setting. Go to a genuine Chinese restaurant and you'll see that the tables are round, not long and narrow like ours. The two tables, and two cultures, are based on different principles, it seems. One sees the purpose of the table in fostering community; another sees the table as a practical place to put food to eat. At a round table all interact as a single organic whole. At a long rectangular table each individual is busy figuring out how best to relate to the nearest one, the furthest one, the one in between.

Others disagreed with this way of speaking. To extend knowledge did not mean to know more about things around you in the world, even if it were a table. It meant, rather, to extend the moral urges within you. Knowledge is to act rightly, not simply to know rightly. It was a matter of a sincere will, not a well-informed head. This way of speaking was much influenced by Mencius. The other way was influenced more by Xunzi. For these Confucians, to extend knowledge was to extend kindness to others, to exercise conscientiousness in all that one does.

This and related arguments raged for several centuries—is the value in things something to be discovered, or do we simply exert our goodwill to all things whatever the situation? But both had long forgotten Confucius' personal understanding of Heaven. Still, for both, Heaven was the ultimate principle of goodness in the universe. It was always spontaneous and creative. Human beings were in a special relationship to this moral activity present in the universe. In fact, Heaven needs us to be its hands and feet. If its urge towards moral perfection is not realized by human beings, then where will it be realized? Certainly not by animals, bugs, or stones. The goal, then, as human beings is to respond to heavenly principle by extending knowledge. This may be done, as some said, by a knowing about things (an informed mind) and acting accordingly or, as others said, by a knowing that simply acts out the moral urges (a sincere will) without relying on external helps such as books and lectures and step-by-step straight-line thinking.

The Third Era?

Something is stirring in East Asia. What it is we do not yet know. For some decades Japan has been the single economic power. But now there are, or were, the four "dragons": Hong Kong, Taiwan, South Korea, and Singapore. And overshadowing all of them is China itself. It could well be that a dominant economic power of the twenty-first century will be in East Asia.

China's encounter with the West has been a difficult and stressful one. The return of Hong Kong to China in 1997 has announced to the world that China can now put the memory of Western colonialism and imperialism behind her and concentrate on the future. But will it succeed? What worldview will guide China as she moves ahead? Communism created a stomachache for the Chinese people, and the Cultural Revolution (1966–1976) was like a bad case of diarrhea. The ideological void left by the failure of Mao-style Communism leaves the way open for a new worldview to guide China. Will it be Confucianism? Or will it be nationalism with some Confucian overtones?

While Mao's wild ideas were raging across China one after the other, Confucian scholars who had left China to escape from Communism gathered in Hong Kong and elsewhere outside of China. They began rethinking the Confucian past. Now most of these groundbreakers have died, but they have left second and third generation followers. Some of these have announced the dawning of the Third Era of Confucianism.

By this I think they mean that Confucianism, as it adapted to the challenge of Buddhism in the past, is now adapting itself to the challenge of the West and of Christianity. It is learning from them and sifting through what will enrich and what will not enrich Confucian commitments. They also mean that the rejection of Confucianism when China opened to modern thought in 1919 and the further rejection by the Communists after 1949 is now past, and the people are ready to take a new look at their traditional values. They mean that Confucian ideas are no longer limited in their value to China, but that, just as these ideas spread throughout East Asia, these ideas have universal value, especially as Western societies experience decay from within and are questioning their own heritage. And finally, they mean that for all the wonderful ideas received from the West, including that of democracy, the time has come in which Western values will be fundamentally reshaped by Confucian values.

Whether this grand vision will bear fruit or not remains to be seen. What one does see is a definite trend toward reinterpreting the world on the basis of Asian, not Western, values and forging an identity that gives East Asians equal dignity with the West in terms of wealth, power, and values. Confucianism is one important ingredient in this mix.

Meeting the Ancestors

It is hard to imagine Confucianism without ancestors. There is perhaps no cult more widely practiced worldwide, excepting much of the Jewish, Christian, and Muslim world, than worship of the ancestors. In parts of the Christian and Muslim world it survives in part as the veneration of saints.

But ancestors are not saints; they are ancestors, my own ancestors. One does not properly worship anyone else's ancestor. In China, were an ordinary person to have worshiped the ancestor of an emperor, it would have been considered an act of rebellion—an attempt to claim imperial status.

Do Confucians worship their ancestors? That may not be a very good way of putting it. In popular religion the ancestors are clearly worshiped. That is to say, they are the direct object of prayers because they are believed to have the power to bless or curse their descendants. We indicated something of this earlier. But it is not so in the orthodox Confucian case. Confucius inherited an ancient ancestral cult, especially as practiced by the emperors of the past. As with so many other things he gave it a new interpretation. Perhaps veneration is a better word here. The ancestors were honored and remembered as those who had given life to their descendants and had been parents to their children. If appropriate, they were honored too for notable achievements in life. Specifically, they were honored through bodily prostration (low bowing), through sacrifices of food and wine (compare flowers at grave sites), and later also through burning of incense, through ritual and prayer.

The outlines of the ancestral cult among the Chinese has three main parts. At the time of death a paper tablet is prepared to remember the deceased. A rectangular piece of paper is attached to a stick and placed on a table in the corner of the living room with an incense pot. On the front side of the paper is written the name of the deceased. On the back are the birth and death dates and the names of the descendants that now honor that ancestor. After one year this paper tablet is burned.

Next a wooden tablet is prepared, with the same information as the paper tablet. It will be placed on an altar that has a prominent place in the living room. The spirit has now transferred from the paper to the wooden tablet. Tablets of earlier generations are usually kept in a drawer of the table. When eventually too many tablets are collected, clan members will get together and build an ancestral hall devoted to honoring the ancestors, and the tablets will be transferred there. These will be worshiped at certain festivals during the year, may be informed of important events in the life of the family, and in homes of the devout will be remembered daily.

Meanwhile, the deceased is also remembered at the tomb. There are various funerary practices and ways of caring for the bones, if buried, or the ashes if cremated. If the family is wealthy, a conspicuous tomb may be built. Once a year, at the Ching Ming (Pure and Bright) Festival the family will go to the grave site, clean the tomb, offer sacrifices, and have a meal together. Typically, the choice of a burial site is determined by geomancy, the skill of discerning a site where the natural forces of wind and water have an auspicious configuration. The popular expectation is that the choice of a good site will result in blessings for the family whereas the choice of a bad site will result in misfortune. If good fortune has been experienced during the year, Qing Ming is the time to give thanks for that.

All these things are matters of great weight within Chinese society generally. Here the boundaries between remembrance and magic very easily break down. Let me offer one example. Many years ago I was involved in a funeral in Hong Kong of a Christian family. I was rather taken aback when at the grave site a loud argument erupted between the family and the grave diggers. The family was upset that the burial plot had been previously used (that was typical then in Hong Kong, bodies being buried for a few years and then exhumed and a new body entombed). The shouting and arguing lasted a good half hour. Finally, the family accepted the inevitable, and permitted the deceased to be buried at the site. The story was then told to me of another Christian family that had buried their loved one at this place, and in the subsequent year had experienced a financial windfall. Accordingly, when they visited the grave site at Qing Ming time they feasted the grave diggers for having selected such an auspicious site.

Whether the ancestral cult is perceived in Confucian terms as a memorial rite to affirm gratitude to one's forbears and to solidify the moral relationships of the community, or whether it embraces more popular and magical understandings as well, this cult is of central importance in Chinese society.

8

MEETING OUR CHINESE NEIGHBOR— AS A DAOIST

‑‑‑‑

Our Chinese neighbor usually includes many influences in her or his worldview. One of these influences is Confucian. We have talked about that in chapter 7. Another influence is that of folk religion. We also touched on that in chapter 2. Yet another influence is Daoism, which we will talk a bit about in this chapter. But influencing them all, is something that has been called Chinese correlative thinking.[1] Yin-yang is perhaps the most commonly known example of this kind of Chinese thinking and, in fact, has become quite popular in some forms of New Age thinking in our own North American context. This chapter, then, will begin with something about Chinese correlative thinking, which has deeply shaped both Confucian and Daoist thinking.

Chinese Correlative Thinking

The other day I bought a book on feng-shui (literally "wind and water," or geomancy) and gave it to my wife for Christmas. This particular book was written by an architect who applies the principles of feng-shui to his work. I gave her this book because one of her research projects is with a person who is studying the relationship of feng-shui to the way people order their lives. While selecting the book, I was surprised at how many books on feng-shui— some truly beautiful books—there were on the shelves at my local bookstore.

Feng-shui is an ancient Chinese idea that there are certain kinds of energies that influence and shape the spaces in which we live and work, and so also the fortunes that we might experience, for good or for ill. In ancient times it was important, as it still is today for many, to orient the grave site of one's parents according to the principles of feng-shui. The goal is to balance the negative and positive energies of the specific burial site so that the best cosmic harmony is achieved. It was this practice that eventually led to the discovery of the compass in China. After all, they were working with real energies—magnetic energies.

Better known to us in the West is the ancient Chinese idea of yin and yang. This deals with what is believed to be a twofold tendency that is present in all things. The idea probably originated in the ancient agricultural society of China—one knows how dependent farmers are upon the twofold tendencies in our world, of light and dark, dry and wet, hot and cold, for instance. In ancient times yin designated the shadow side of a mountain and yang the sunny side. As the sun moves through the sky the shadowy side becomes sunny and the sunny becomes shadowy. Everything in the world changes in this way. The change is gradual and always balanced. When, for instance, the sun is at high noon, all sides of the mountain are sunny. But there is still some yin, or shadowy character, hidden in there, because rocks and trees and other things cast a shadow, so it never becomes entirely sunny even though it seems to. At night the yin is at its extreme—all seems to be shadow—yet there is the light of the moon, or if that is gone, the light of the stars. Animals run around the mountain at night—they can see even if we cannot. Everything is correlated. Hidden in yang is some yin, and hidden in yin is some yang (therefore the contrasting dots in the pollywoglike figures below). There is always a balance: 10 percent yin and 90 percent yang makes 100 percent just as 50 percent yin and 50 percent yang makes 100 percent. Yang rises to its highest, and then yin begins to increase; yin rises to its highest, and yang begins to increase. The universe is an active matrix of continual change in this manner.

Over time yin and yang have been correlated with almost anything there is in the universe. Yin is associated with moon, feminine, weakness, darkness, dampness, poverty, odd numbers, north, west, smooth, foods that are "cool" or easy to digest, the earthly soul (*po*), and so on. None of these are bad as such, just one aspect of the way things are. Yang is associated with sun, male, strength, light, dryness, even numbers, wealth, east or south, hardness, harder-to-digest foods that tend to give a sort of "heat," and the heavenly soul (*hun*). The yin and yang then correlate with the five energies (metal, wood, water, fire, earth), and these in turn with other schemes, resulting in enormously complex systems.

These correlations are *not* static but dynamic, always moving and changing. In fact, one of the most ancient Chinese texts, the Yijing (also spelled I Ching), means exactly that—"the classic of changes." Confucius himself revered it as a most insightful text. Daoists, too, have incorporated it into their thinking. In popular Chinese thought it has always been a text of fortune-telling. In our bookstores today, we can find many interpretations of it for people who want to govern their lives according to holistic principles. The Yijing, thus, is another example of correlative thinking among the Chinese. Since so many of our youth are interested in it, we will say a few things about it.

It is a book of dynamic correlations, based on two kinds of lines that represent two kinds of possibilities. One is a broken _____ _____ line and the other a solid _____ line. These can be correlated with the yin and the yang. If a third line is joined to the two, called a trigram, the result is eight possible combinations (see below). If two trigrams are joined, the result is a hexagram of six lines. This allows sixty-four possible combinations.

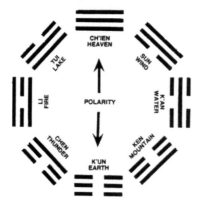

The images represented by these abstract lines are very concrete. Thus, three or six solid lines one above the other represent Heaven or activity. As a guide to behavior it might mean something so simple as "work steadily and you will achieve favorable results." Three or six broken lines represent Earth or receptivity. It can mean something so simple as "Do not force matters but go with the flow." From here on things get very complicated. Each of the six lines has a number and a significance, and the relations among the lines change as well, so these relations also need to be read to get the full message. Whether a hexagram comes before or after another hexagram will also affect the meaning.

Tranquillity is three broken lines on top of three solid lines:

Stagnation is three solid lines on top of three broken lines:

Compare this to an active volcano. Before it blows its top, we could say it is constipated. Stagnation would symbolize the situation well—liquid (soft) beneath the solid (hard). After it erupts, there is tranquillity as the mountain settles down. Now the solid is below and the top is open with three broken lines. Have you seen Mt. St. Helens? I camped with my wife in the tranquil world of ash beneath the blown top. The Yijing interprets all phenomena of nature and society in terms of these changing configurations. Many believe that by observing these configurations one can give moral counsel or even predict fortunes.

This bias towards such correlative thinking is present in virtually all traditional Chinese thought. It is a way of thinking that doesn't go from point A systematically to point B and then in a logical way to C. This straight-line thinking is very common for us in the West. Instead, it takes note of wholes, and then looks at the parts as correlations within the larger whole. Earlier we talked about the importance of paired relationships like parent-child. This is more like correlative thinking than straight-line thinking. You don't just act rationally, in a straightforward fashion; you act relationally, in a more indirect and roundabout way. Rather than going straight ahead one goes back and forth, and around and around. This makes it easy for people from East Asia and the West to misinterpret each other. This is why Westerners sometimes think that East Asians are dishonest, and East Asians sometimes think Westerners are rude.

A Daoist Sense of Things

Correlative thinking, as I mentioned, has influenced both Confucian and Daoist thinking. The proper Confucian usage, however, is to aid a person in making moral judgments. It is not for fortune-telling. In Daoism, correlative thinking can become a pattern that influences all facets of life.

Daoism, however, is a word that refers to many things. The word *Dao* is composed of two Chinese symbols. One symbol signifies a head—it is written 首. The other symbol is written thus 辶. It simply indicates the idea of movement. If one puts the two together, then one has the character *Dao* 道. This means Way, or Path—a head in movement in some direction, and by extension Word or Idea or Truth. When translators of the Bible wanted to find the right word to translate John 1:1, "In the beginning was the Word," some chose the Chinese word *Dao*. It was a good choice, having just as rich a set of meanings as the original Greek word *Logos*. In fact, any system of thought or practice in China can be referred to as *Dao*, including Confucianism.

We will comment here only about one of the many important movements referred to as Daoism. This is a worldview that was given shape in the two to three centuries both before and after Christ. Laozi (Lao-tzu) and Zhuangzi (Chuang-tzu) are names always associated with this worldview. But there are other movements that also go by the name of Daoism. We will just mention them here but not discuss them. One kind of Daoism was interested in alchemy. It was hoped, for instance, that the king, by ingesting gold and mercury or certain other metallic substances could become as changeless as they were and so be immortal. Several Chinese emperors and others died in such experiments. Later the quest for immortality became a technique of meditation and control of the *Qi* (ch'i) or primal energy or breath. Through breath control, or even through the retention of semen at the moment of orgasm, it was believed one could nurture the eternal infant within oneself and, in this way, attain immortality. Then again, Daoism refers to a movement of religious fervor and practice. The earliest known manifestation of it was around the third century B.C.E. when there arose a faith in the Queen Mother of the West (that is, from the high mountains on the western fringes of China), or Xi Wangmu. Through faith in her, and by use of charms in her name, all sorts of benefits could be gained.[2] In subsequent centuries there were similar types of religious enthusiasm that took place. Eventually there arose a very elaborate system of gods and goddesses, with highly complex rituals, a wide variety of beliefs, and a very careful attention to affects of good or evil deeds, and charms of every kind, with trained religious specialists, and transmission of authority from one generation to the next, not unlike papal succession. When some speak of Daoism, they mean this elaborate religious system. In fact, all these movements I have mentioned interconnect in a variety of ways. But we shall limit ourselves to the early rise of a particular worldview that formed a striking contrast to the Confucian worldview and continues to be influential to the present day.

The foundation text for Daoism is the *Daodejing* (*Tao-te-ching*). The supposed author is Laozi (Lao-tzu). In fact, the author is unknown, and the formation of the tradition that led to its writing is hidden in the obscurities of history. An early Chinese historian, Sima Qien, writing around 100 B.C.E. about the possible authorship of the text concludes that "no one in the world can say whether all this is true or not. Laozi was a hidden sage."[3]

Daoism and Confucianism relate to each other like yin and yang. I referred to this tension in chapter 1. Daoism is a naturalism that counters the Confucian emphasis upon society. The same historian referred to above tells the tale, doubtless without historical basis, of a meeting between Laozi and Confucius. Confucius, always fussy about ritual and right procedure, asks Laozi "to instruct him in the rites." Laozi does so, but not in a way that Confucius might have anticipated. He informs Confucius that "a good merchant hides his wealth and gives the appearance of want" and that "the superior man has the outward appearance of a fool." Then, rebuking Confucius, he adds: "Get rid of that arrogance of yours, all those desires, that self-sufficient air, that overweening zeal; all that is of no use to your true person. That is all I can say to you." Confucius, a gentleman to the end, later confides to his disciples that "the dragon is beyond my knowledge; it ascends into heaven on the clouds and the wind. Today I have seen Lao Tzu, and he is like the dragon!"[4]

The message of the *Daodejing* is summed up in these words in chapter 25: "Humanity conforms to earth; earth conforms to heaven; heaven conforms to Dao; and Dao conforms to self-so-ness." In these few words the relationship among all things in existence is summed up.

What does it mean that "humanity conforms to earth?" We have spoken of Daoism as a naturalism. This means at least two things. First of all, everything is rooted in nature. Human existence is not higher than nature, just a part of nature. Zhuangzi referred to nature as "the great clod."[5] Thus, as we noted in an earlier chapter, when Zhungzi's wife died he comforted himself with the thought that she had now entered into the eternal transformation of things, into nature, into this great clod. Secondly, it means that human life is not something that is to stand out from and dominate or control nature but is to learn from and pattern itself after nature. The ancient Daoists would be horrified at our modern industrial society that cuts and chops and hacks the earth to pieces, all the while filling the air with noxious fumes.

So what does it mean for one's life to conform to the ways (*dao*) of earth? Earth here does not just mean matter, but the way earth as a complete entity functions. For example, one can look to the way water and earth interact. Water always follows the contours of the earth to the lowest place. Water always seeks out the gaps and valleys, the rifts and cavities of the earth. It flows down. It seeps down. It does not climb to the tops of mountains and there proclaim its greatness. Water, in other words, is "humble" and "meek." "The valley spirit never dies," says the *Daodejing*.[6] This humility is forever.

Or, again, we can see another way in which water acts upon the earth. The waters clash and thunder against the coast, and it seems that the rocks have the power to split the water into shreds and spit it back to the sea in tiny droplets. Nevertheless, the water always comes back together again as the same body of water, and over the centuries the coastline is chiseled and whittled away. "That which under heaven is the most soft," we read, "overcomes that which is the hardest."[7] "Thus," we read again, "the soft and weak are the disciples of life; the hard and forceful are the disciples of death."[8]

If humans are to conform to the way earth functions, the next phrase adds, "earth conforms to heaven." What might this mean? The U.S. state of Montana prides itself as "big sky country." It is big sky in part because with few trees one can see the large sky punctuated by mountain peaks on all horizons. In other words, heaven stretches over all. It lends continuity to the whole. As it lays its canopy over all, each particular thing finds its special place.

In other words, heaven introduces a unifying principle to all things. One is not just dealing with a world that is a chaos of particular things. Water naturally tends downward. Trees naturally grow up and sink their roots into the soil. The sun rises and sets. The moon goes through its phases. The stars carry on their eternal dance around the North Star—as far as we see the night heavens. There is order, unity, wholeness, and predictability to things. Apples fall; steam rises; bees buzz and make honey. There is a universal rhythm to the way (*dao*) all things work.

Heaven itself, however, is not the end of the line. "Heaven," we read, "conforms to Dao." The Dao is before all things and present in all things. It is the source of inexhaustible activity. The heavens do not push the sun around. There is an energy latent from the very beginning of things that creates the dynamism of our solar system, of all the galactic systems. Dao births the cosmos. We read:

> The Dao gives birth to the one.
> The one gives birth to the two.
> The two gives birth to the three.
> And the three gives birth to the Ten Thousand Things.
> The Ten Thousand Things carry yin,
> And embrace yang;
> And achieve harmony by the mixing of *qi*.[9]

The Dao, then, is a primordial wholeness (one) that carries within it the power for differentiation (two) and yet maintains continuity (*qi* or breath, energy) amid the multiplicity making, thereby, a fecund and richly diverse world (ten thousand things). But what is the Dao itself?

> That thing which is the Dao is eluding and vague.
> Vague and eluding, within it are the forms.
> Eluding and vague, within it are things.
> Deep and obscure, within it is the life force.
> This life force is truly real; within it are the evidences.[10]

Above we mentioned the biblical translation of the word *logos* or Word in John 1:1 with Dao. There we learn that "the Dao became flesh and lived among us."[11] We also hear Jesus say, "I am the Dao, the Truth and the Life."[12] Not so, however, in Daoism. Here we find that "The Dao that can be spoken of is not the eternal Dao. The name that can be named is not the eternal name." We then read:

> That without name is the origin of heaven and earth.
> That with name is the mother of the Ten Thousand Things
> These [the "without name" and the "with name"] proceed from the
> same source, yet have different names.
> Both together are called the dark.
> Dark and even darker,
> It is the gate of all hidden-wonders.

This leaves us with an unnamed obscurity that is the ground and principle of the birthing of all things. It is beyond conception. It is utter mystery. Since this is so, we are perhaps not so surprised to hear the next and final phrase indicate that the Dao is not even itself the end of the line, but that "the Dao conforms to *Ziran* [Self-so-ness]."

Not only is the Dao the source of all things, hidden in its eternal power and mystery, but it is rooted in absolute freedom. *Ziran* can be translated "nature." But it does not mean "nature" in the way we often use it. When we speak of nature we generally think of the material world around us that we can shape according to our own design. We know, of course, that in the end we can't reshape nature thoughtlessly, for nature will get back at us. *Nature* comes from the Latin word *natus* ("born" or "birthed") and indicates the inner essence of a thing. But *ziran* means more than this. It means pure spontaneity. There is no first cause. There is no creator God. There is simply "self-so-ness," the spontaneous origin of all things. Dao is rooted in this ultimate realm where freedom and spontaneity are the final principle.

In this brief summary, we have traveled from the way of human activity to this ultimate principle of spontaneity, a very long way indeed.

An Alternative Social Vision

The Daoist sense of things has always formed a counterpoint to the Confucian sense of things. This is seen most clearly in the social visions offered. In the preceding chapter we have seen something of the Confucian social vision. In contrast, here is a characteristic presentation of a Daoist social vision:

> Let there be a small country with few people.
> Let there be ten times and a hundred times as many utensils but let them not be used.
> Let the people value their lives highly and not migrate far.
> Even if there are ships and carriages, none will ride in them.
> Even if there are arrows and weapons, none will display them.
> Let the people again knot cords and use them [in place of writing].
> Let them relish their food, beautify their clothing, be content with their homes, and delight in their customs.
> Though neighboring communities overlook one another and the crowing of cocks and barking of dogs can be heard,
> Yet the people there may grow old and die without ever visiting one another.

This is quite a social vision—pure contentment! Its principle is rooted in living not against nature, but with nature.

Daoists never tired of mocking the Confucian attempt to order the world according to their own Confucian prescription. Here are some more examples:

> Banish "wisdom"; discard "knowledge,"
> And the people will be benefited a hundredfold.
> Banish "benevolence"; discard "morality,"

And the people will be dutiful and compassionate.
Banish "skill"; discard "profit,"
And thieves and robbers will disappear. . . .[13]

All of the words with quotation marks above represent the values of those who want to organize society for their own well-intentioned but, according to the Daoist, illusory ends. All of these things are evidence of the loss of spontaneity. Thus:

It was when the Great Dao declined
That "benevolence" and "righteousness" arose;
It was when "knowledge" and "wisdom" appeared
The Great Lie began.
Not till the six near ones [i.e., family members] had lost their harmony
Was there talk of "filial piety,"
Not till countries and families were dark with strife
Did we hear of "loyal ministers."[14]

Not one of these humanly constructed institutions actually serves the people; they only enrich the powerful. After describing the favored primitive collectivism of Daoism, another ancient Daoist text goes on to indicate the destructive results of setting up these institutions:

The mountains and streams were divided with boundaries and enclosures, censuses of the populations were made, cities were built and dikes dug, barriers were erected and weapons forged for defense. Officials with special badges were ordained, who differentiated the people into the classes of "noble" and "mean," and organized rewards and punishments. Then there arose soldiers and weapons, giving rise to wars and strife. There was the arbitrary murder of the guiltless and the punishment and death of the innocent. . . .[15]

The solution to all these problems is both simple and drastic:

Block up the "apertures,"
Close the "doors" [which open to all these untoward influences]
Blunt the edges [of weapons],
Dissolve the feudal class-distinctions
Harmonize the brilliances [the talented who become subservient to the community],
Unite the dusts [the ordinary people of the community]
This is called the mysterious Togetherness,
[For in this community] there can be no likings nor dislikings,
No private profit and no loss,
There can be no "honorable persons" and no "mean ones,"
And therefore it is the most honorable thing under Heaven.[16]

Return, in other words, to simplicity. As it says again:

> In olden times the best practices of the Dao
> Did not use it to awaken the people to "knowledge,"
> But to restore them to "simplicity."[17]

The literature is full of this call to simplicity. For all that, this Daoist social vision is a thoroughly impractical one. No human society could long exist were this vision to be radically carried out. Yet, it has persisted as one vision among many. Wherein lies its enduring appeal?

First, it is the vision of protest. It acts as a counterpoint to the agendas of all those who believe they are wise enough to tell the rest of the world how to live. No government, as we well know, has yet been fully successful. All attempts at justice are merely that, less or more bad attempts. This vision is the perpetual shadow of society's ills. Second, it appeals to the priority of individual contentment over a forced communal contentment. It gives voice to the vital energies of the individual and to the desire for untrammeled freedom and spontaneity of expression. It has a powerful sense of our bodily reality and its participation in the larger natural rhythms of life. It was doubtless due to the powerful attraction of these basic themes that philosophers, artists, shamans, priests, and magicians, those thirsting for immortality, even the rebellious, the political outcasts, and the social misfits, were drawn in.

Chinese history has been shaped in important ways by this counterpoint of Daoist and Confucian sentiments. The one seeks to make and construct a social world with a responsible government. The other seeks to unmake all these human constructions and let human society reflect what are seen to be the natural rhythms of life. Somehow, this counterpoint has always belonged together in Chinese history: the devoted official serving the people and the state; the contented recluse living the simple life. Daoism in this philosophical mode remains a continuing influence in many aspects of Chinese sensibility. As the early Daoist dictum puts it, "Act not, and all acts happen." That is to say, if one ceases from artificial efforts to make things conform to one's own idea of the way things should be, things will happen in a natural and unconstrained way, following the dictates of nature.

9

MEETING OUR HINDU NEIGHBOR

W ho is our Hindu neighbor? Many images and impressions might parade before our minds: a wild-haired guru that we have seen or read about; a singing, dancing, and mostly shaven-headed Hare Krishna group; a million or more people pressing forward to bathe in the holy but filthy waters of a sacred river in India; theosophy and the teaching that all partial truths are the manifestation of a supreme truth that transcends them all; yoga; caste; Gandhi and *ahimsa*; gods and temples. . . . Mark Twain said this about the image worship he observed while on a visit to India: "And what a swarm of them there is! The town is a vast museum of idols—and all of them crude, misshapen, and ugly. They flock through one's dreams at night, a wild mob of nightmares."[1]

These and much more pass through our minds. All of these are a bit of what Hinduism is about, in a crude sort of way. The word *hindu* in fact is not the name of a religion, really. It is simply a form of the word *Indus*, a river that runs through Pakistan.[2] It is used today to refer to the indigenous culture of India.

Nevertheless, there are ways in which these diverse practices and beliefs have connections with each other, however much they differ. What we call Hinduism is more than a tangled jumble of nonsense. Let us see if we can untangle it a bit.

To make something very complicated as simple as possible I will survey Indian religions in the light of three periods. These are the periods of Vedic religion, a time of Transition, and Hinduism proper.

VEDIC PERIOD   TRANSITION   HINDUISM

The Vedic Period

The Vedic period stretches all the way from before the time of Abraham (2000 B.C.E.) to the time of Israel's exile (around 500 B.C.E.). This period had a very definite start when various Indo-European peoples immigrated into the regions of northwest India and today's Pakistan, probably from west central Asia. They were nomads, who probably came in waves, much like the Israelites who immigrated into ancient Canaan.

Little is known about this period of time. There was an ancient civilization that preceded the arrival of the Aryans, as these people were called, in the flood plains of the Indus River. They had large ceremonial urban centers and had a written language. But their language has never been deciphered, and all that is left are some small artifacts, mostly images and seals. The seals typically depict a male figure in a yogalike posture with an erect penis, surrounded by animals. Maybe he is the precursor of the later Hindu god Siva. There are also female figurines, some pregnant or with children in their arms and their sexual features exaggerated. There are depictions of trees, perhaps sacred trees. Associated with the layout of the cities are large baths, possibly used for purification rites, not unlike in present day India. Whatever these things mean, it is clear that they depict a worldview in which nature, deities, and the human world share in a common cosmos in which themes of fertility, religious discipline, and purification are prevalent.

This civilization disappeared suddenly, either because of the arrival of the Aryans or possibly before their arrival. We don't know if the wealth of that civilization attracted the Aryans, or whether there was just a power vacuum that allowed them to enter that region.

In any case, the language of the Aryans was Sanskrit, and their beliefs have come down to the present first through elaborate oral traditions and then also through written collections of their beliefs. These are collected in the *Vedas*, a word that means knowledge. For us the most interesting of these texts is the Rig-Veda, a collection of hymns not unlike Psalms. Other texts dealt with ritual, magic spells, and the like. The hymns show that the people believed in a colorful pantheon of gods, similar to the Greek, Roman, and even Iranian traditions, as well as the Germanic and Nordic pantheon. In fact, some of the names of the deities are related. One of their more colorful gods was Indra, a bellicose god of the storm, full of energy and bravado, like Thor. Varuna was a somber deity who silently governed the rhythms of the universe, being associated with time and destiny. There was Agni, the god of the sacrificial fire; there was Soma, the god of the ritual drink, a hallucinogenic drug perhaps made of a mushroom. There were the Adityas, beautiful goddesses of the dawn. Many other gods and goddesses filled out the pantheon, symbolizing celestial, atmospheric, and terrestrial powers. There had been battles and disturbances among the gods, most notably the destruction of an ancient monster, Vrtra. (Incidentally, Vrtra has a counter-part in the ancient Sumerian deity, who is reflected in the Hebrew word *tehom*, or "chaos," in the Bible.) Vrtra was destroyed by the exuberant Indra, bringing boon to gods and humans alike.

The hymns are particularly interesting. They are addressed to one or another deity, singing their praises. The tendency of these hymns was to address each deity as if it were the one and only deity. One deity would be praised in this way; but then they would turn around and praise another deity with a similar string of exalting epitaphs. Here is a verse from a typical hymn, this one addressed to Agni:

> You, O Agni [Fire], are Indra, the bull [strongest] of all that exists; you are the wide striding Visnu, worthy of reverence; you, O Lord of the Holy Word, are the chief priest who finds riches [for the sacrifice]; you, O distributor, are associated with munificence.[3]

Here are three stanzas taken from a hymn to Varuna:

> I hymn the self-luminous wise Lord
>   to be praised and glorified above all forever
> Varuna the mighty! I beg him for renown,
>   the God who shows love to all those who adore him.
>
> With reverence and care we sing your praises.
>   Happy we feel in your service, O Varuna!
> We hymn you like the fire that arises each dawn
>   to usher in the day with its promise of riches.
>
> O Leader of heroes, whose words reach far,
>   may we ever abide in your shelter, O King!
> O sons of the Infinite, Gods ever faithful,
>   forgive us our sins; grant us your friendship.

It is evident from these hymns that the Vedic religion was very much centered on the concerns of this life rather than an escape from this life. Wealth, health, fertility, herds, and well-being were its concerns, and the gods were a living part of that whole.

Vedic religion itself was an evolving worldview. There were later texts, called *Brahmanas*, which were ritual commentaries on the earlier Vedic texts. These in turn were followed by further commentaries that were highly philosophical and meditative in character called the *Upanishads*.

As Vedic religion gradually evolved from a this-worldly cult to an increasingly sacrificial and then knowledge-focused cult, there was an accompanying change in beliefs and ideas as well. For instance, during the sacrificial phase, ritual and the priest became increasingly important. One result was that the gods began to recede into the background. In fact, the gods became dependent upon the sacrifices conducted by the priest who manipulated sound, visible objects, colors, and numbers. The whole universe was conceived as a sacrificial process, a divine ecology—the gods give rain and sun, which strengthen nature; we eat the food provided by nature and are made strong; the sacrifice in turn is performed by humans to once more reinvigorate the gods so that they can continue to give rain and sun.

But already questions were beginning to be asked. On the one hand there was a quest for some original integrating principle, a One that could unite the multiplicity of the world. Are the gods simply many, or is there one God or one principle behind them all? On the other hand, it seemed that everything was impermanent, the gods themselves even being dependent upon the sacrifice. The question was asked: "Since everything here is overtaken by death, since everything is overcome by death, whereby is a sacrificer liberated beyond the reach of death?"[4] That is to say, what benefit does the sacrificer gain from the sacrifice? He will himself die eventually, as does everything else. A sage by the name of Yajnavalky, using the language of the primeval sacrifice, asks pointedly:

> When the voice of a dead man goes into fire, his breath into wind, his eye into the sun, his mind into the moon, his hearing into the quarters of heaven, his body into the earth, his soul [atman] into space, the hairs of his head into plants, the hairs of his body into trees, and his blood and semen are placed in water, what then becomes of this person?[5]

It was this sort of questioning and speculation that led into the second period, which we have termed the transitional period.

The Transitional Period

By the time these questions were arising in a serious way, around the eighth century before Christ, some other developments had taken place that were to help shape the fresh effort to find answers. It is not entirely clear to what degree these developments resulted from internal factors in the Vedic tradition itself and to what degree it was the influence of outside elements, such as submerged older, pre-Vedic traditions, which began to emerge into the dominant Vedic tradition and reshape it. It was probably a mixture of both.

As we have seen, the first stage of Vedic religion was praise of the gods in the context of sacrifice, but they were many and it wasn't certain which was really God. It left the puzzle whether there might actually be a One behind the many. The next stage was a turn to sacrifice, which brought gods and humans and sacrificial action all into one big cosmic ecology. The emphasis was on the efficacy of regulated, outward ritual action. But, as we have seen, this outward action did not answer questions such as those about death and finitude. With these two questions, there is a turn inward, in search of a final principle to things that is autonomous, unchanging, uninfluenced by the flux of circumstance, something that is the inner essence and foundation of all things. This principle was eventually called Brahman, now meaning not the outward action of sacrifice, but the inner soul of all things, the Absolute Self that lay hidden behind all phenomena.

Meanwhile, other developments had also begun to take place, changing the worldview within which the questions were asked and answers given. By the sixth century before Christ a pan-Indian worldview had developed. All subsequent religious answers in India deciphered the riddle of life in these terms. Three words sum up this worldview: *samsara*, *karma*, and *moksha*.

Samsara means "passage" and came to refer to the endless cycle of lives that all beings go through. Closely associated with it was the idea of rebirth. Every living being has had an endless number of previous existences, and this life leads forward into an endless series of future existences. Existence itself is divided and subdivided into many realms—there are the gods, humans, spirits, animals, hell, and so on. Rebirth can take place in any one of these. One time I may be human, another time an animal, yet another time a god.

Karma is the dynamo that keeps rebirth going. Karma means simply "action." Sacrifice itself, for instance, is an action, an action that brings about a result—or so it was hoped. Eventually the term *karma* became applied to any action that brings results, especially actions of intent, will, desire. In one of the most important Upanishads we read these words:

> According as one acts, according as one conducts himself, so does he become. The doer of good becomes good. The doer of evil becomes evil. One becomes virtuous by virtuous action, bad by bad action.
>
> But people say: "A person is made [not of acts, but] of desires only." [In reply to this I say:] As is his desire, such is his resolve; as is his resolve, such the action he performs; what action [karma] he performs, that he procures for himself.[6]

Every thought, word, and deed brings about a result, an energy or force that leads to another event, and ultimately to another existence. Our rebirths are endless, for our thoughts and deeds are endless.

Now, this endless cycling of rebirths was not looked upon as desirable, for rebirth also meant new forms of suffering. Even to be reborn in the divine realm involved suffering, for that too would end. Samsara, this continual passage, was a dreary prison of endless new forms of suffering. This awakened a profound desire for liberation from this dreary cycle into a realm of permanence and changeless bliss. *Moksha* means deliverance.

With these ideas we have passed from the world of Vedic religion into the world of Hinduism. It is a world of religious thought dominated by the ideas of samsara, karma, and moksha. However, unlike Buddhism, which repudiates the Vedas, Hinduism as a whole retains a respect for the Vedas and its later interpretations in the Brahmanas and *Upanishads*, something like Christianity's view of the Hebrew Scriptures as an Old Testament.

Hinduism

Hinduism, as we suggested earlier, is not one thing but a great many things with rather loose and unstable connections. We suggested that the acceptance of a common worldview that sees our world as a dreary cycle of passing from one life to the next and from which one seeks deliverance is one connecting link. Another is that the Vedas are accepted, or at least not rejected, as the Buddhist and Jains reject them. Given this, Hinduism can be almost anything one might imagine.

We also suggested that there were doubtless submerged traditions that ran parallel to the Vedic tradition and that went back to great antiquity, perhaps even pre-Vedic times. We can indicate this relationship in the following diagram.

Aryan Invasion (ca. 1500 B.C.E.)		(ca. 600 B.C.E.)	Buddhism
Indus Valley	Vedic Religion	Transition	Hinduism
Civilization	Vedas----Brahmanas----*Upanishads*		
	polytheism sacrifice atman/brahman samsara		path of works
	yoga	karma	path of knowledge
		moksha	path of devotion
			Visnu
			Siva
			Devi

Within Hinduism various new scriptural traditions developed. The *Agamas* (literally "scriptures") and *Puranas* (literally "ancient") were vast collections of stories about the gods, about human history, about beliefs and practices, with detailed information on temple building, image making, festival celebration, and much more. Like the Vedas, it is claimed that they were revealed by one or another god. In fact, it is really these non-Vedic texts, including the great epics (the *Mahabharata* and *Ramayana*), sometimes called the "fifth Veda," that actually shape the cultural and religious life of the vast majority of people in India. As one writer comments:

> If one wishes to understand Hindu religious and theological terminology, one has to turn to these books constantly. They have become the medium of imparting secular knowledge as well: they are the sources for much of Indian sociology, politics, medicine, astrology, geography, and so on. . . . Many Indians bear the names of the heroes and heroines . . . . Most are familiar from early childhood with the stories in them. . . . School readers . . . are full of tales from them. Countless films and dramas take their subjects . . . from these ancient books. . . . Broadcasting, printing presses, films, and musicals keep this "true history of India" alive, a "history not of events, but of the urges and aspirations, strivings and purposes of the nation." . . . Anyone interested in the real religion of the Indian people today would find the Itihasa-Purana the best source for all aspects of the contemporary living religion of the masses.[7]

Perhaps the easiest way to describe Hinduism as it exists today is to follow the traditional idea of the three ways of practice in which all Hindus engage. These are the path of works (*karmamarga*), the path of knowledge (*jnanamarga*), and the path of devotion (*bhaktimarga*).

The Path of Works

This way of being Hindu is most interested in how this life is understood and lived. We mentioned that in the earlier Vedic period the religion was very this-worldly, and much attention was given to sacrifice. This way continues those concerns. For instance, one's social identity is fixed by caste, one's passage through life is packaged into four stages, and one's daily life is heavily influenced by ritual.

One's social identity is fixed by caste. Caste or, more correctly, *varna* (literally "color," indicating a racial basis) is not some set of rules that people set up, but goes back to the very way things came to be. In the collection of Vedic hymns we mentioned, one speaks of creation as the sacrifice of a cosmic giant called Purusa (later the term for person). The different parts of the giant's body became the features that make up our universe. Caste was one of these original features:

> The *brahmin*[8] was his mouth
> His two arms became the *rajanya* [or *ksatriyas*]
> His thighs are what the *vaisya* is;
> From his feet the *sudra* was produced.[9]

Of these four the Brahmin, or priestly caste, was the most noble, and for them priestly duties were primary. The Ksatriyas, or ruling caste, came second, and their responsibilities had to do with governing and administration. Next came the Vaisya caste, who were the farmers, business people, and others who made economic and social life function on a day-to-day basis. At the bottom were the Sudras, laborers and servants, who were assigned the most humble tasks, as is indicated by their birth from the feet.

Not mentioned is the large group of outcastes, which makes up about one-fifth of India's population even today. These were castoffs from society by birth, or became such by violating caste laws. At best, they did the dirty jobs, like cleaning toilets or butchering. They could not use the same well water as caste people, and even their shadow was not to fall upon the Brahmin. They could be mistreated, raped, or even killed with impunity. They were treated worse than cattle because, according to traditional law, they ranked below these bovines. In this system there is no such thing as human rights, only caste rights, and if you are an outcaste, tough luck. Though modern India has made laws granting them equal political rights and even certain privileges, such as in education, much of rural India still lives by the ancient rules.

These castes, in turn, are divided up into an almost infinite number of subgroups, which are based largely on occupation. Rules govern the relations among these groups, including with whom one eats and who can marry whom. In such a society everybody knows one's place, and is obligated to live according to one's status. It is certainly one of the most enduring features of Indian society. One's birth into a caste, or as an outcaste, is, of course, due to karma. By living willingly in one's appropriate station in this life one can gather favorable karma for a future life.

Also as a part of this path are the four stages of life. First is the youthful stage of student, when boys aged from eight to twelve in the three upper castes are supposed to find a teacher and undergo an initiation so that one could study the Vedas. They are then called the "twice-born." Such boys might even live with their teacher as they learn the sacred texts. Next is the householder stage when young men are to marry and take up the duties of providing for a household and raising a family. For women, of course, the situation is different. "In childhood a female must be subject to her father, in youth to her husband, and when her lord is dead, to her sons; a woman must never be independent,"[10] say the ancient texts. Upon retirement there is entry upon the "forest-dwelling" stage, when the elderly withdraw from daily responsibilities and devote themselves to religious duties. The fourth stage is an even more rigorous renunciation, as one becomes an ascetic, gives up all possessions, departs from home for a wandering and begging existence, and engages in meditation. Few may do this today, preferring to defer this stage to a future life, but this stage of *sannyasa*, or renunciation, is essential for all who aim for the final salvation.

Life, finally, is governed by ritual. For a devout family there are rites that follow throughout life's passage. Thus, for instance, for those particular about ritual, there is a rite of impregnation at conception, a male-producing rite at the fourth or fifth month of pregnancy (too late, we might say!), a rite of parting the hair to protect the pregnancy from evil spirits, a birth ceremony, a naming ceremony, a feeding ceremony when the baby takes the first solid food, a first-haircut ceremony, an initiation ceremony between the ages of eight to twelve already mentioned above, the wedding ceremony, and of course a funeral ceremony and postmortem rites.[11] Besides this, of course, there are the various daily ceremonies—rites associated with image worship called *puja* are the most common (we will touch on them later)— held either at home or in the temple, ceremonies for special occasions in life such as moving, and the festival activities that occur throughout the year. One common rite in the homes of devout high-caste Hindus is the dawn meditation. After arising at the crack of dawn, bathing, drinking a few swallows of water, and placing a mark called a *tilaka* on the forehead, which indicates one's particular sect, one will practice breathing exercises (yoga) for a while, and as the sun appears stand and recite these words:

> Let us meditate upon that excellent glory
> Of the divine vivifying Sun;
> May He enlighten
> Our understanding.

After the recitation, water is poured out to the sun from cupped hands, the ritual is complete.[12]

Thus it is that in the path of works the whole of one's life, whether social, personal, or religious, is given order and meaning. One's religious duty is to live to the best of one's ability within these structures, being both dutiful while also enjoying the good things of life. How one conducts oneself in these ordinary matters determines one's future existence.

The Path of Knowledge

We usually think of knowledge as knowing many things. Knowledge, at the very least, is knowledge of *something*. That is not what knowledge means here. It is simply awareness itself. If I look out the window at the forest outside, I will see many trees and be able to name them. That is to know something. But if I had the knowledge we're talking about here, I would simply be aware of the panorama and not have any thoughts about it. The Oneness of reality and its manifoldness merge into a single whole, without separation.

We have already mentioned the Upanishads several times. These writings and their interpretation are often referred to as Vedanta, the end or completion of the Vedas. It is these texts that talk about this kind of knowledge. It is finally a knowing that one's individual self, the atman, is no different from the universal self, Brahman. They are one. It is something like a drop of water and the ocean. The drop of water is separate, it is lost, so to speak. The ocean is a vast oneness. When that drop enters the ocean, it shares in that oneness. It is no longer alone, fragmented. Or imagine dewdrops in the light of the morning sun. They glisten as they pick up that light. The light of the sun and of the dewdrops is ultimately one, not many—light from light, we might say. Numerous metaphors could be used to describe this union of like with like.

This knowledge is gained not by saying yes to the world, as one does in the path of karma, but by saying a persistent and unrelenting no. The quest is for the true self. Where is it to be found? It is not to be found in my daily life; it is not to be found in my body; it is not to be found in my mind; it is not to be found in anything I can see, feel, or think. As soon as I think my real self is this or that I must quickly say "no, no, it is not this, it is not that," for it is deeper than this or that can ever be, it is beyond all thoughts in the mind.

The ordinary self of everyday life, in this view, is conceived as a layered self, not a single or simple self. The outermost layer is the bodily self, the self that desires and eats food. Within this is the psychic self, the self that breathes and feels, our living self. Within this, again, is the self of mind, our sensory mind that awakens our internal mental states. Within this yet again is the mind of understanding, the contents and images by which we know things. Within this, finally, is the self of pure bliss. This self is beyond food, life-breath, mind, and understanding. It is beyond all words and concepts. It is the innermost center of awareness that in its purity is experienced as bliss. When the outer spheres have been cast off, like the spent boosters of a rocket, this inner self of bliss then becomes like a drop in the ocean of Brahman, or like a dewdrop that responds perfectly to the sun, light to light. This is liberation, moksha.

The way of knowledge is, really, a way of techniques to get through these several layers of the outer selves to the unchanged, unchanging, characterless self of bliss at our personal core. Yoga in its many forms is the primary technique. As one follows these techniques, one passes from the lowest stage of normal awareness in which one only sees external things, through the dreaming state in which one now sees internal objects of the mind, through a dreamless state in which, as one looks at the panorama of the forest for instance, the separation of subject and object is overcome in a single unitary consciousness, to finally the highest state in which there is neither inner nor outer, content or container, but only awareness as a timeless bliss.[13]

There are many kinds of yoga. Yoga is related to our English word *yoke*, and means to join, unite, fix, concentrate. Common forms of yoga include *Raja-yoga*, the "Royal" or classical form, *Hatha-yoga*, or "forced" yoga, which is most widely practiced now in the West, especially as calisthenic techniques, and *Kundalini-yoga*, or "serpent" yoga. Serpent yoga envisions a serpent coiled at the base of the spine, an image of vital energy. Through meditation techniques, the serpent is aroused, and its energies move up the spine, through several centers, until it finally reaches the top of the head and may, according to some, burst out into union with the female deity that is often associated with this kind of yoga. Thus, one might say, sexual energy has been transmuted into the liberating experience of union with deity.

Here we will comment briefly on the Royal yoga. The human problem, we might recall, is that the true self within, the atman, is separated from the universal self, or Brahman, by several layers of grosser kinds of self. Yoga enables one to peel these outer layers away and reach to the innermost self, which then experiences union and identity with Brahman from which it has been separated.

There are traditionally eight steps. One can see these as techniques of progressive withdrawal from the outer layers to the innermost. The first step is called *yama* (self-control), followed by *niyama* (observances). These have to do with ethical guidance, prohibitions of wrong thoughts and actions, and the cultivation of proper behavior, including ritual behavior. It is above all the trinity of greed, delusion, and anger that lead us astray. These exercises are followed by *asana* (bodily postures). In the first two, one begins to withdraw from the outer world dominated by greed and the like. Now one begins to bring the body under control and withdraw from ordinary action. Hatha-yoga is an elaborate orchestration of these bodily postures of body control. Next comes *pranayama* (breath control). One now brings one's breathing itself into control by being fully attentive to it. One is beginning now to move inward. This is followed by *pratyahara* (withdrawal of the senses), which is the use of various techniques to isolate oneself from uncontrolled response to sense stimuli. *Dharana* (concentration) deepens this removal from sense stimuli, letting now the inward states control the outward, and not the other way around. One then enters into deeper or higher levels of meditation (*dhyana*) and finally attains full inward self-identity in *samadhi*. This is the end of the path and unites one with the universal self, Brahman. Along the way, one may acquire all kinds of miraculous powers, such as prediction of the future, vision of past lives, telepathy, invisibility, levitation, and the like. However, one is not to pursue these but leave them behind, because they still belong to the world of multiplicity. Having attained the end, one could conceivably depart from this physical life. More likely, though, one lives out one's life while these moments of breakthrough remind one of the final liberation that one now looks forward to.

The Path of Devotion

If one wants to describe the piety of the ordinary Hindu, the devotion to God in the form of an image, in which God is embodied, is most what it is like. We earlier cited the humorous description of Mark Twain—"a vast museum of idols." Before we speak more about them, however, a word should be said about the gods that are embodied in these images.

Three Gods

Three gods, Visnu, Siva, and Devi, receive most of the attention in India. The followers of each of these gods consider the one they worship to be the one and only God, with the others subordinated at best. Worshipers of Visnu are called Vaishnavas; worshipers of Siva, Saivas; and of Devi Sakta, Sakta, meaning the power or divine energy of the god. Sometimes there is reference to the threesome of Brahma, Visnu, and Siva, as creator, preserver, and destroyer (though few actually worship Brahma). Beyond these there is an endless host of lesser deities, many of which are taken as manifestations (*avatara* or associates) of Visnu, Siva, or Devi.

These three divinities each have both frightful and kindly aspects to them. Siva, for instance, is the superlative ascetic who has forsaken the world and in whom reside all the destructive powers of the universe. At the same time he is a lustful and passionate lover, often depicted with an erect penis, whose most important symbol is the lingam or phallus. Central to all Siva worship is the joined lingam and yoni, the male and female sexual organs. Siva is often depicted while doing a cosmic dance. Siva is also associated with one or another female deity and is himself sometimes depicted as half male and half female.

One of the most entrancing depictions of Siva is in his dance of creating the world. He has four hands. In one hand is a drum, a symbol of creation, in another a flame, a symbol of destruction. One hand makes a sign of peace, while another points to his feet where he dances upon the prone figure of the dwarf that had been sent to destroy him and where the devotee might find salvation. As long as he continues the wild dance, the worlds remain. Should he cease, they would disappear. Showing his destructive nature Siva haunts the cremation ground, his body smeared with ashes of the dead. He wears a necklace of skulls. Myths tell of his many destructive acts. Devoted followers, to show forth this side, might dwell in cremation grounds themselves, perform bloody sacrifices, and beg with skulls as bowls.

Siva's ferocious side is balanced by his kindly side. In ancient mythology, he was known as one who handled poisons. Later a story developed in which the gods churned a Sea of Milk in an effort to extract from this churning froth an elixir of immortality. A mythical serpent was wrapped around the churn and pulled back and forth to stir up the Milk. Unfortunately, under such rough treatment, just as this elixir was to form the serpent took sick and vomited from its thousand heads a venom so deadly that it threatened the lives of the gods themselves. When Siva got wind of this, he came and skimmed off the poisonous dark blue froth that was the poison and drank it all up. The gods were saved, but Siva had a blue stain on his throat forever after. Worshipers remember in gratitude this self-sacrificing love.

Even more dramatic, if that were possible, is the Devi in her many forms: Durga, Kali, Parvati, Candi, and others. She is a symbol of creative power, and her association with Siva in fact gives him the power of creation. She is worshiped in her own right. Kali is perhaps the most terrible of all, running around with disheveled hair, a necklace of skulls, eating human flesh, drinking blood out of a skull cup; she bears fierce weapons and might even hold a severed head in one hand. She is also the bearer of disease. Often worshiped by bloody sacrifice, she stands triumphant over the prone body of Siva. Durga, both beautiful and fierce, is also prone to violence, but her violence has brought a boon to humanity in her destruction of a buffalo-demon. On the kindly side, however, these goddesses are often depicted full-breasted and with a child, upon whom they look down with great tenderness.

Sakti worship is concerned primarily with the blessings of this life—fertility, health, and wealth. But it also recognizes the sufferings and tragedies of life as signified by her terrible side. Even so, devotees accept the troubles of life as themselves a divine boon. One hymn writer honors Kali in this way:

> Though the mother beat him, the child cries, "Mother, O Mother!"
> and clings still tighter to her garment.
> True, I cannot see thee, yet I am not a lost child.
> I still cry, "Mother, Mother." . . .
> All the miseries that I have suffered and am suffering, I know, O Mother,
> to be your mercy alone.[14]

In its most extreme form the worship of Sakta violates all norms of society, most especially seen in its indulgence in sexual rites (sometimes called tantrism), seeking liberation by fighting fire with fire, so to speak.

Krisna

One of the most widely worshiped gods is Visnu, especially in the form of Krisna. Here too we see the duality present in so many of the gods. On the one hand is the playful, licentious Krisna who enjoys affairs with all the women of the town. On the other hand is the supreme Krisna, lord of heaven and earth, who in his unapproachable holiness is both the source of all as well as the one who devours all.

Numerous tales recount the exploits of Krisna, the avatar, or earthly manifestation, of the God Visnu.[15] These tales fall generally into three cycles: those associated with his infancy and birth, those with his youth, and those with his role as a warrior.

Both the terrible and the lovable are already evident in him in his infancy. The ruler had been warned that the birth of this child would be his downfall. Therefore, in an attempt to eliminate him he sent a female monster, which impersonated a beautiful and kindly nursemaid, to destroy him. This mischievous child, given to such things as stealing butter from the churn and generally making a nuisance of himself, was visited by the nursemaid. She offered him her breast—which she had filled with poison—but the infant Krisna sucked heartily, and having sucked out all the poison continued to drink until the very life of the monster was sucked out and it died.

As a youth he became the rage of all the women. The family had moved to the Vrindavan region. Once in his mischievousness, when the village girls were bathing in a stream, he stole all their garments and made them come to him one by one naked to get them back. On another occasion he went into the woods and played his flute. All the women of the village, married and unmarried, entranced by the music made their way into the woods. For two months they frolicked as he made love to everyone. This adulterous love, of course, symbolizes the turning of the women away from the world as they forgot hearth and home and showed a pure devotion to Krisna alone.

One of the greatest religious texts of Indian religion, *Bhagavad-Gita* ("Song of the Lord"), which comes in the midst of the great epic *Mahabharata*, shows Krisna in his human disguise manifest the truth about himself to his friend and associate, Arjuna. We learn, for instance, that Krisna periodically appears on earth to bring help:

Though I am an eternal unborn Soul,
the Lord of Beings,
relying on my own materiality
I enter into phenomenal being
by my own mysterious power [maya].
Whenever righteousness declines
and wickedness erupts
I send myself forth, O Bharata [Arjuna].
To protect the good and destroy evildoers
and establish the right, I come into being
age after age.[16]

This instruction comes in the lull before two armies enter into battle. Arjuna is a warrior, and Krisna his charioteer. Arjuna has asked that Krisna drive them into the no-man's-land between the armies before the battle. Surveying the enemy Arjuna loses heart. He cannot enter into battle for he sees that he will be fighting his own kith and kin—his own cousins are among his enemies contending for the throne. When Krisna hears of his plight, he seeks to instill courage. He tells him that it is his duty as a member of the ruling caste to uphold righteousness. If he turns from battle, the resulting chaos will be worse than the killing of his family and friends.

Krisna then goes on to explain that killing the body does not touch the soul:

> As leaving aside worn-out garments
> A man takes other, new ones.
> So leaving aside worn-out bodies
> To other, new ones goes the embodied [soul].
> Swords cut him [the soul] not,
> Fire burns him not,
> Water wets him not,
> Wind dries him not.[17]

He continues to teach, and after some time Arjuna realizes he is speaking with someone special, someone who is his friend yet whom he doesn't really know. In puzzlement Arjuna asks Krisna, "Show yourself!" He soon realizes Krisna is divine and asks further: "Fain would I see the form of You as Lord, O All-Highest Person. . . . Show me, Lord . . . [this] Self." Krisna agrees, but with this provision: "Never will you be able to see Me with this your [natural] eye. A celestial eye I'll give you, behold my power as Lord!"

With that there follows one of the most marvelous theophanies (God manifestations) in religious literature. The power of Krisna manifests itself as a devouring, destroying reality. Terror-struck, Arjuna calls out: "I see your mouths with jagged, ghastly tusks reminding [me] of Time's [devouring] fire: I cannot find my bearing, I cannot find a refuge; have mercy, God of gods, home of the universe!" Finally, Arjuna begs for the theophany to cease and for him to return to his original human form:

> On every side You lick, lick up, devouring—worlds, universes, every-
> thing—with burning mouths. Visnu! your dreadful rays of light fill the
> whole universe with flames of glory, scorching [everywhere]. Tell me,
> who are You, your form so cruel? Homage to You, You best of gods,
> have mercy! Fain would I know You as You are in the beginning, for
> what You are set on doing I do not understand.

"Time am I, wreaker of the world's destruction," Krisna answers. He then gives counsel to Arjuna and calls upon him to assume his own dreadful responsibility of fighting for the right. Arjuna, meanwhile, in astonished humility recognizes how he had treated Krisna as no more than a familiar friend—"Hey Krisna, hey Yadava, hey comrade!" he would say. "I crave your pardon, O [Lord,] unfathomable, unfallen!" When, finally, Krisna resumes his familiar human form, he informs Arjuna:

Not by the Vedas or grim ascetic practice, not by the giving of alms or sacrifice can I be seen in such a form as you did see Me; but by worship-of-love addressed to [Me,] none other, Arjuna, can I be known and seen in such a form and as I really am: [so can my lovers] enter into Me.[18]

Images

The most frequent way in which all of these gods are worshiped is through images. The common word for image is *murti*, which means literally "embodiment." These images made of metal, wood, or stone are taken to be actual embodiments of God. They are not just symbols, but embodiments. When, for instance, the Bible makes fun of the nations around Israel for worshiping idols, the Hindu thinks the Bible misses the point. For instance, we read in the Bible:

All who make idols are nothing. . . . Who would fashion a god or cast an image that can do no good? . . . The carpenter . . . makes it into a human form, with human beauty, to set up in a shrine. He cuts down cedars or chooses a holm tree or an oak. . . . Part of it he takes and warms himself . . . and says, "Ah, I am warm, I can feel the fire!" The rest of it he makes into a god, his idol, bows down to it and worships it; he prays to it and says, "Save me, for you are my god!" They do not know, nor do they comprehend; for their eyes are shut, so that they cannot see, and their minds as well, so that they cannot understand.[19]

In fact, the Hindu does just this and finds it meaningful. An image is made according to certain specifications, it is consecrated in a special way, and then it is deemed to be the place where the God makes God-self available to the worshiper.

The Hindu believes that all of reality is a manifestation of God. The world is in some sense God's body and God is its soul. God can be revealed in the depths of the heart. And God is also present in a properly consecrated image. God is never thought of as actually himself or herself stone or wood, but personally present through that medium—a sacramental presence. It is God's mercy that God in this way becomes approachable and no longer distant. God is available here, but not limited to this image.

Indeed, the most characteristic form of Hindu worship is the act of *darsan*, seeing God and being seen by God. In the image God is visible, palpable, present to one's senses. What we call an "idol" receives all the attention that a beloved ought to receive—gestures of respect and humility, signs of subservience, care for daily needs. In what one could call a "dollhouse religion," the image is to be awakened, bathed, dressed, fed, entertained, put to sleep. Such actions characterize the worship of the Hare Krishna group, for instance.

Here is how one Indian theologian of the past put it:

> This is the greatest grace of the Lord, that being free He becomes bound, being independent He becomes dependent for all His service on His devotee. . . . Behold the supreme sacrifice of Isvara [the Lord], here the Almighty becomes the property of the devotee. . . . He carries Him about, fans Him, feeds Him, plays with Him—yea, the Infinite has become finite, that the child soul may grasp, understand and love Him.[20]

Again, we read:

> Although omniscient, [Visnu in his image] appears unknowing; although pure spirit, he appears as a body; although himself the Lord he appears to be at the mercy of men; although all-powerful he appears to be without power; although perfectly free from wants, he seems to be in need; although the protector of all he seems helpless; although invisible, he becomes visibly manifest; although unfathomable, he seems tangible.[21]

Most of the time the place where these images are worshiped is in a shrine at home. The worship, as described above, is called puja. The worship is also done in shrines in public places. The most elaborate setting for these rituals is the Hindu temple itself.

Conclusion

We have described some of the core beliefs and practices of Hindus and suggested how they fit within a larger history of Indian religion. The twentieth century has been a dynamic one for Hinduism. During the nineteenth century, Westerners, including missionaries, looked at Hinduism and decided it was hopelessly corrupt and was on its way to dying out. The poverty of India, the oppressions of caste, holy cows running free in city and country, sati or the self-immolation of widows on the death of their husbands, temple prostitution of young girls, and on and on seemed to be inextricably linked to Hinduism. In fact, the twentieth century has seen a renewed strength in Hinduism. Hinduism is also having a significant effect in the West as well.

There have been numerous reformers and reform movements in Hinduism. We cannot begin to list these here. These reforms have gone in two directions. One direction treats Hinduism as a way of knowledge that is tolerant of other religions and that allows many paths to the same truth. Meditation and yoga remain important values. At the same time the concerns for social reform inherited from the West are taken into Hinduism and become a part of its worldview. Names such as Ram Mohan Roy, Keshub Chandra Sen, Swami Dayananda Sarasvati, Ramakrishna, Swami Vivekananda from the nineteenth century, and Rabendranath Tagore, Sri Aurobindo Ghose, Mahatma Gandhi, Sarvepalli Radhakrishnan, Krishnamurti, not to mention many swamis and gurus, represent the great diversity of these reforms.

The other direction has been to reaffirm the nationalistic fervor of Hinduism as specially and uniquely Indian. These movements are having a continuing impact within India itself, seeking to make India into a truly Hindu nation.

Where all of these movements of renewal will come out in the end is anybody's guess. One writer suggests that, as far as the worldwide appeal of reform Hinduism goes, "It would not be surprising to find Hinduism the dominant religion of the twenty-first century." Already many basic Hindu beliefs, such as reincarnation, many gods and spirits, meditation, karma, the role of a guru or spiritual leader, the idea that many religious paths lead to the same religious goal, and karma are now common currency in the West. "All of us," he adds, "may be already much more Hindu than we think."[22]

PART III
A SPECIAL CASE—
MEETING OUR JEWISH NEIGHBOR

✳ ✳ ✳

In part 1 we indicated the main themes that should inform our attitude and behavior as Christians in our relationship with people of different faiths. In part 2 we gave brief descriptions of certain religious communities and worldviews. Not included in part 2 was one very important religious community, the Jewish people.

The relationship Christians have with Judaism is unique. More so than with any other religious community, with Judaism it is difficult to talk about our relationship as Christians with that faith without also talking about our historical relationship with it. In this section, then, we attempt to do this. The first three chapters explore various stages in that historical relationship. The last chapter suggests a way to understand our faith relationship with the Jewish people. All chapters attempt to apply the kinds of attitudes and concerns that have been identified in part 1. We are applying those concerns in a somewhat more detailed treatment of one religious community, the one that is closest to Christians.

While Judaism is a rich religious tradition with great variety, the focus here is upon Rabbinic Judaism. I won't try to discuss many other movements such as various messianic movements, Jewish mysticism, or the form of pietism referred to as Hasidism. Rabbinic Judaism is taken to be the backbone of Jewish identity, and without its development there might not be today a distinct and recognizable Jewish people.

No Christian relationship with Judaism can ignore Rabbinic Judaism, even when the contemporary relationship is with the Reform, Conservative, or Orthodox forms of Judaism today. The relationship is not an easy one. It is fair to say that our relationship with the Jewish people is more important for us theologically than our relationship with other religious communities. How we understand this relationship the Jewish faith will decisively shape the understanding with which we approach every other situation.

The Faithfulness of Judaism

⟶

The Christian faith has a relationship with Judaism that is different from its relationship with all other religions. Our relationship with our Jewish neighbor is therefore also different. If, as Christians, we want to understand something of Judaism, it is necessary at the same time to discuss our relationship as Christians with Judaism. This is not the case with the other religions.

The Jewish people are the elder brothers and sisters of gentile Christians. Or, to put it a bit differently, they are God's chosen people by birthright; gentile Christians are God's chosen people by adoption. Paul uses the image of an olive tree (Israel) and a wild olive (gentile Christians). The wild olive branches are grafted onto the natural olive tree.[1] Yet another way that Paul refers to this relationship is implicit in the phrase, "the Jew first and also . . . the Greek."[2]

The earliest Christians (and a few Christians even today), however, were themselves Jewish people. As Jews, they too are the elder brothers and sisters of us gentiles. It is through them that we gentile Christians find an historical connection with the Jewish people because the first Christians were Jews. Even more important, we gentile Christians join the early Jewish Christians through Jesus the Messiah in becoming inheritors of the promises given long ago to Israel.

Judaism and Christianity are sister faiths since they are two different interpretations of the faith of Israel. For Judaism, the Torah (the revelation given to Moses) included both the written Torah (law or teaching) of the first five books of the Bible (which Christians also accept) and the oral Torah, also first given at Sinai and believed to have been passed down by word of mouth from rabbi to rabbi (which Christians do not accept). This dual Torah was the basis for the interpretation of the faith of Israel in Judaism. For Christians Jesus is the basis for the interpretation of the faith of Israel. The Torah is central to Judaism in a way that Jesus is central to the Christian. For Christians Jesus is the Torah in the flesh, both the written and oral Torah.

Both Jew and Christian believe that their understanding of the faith of Israel is the authentic one. We will talk more about that question later. But for now it is important not to forget this parallel origin of Judaism and Christianity. Nevertheless, the relationship is not equal. Christianity cannot understand itself apart from Judaism; Judaism insists on understanding itself without reference to Christianity.[3] Controversy is at the very birth of our two existences.

The Beginnings of Judaism

The history of Judaism is not quite the same as the history of Israel, or even the history of the Jewish people. The story recorded in the Bible, of course, goes back to creation, but the story of what was to become the Israelites begins with the call of Abraham. With Abraham God established a covenant, continued through Isaac and then Jacob. It was Jacob who, when he wrestled with the angel at the river Jabbok,[4] was given the name Israel. His twelve sons became the heads of the twelve tribes of Israel. But the Israel of David's time was later divided into the ten tribes of the north, or Israel, and the two tribes of Judah and Benjamin of the south, or Judah. When in 722 B.C.E. the Northern Kingdom was destroyed, only the inhabitants of the kingdom of Judah, the Judeans (*Yehudim*), remained. From them comes both the term *Jew* (*Yehudi*) and *Judaism*, and they came to refer to what formerly was called Israel as well.[5]

The terms *Jew* and *Judaism* do not mean the same thing either. *Jew* today normally refers to a person who is born of a Jewish mother, and is therefore an ethnic designation.[6] It can also refer to a person who has converted to the Jewish faith and who takes on the ritual obligations that identify one with the Jewish people. *Judaism* typically refers to a network of ritual, communal, moral, and faith commitments. Only Jews can hold these commitments, but not every Jew does.

Judaism, as this network of ritual, communal, moral, and faith commitments, goes back to the time of the Second Temple. In 586 B.C.E. the first temple had been destroyed, along with Jerusalem, and the people taken into exile to Babylon. Around 500, small groups began to return, and the temple was rebuilt under Zerubbabel around 450. Under the leadership of the priest-scribe Ezra, national life was organized around the written Torah with a determination and thoroughness that had never been seen before. This renewing of the covenant was celebrated in a public reading of the Torah on New Year's Day in 444 B.C.E. From then on the Jewish faith was centered on faithfulness to the Torah. Somewhat later, under the leadership of Nehemiah, the walls of Jerusalem were rebuilt. Judaism was born.

It was this Judaism that was being practiced in Jesus' day. Of course, over the centuries many, many changes had taken place, and things were still changing even during Jesus' time. A decisive turning point was the destruction of the Second Temple in c.e. 70. With the temple and the sacrificial rites no longer in existence, a fundamental reinterpretation of the Torah, which had talked so much about temple and sacrifice, came about. How was there going to be Judaism without these? This was the birth of rabbinical Judaism. It is this Judaism, and its successor forms today, that is our concern in this chapter. Both it and Christianity (Jesus was crucified around c.e. 30) arose at about the same time, both having been born out of the womb of an earlier Jewish faith.

Decisive for Rabbinic Judaism was the place given to the oral Torah. Readers of the New Testament will be familiar with the Pharisees, the Sadducees, and the scribes. The scribes were professionals devoted to the study of the Torah and its teaching and who prepared legal documents that applied the teachings of the Torah to life. Some of these professionals would have been Pharisees in Jesus' day. Sages, also called rabbis, formed a religious movement characterized by a deep piety and devotion to the Torah, both written and oral. They tried to interpret the Torah in the light of the lofty moral ideals of the prophetic tradition. The deep commitment to the moral core of the Torah is evident in Hillel, a Pharisee at the time of Jesus' infancy. He was asked by a gentile to define Judaism while standing on one foot. He replied: "What is hateful to yourself do not do to your fellow man. That is the whole Torah. All the rest is commentary. Now go and study."[7]

One will also recall from the New Testament Gospels that the Pharisees held the oral Torah, the teachings of the elders, in very high regard. This became the occasion for considerable controversy between Jesus and the Pharisees.[8] One will also recall that teachers of the Torah were called "rabbis." This was a term of respect. Jesus was often referred to in this way. The Sadducees, as we also know, were opponents of the Pharisees. They disagreed with the attachment of the Pharisees to the oral tradition and rejected what they considered to be their innovations, such as a belief in the resurrection.[9] Later Rabbinic Judaism was a continuation of the interests and commitments of the Pharisees, to which it gave a definitive form. Included in these commitments were the centrality of the moral teachings, the importance of the oral Torah as well as the written, and the application of these teachings to the whole of both personal and communal life.

The Faithfulness of Judaism

The passion to be faithful to God, who had a special love for the Jewish people and gave them the land, is well expressed in the Jewish prayer book. Liturgy, worship, is indeed central to the life of Judaism. Consider, for example, the prayers associated with the grace after meals. On weekdays the psalm preface is taken from Psalm 137:

> By the rivers of Babylon we sat down and wept
> > when we remembered Zion. . . .
> If I forget you, O Jerusalem,
> > let my right hand wither away;
> let my tongue cling to the roof of my mouth
> > if I do not remember you,
> if I do not set Jerusalem
> > above my highest joy.[10]

On the Sabbath or a festival it is taken from Psalm 126:

> When the Lord brought back those that returned to Zion,
> > we were like dreamers.
> Our mouth was filled with laughter,
> > our tongue with singing. . . .
> Restore our fortunes, O Lord,
> > as the streams in the dry land.
> They that sow in tears
> > shall reap in joy.[11]

In this grace after meals, the psalms are then followed by several paragraphs that strike a variety of themes acknowledging God's lordship:

> Blessed art Thou, Lord our God, King of the Universe, who nourishes all the world by His goodness, in grace, in mercy, and in compassion. . . .
> We thank Thee, Lord our God, for having given our fathers as a heritage a pleasant, a good and spacious land. . . .
> O Lord our God, have pity on Thy people Israel, on Thy city Jerusalem, on Zion the place of Thy glory. . . .
> Blessed art Thou, Lord our God, King of the Universe, Thou God, who art our Father, our powerful king, our creator and redeemer. . . .[12]

As we will see later, Jewish history has been marked by a relentless sequence of crises and disasters. Judaism has been forged in response to such crises. Let us examine Judaism's faithfulness in its response to the devastating destruction of the Temple, first in 586 (the First Temple) and then again in c.e. 70 (The Second Temple), about forty years after the death of Jesus.

From the outset, it is well for us to take note that two interlocking themes become central to this faithful response. The one theme is that of "peoplehood." The Jews are a people specially loved, or specially chosen by God (as seen for example in the Exodus), who have been given special obligations through God's revelation to Moses at Sinai. These events formed them as a single people. The second theme is the twin notions of Exile and Return. The pathos of Jewish history is measured by the repeated vulnerability of the Jews to Exile and the perpetual longing, a longing sometimes partially but never finally realized, for Return. Judaism lives out its faithfulness to God from its sense of peoplehood and its experience of the rhythms of Exile and Return.

Judaism of the Written Torah

It was in 538 that Cyrus gave the Jews exiled in Babylon (present-day Iraq) the freedom to return. Over the succeeding decades, a number did return. These events are recorded in the biblical books of Ezra and Nehemiah, who were prominent leaders in this return. Ezra, as both a leader and a priest, was particularly important for the response of the Jews to the political event of the return. It was probably at this time, or shortly thereafter, that the books of the Old Testament were gathered roughly into their present shape. The first five books of Moses (the Torah) were given special prominence. This reflected the priestly commitments of the religious leaders of the day. They had learned the lesson of exile well. Their sin as a people had led to the destruction of their nation and their temple. The prophets had called Israel back to faithfulness. Now, once and for all, they would choose faithfulness to God's covenant, to the revelation given at Sinai. Despite many trials and difficulties, the temple was rebuilt, though not so grand as the original one. By 444 B.C.E. they were in a position to hold a rededication service based on a renewed commitment to Torah faithfulness.

Something of the passion that accompanied this process can be seen in the incident connected with marriage to foreign women recorded in the book of Ezra. Some of the returnees, perhaps having difficulty finding wives among the returnees themselves, had married women from the surrounding countryside. While the local people may have had some Jewish roots, they had intermarried in the intervening years with non-Jewish inhabitants and so had lost their Jewish identity. "Thus the holy seed has mixed itself with the peoples of the lands, and in this faithlessness the officials and leaders have led the way."[13] Upon discovering this, Ezra became distraught: "I tore my garment and my mantle, and pulled hair from my head and beard, and sat appalled."[14] At the evening sacrifice he fell on his knees in prayer to God: "O my God, I am too ashamed and embarrassed to lift my face to you, my God, for our iniquities have risen higher than our heads, and our guilt has mounted up to the heavens."[15]

As he thus "prayed and made confession, weeping and throwing himself down before the house of God,"[16] the people gathered about him. They acknowledged their wrong and a procedure was worked out whereby they would deal with the issue. One by one their cases were dealt with. All the non-Jewish women were divorced from the men, and "they sent them away with their children."[17] In this and related ways a passionate attachment to Torah faithfulness was inculcated among the people.

There was, of course, much history to follow. There were the victories of the armies of Alexander the Great (336–323 B.C.E.); there were the successor rulers, the Ptolemies (from 301) and the Seleucids (from 223). These last, under Antiochus IV Epiphanes, tried to suppress Jewish religion, including desecration of the temple. This led in 167 to the rebellion of the Maccabees, belonging to the Hasmonian lineage that claimed descent from Aaron, and led to Jewish independence in 142.[18] In 63, Rome was able to assert power over Judea, which they ruled through their puppets, Antipater and the Herods, and then later directly through Roman procurators, such as Pilate. But through it all, the reforms of Ezra and Nehemiah had set a tone of Torah faithfulness that found a rich response among various sectors of the population, most notably among the Pharisees, but even in separatist movements such as the Essenes. The history of these centuries—from Ezra and Nehemiah to the time of Jesus—is far too tumultuous, both politically and religiously, for us to explore in detail here. But what had been defined from Cyrus on was an idea of faithfulness to God understood as faithful adherence to the ritual, communal, moral, and faith requirements of the Torah. It was within this tradition that Jesus was to grow up, live, and teach.

The issue of foreign wives, referred to above, was not a trivial issue. At the heart of this, as of other issues, was the question, Who is Israel? Through Exile they had learned who they were not to be. But now, who were they to be?

It was the Torah, the first five books of Moses,[19] that gave the answer to this question. Who was the Israel that God had delivered from Egypt way back then? "If you obey my voice and keep my covenant, you shall be my treasured possession out of all the peoples." And what did this mean? "You shall be for me a priestly kingdom and a holy nation."[20] That was Israel's destiny; that was her identity—to become a sanctified people. Once they had failed. This time they would not. This question of self-definition has ever since remained the underlying question of Judaism.

Israel's destiny, then, was to holiness, to sanctification. This holiness centered on the altar located in the temple. Linked to this central point of holiness, the people were to reflect this same holiness in the food they ate, in the conduct of their lives, and in the separation from all that was not holy, including unholy people.

Judaism of the Dual Torah

The next decisive moment in the formation of Judaism was the destruction of the Temple in C.E. 70. The Jewish people, suffering under Roman domination and provocation, rose in armed rebellion. After years of war, Titus conquered Jerusalem. The failure of the Bar Kokhba rebellion in 135 sealed the defeat.

With the fall of the Temple, until today never rebuilt, priestly definition of Judaism came to an end. It was the Pharisees who above all were in a position to carry the tradition forward. Even before the destruction of the Temple, in C.E. 68, the Roman general Vespasian, father of Titus[21] and soon to become emperor, had granted to the Pharisee, Yohanan ben Zakkai, the right to open an academy in Jabneh to perpetuate the religious teaching of the Pharisees. According to one tradition, opposed to the rebellion and already aware that the Temple cult was doomed, he lay in a coffin feigning death and so was safely brought out of the city surrounded by Roman troops. He then made his way to Vespasian.

Among his associates was Gamaliel, grandson of the Gamalial mentioned in Acts 5:34, who became the first nasi (leader) or Sage of the Sanhedrin that had been installed by Yohanan in Jabneh. Eventually, the Romans reverted to their old policy of ruling through local people instead of directly. This was accomplished by investing the politically compliant Jewish Sage with authority over Palestine, designating such persons as patriarch. The Romans recognized the apolitical Pharisees, from whom the Sages came, as the movement among the Jews most likely to contribute to peace and stability. In fact, their influence became pervasive among the Jews in Palestine for the next two or more centuries.

The task of framing a Jewish response to the destruction of the Temple and temple cult fell to these Sages, also called rabbis. They were of course joined in their task by the professional scribes and sympathetic priests who, having lost their religious function, still had their memories. What emerged was Rabbinic Judaism, or the Judaism of the dual Torah. It was a Judaism initially designed to give a religious shape to the governance of the people. It was designed to form a holy people apart from the temple cult. No longer could priests in the Jerusalem temple exemplify Jewish holiness; the people themselves were to become the holy ones. Holiness of life substituted for the sacrifices of the altar. This holiness was attained by carrying out the commandments (*mitzvot*) of God and by performing deeds of kindness over and beyond the commands (*maasim tovim*). [22]

The frame of mind at work is well represented in this record of a conversation with Yohanan:

> When a disciple of Yohanan ben Zakkai wept at seeing the Temple mount in ruins, Yohanan asked him, "Why do you weep, my son?"
>
> "This place, where the sins of Israel were atoned, is in ruins, and should I not weep?" the disciple replied.
>
> "Let it not be grievous in your eyes, my son," Yohanan replied, "For we have another means of atonement, as effective as Temple sacrifice. It is deeds of loving kindness, as it is said, 'For I desire mercy and not sacrifice.'"[23]

There were several stages to the formation of full-blown Rabbinic Judaism. The all-important first stage was the writing down of the Mishnah, completed by about c.e. 200.

The Mishnah was a highly condensed law code that set forth in sixty-three tractates in six divisions the rules governing decisions on matters of behavior for all kinds of possible situations. Much of it had no practical application but rather gave rules for an idealized situation. Thus, for instance, the many rules governing the temple cult in "The Division of Holy Things" treats matters concerning a situation that no longer existed. Much, however, dealt with actual situations. "The Division of Agriculture," for example, sets forth rules governing the use of land. Its point is that the land is holy because God lays a claim on it and its use. "The Division of Appointed Times" deals with days of special significance, such as the Sabbath. Life in village and family become extensions of the holiness that governed affairs in the now defunct Temple. "The Division of Women" treats mainly the ins and outs of marriage and divorce. Only an orderly social world can correspond to the holiness proper to heaven. "The Division of Damages" deals with the ordinary affairs of civil society, commerce, trade, property, administration, and the like. The goal is perfect stability in society without unbalanced relations leading to instability and collapse. "The Division of Purities" sets out the rules governing what makes things and people clean or unclean. Only the pure is truly holy. In sum, the Mishnah puts forward an ambitious program for guaranteeing the holiness of a whole people, a holiness that comes about by a meticulous conformity to the divine arrangement of things.

We have already commented on the dual Torah. The written Torah was the five books of Moses, although sometimes the word was used to refer to the Hebrew scriptures as a whole. The oral Torah, also supposedly given at Sinai, was finally compiled in the Mishnah. Subsequently other texts were added to it. The Abot (the Fathers), for instance, linked the authority of the Mishnah to Sinai by devising a chain of authorities reaching from Sinai to the sages (or *tannaim* as they are called) who speak in the Mishnah. It begins with these words:

> Moses received the Torah from Sinai and transmitted it to Joshua,
> Joshua to the elders, and the elders to the prophets, and the prophets
> transmitted it to the Men of the Great Assembly.[24]

"Great Assembly" presumably referred to the authoritative assembly originally established by Ezra. Its successor was to be in the Sanhedrin, familiar to us from the New Testament and later reestablished in Jabneh.

While the text of the Mishnah is dry in the extreme and so terse that only the informed can really understand it, it does convey an important message. In the Abot appended to the Mishnah, Rabbi Simeon ben Gamaliel says, "The decisive thing is not study but the deed," and again, "The world rests on three things: truth, justice, and peace."[25] Jacob Neusner writes,

> The Mishnah's system had one fundamental premise: Israel the people
> was the medium and instrument of God's sanctification. What
> required sanctification were the modalities of life lived in community.
> . . . The system then instructed Israel to act as if it formed a utensil of
> the sacred.[26]

Another way of putting it is that humans are created in the image of God. God has therefore made humans an active power in the world. As image, humans are God's counterpart on earth. Sanctification is not a given, but arises through deeds; it arises by using the things of the world in a way that fits with and fulfills God's intentions. A people without deeds are an unclean people. Truth, justice, and peace are the fruit of human doing, God's will for us. The Mishnah presented instructions, *halakhah* (root meaning "to go" or "way"), carefully argued guidelines for living life in this holy way.

Of course the Mishnah was not the only thing that the rabbis and Sages were doing during these years up to c.e. 200. An extensive body of Bible interpretation (Midrash) and preaching, stories, and encouragement of all kinds (*aggadah*, meaning narrative) also developed. But the Mishnah, this code of laws, this now written down oral Torah, was the kingpin of Rabbinic Judaism.

It naturally led to many other writings as well. Not least important was a vast collection of the additional discussion rabbis had on the Mishnah, including much of the biblical interpretation and preaching materials. This collection was called the Gemara, meaning "completion." This together with the Mishnah became the main components of the Talmud ("learning"), which was completed around c.e. 500.[27] If anything characterizes the piety of Rabbinic Judaism, it is the study of the Talmud.

But the Talmud itself was so vast that few could ever even read the whole thing, much less study it thoroughly. It comprises some 2.5 million words in its standard form, with some eleven to twelve thousand large pages. It therefore in turn led to an endless stream of interpretive literature in the following centuries. Some elaborated further on it; some trying to simplify it. The book that was the most successful in accomplishing this latter goal was the *Shulhan Arukh*. It was written by a Jewish refugee from Spain in Palestine and published in 1565.

Thus it is clear that the Talmud points to a way of life in which action is all important, and at the heart of that action is a deep moral sense. Perhaps the following conveys its fundamental underlying principle:

> Rabbi Hama, son of Rabbi Hanina, said: "Follow none but the Lord your God" (Deuteronomy 13:5). But can man follow God? It means that we must follow God's acts. As He clothes the naked, so shall you clothe the naked (Genesis 3:21); as the Holy One—Blessed be He— visited the sick (Genesis 18:1), so shall you visit the sick. Even as He . . . comforts those who mourn (Genesis 25:11) so shall you comfort those who are in mourning. As the Holy One . . . buries the dead (Deuteronomy 34:6) even so shall you bury the dead. . . . The Torah begins with deeds of kindness—as God made clothes for Adam and Eve—and it ends with kindness, as it is written: "He buried [Moses] in the valley."[28]

The Fateful History of Judaism

The year c.e. 313 was a fateful year in the history of Judaism: Emperor Constantine declared Christianity a protected religion in that year. The result was that Christianity became the privileged religion, and it was not many years after that that it effectively became the religion of the empire. Henceforth, Judaism would have to live under the stigma placed upon it by a triumphant and politically influential Christianity.

While there is no straight line running from Constantine to the Holocaust, Christianity as it developed in Europe paved the way for the violent and unimaginable evil of that event. In fact, several tendencies worked together to place the Jewish people at a distinct disadvantage in the following centuries. There were the leftovers of anti-Jewish sentiment in the pagan Roman Empire, crystallized by the wars Roman legions had to fight against Jews in the Jewish rebellions of c.e. 70 and from 132 to 135. There were theological reasons drummed up by Christian theologians and leaders who never wandered far from blaming Jews for the crucifixion of Jesus. There was the perceived clannishness of Jews who ate differently, believed differently, and sometimes spoke and dressed differently. Such marks of difference, as always, tend to create suspicion in the minds of the dominant population.

The Jewish people have had a bumpy ride, to say the least, since the ascendancy of the church. We may picture the history of this bumpy ride as follows:

The History of Jewish-Christian Relations

200–600	Basic anti-Jewish ideas developed by Church preachers, teachers, and leaders
600–1000	Relatively stable era with minimal restrictions on Jewish communities
1000–1800	Anti-Jewish practices by church and rulers leading to expulsions
1800–1950	Emancipation/Holocaust/Land of Israel
1950–present	Leading roles of Israeli and American Jews

The anti-Jewish sentiment in antiquity (the three or four centuries both before and after Christ) was largely based on the desire of Jews to be a separate people. Scattered in various large cities they nevertheless gathered in more or less exclusive communities. This was largely due to their habits, religiously-based, of eating certain foods prepared in a special way and other laws that made sharing an intimate life with gentile people difficult. With the Jews isolated from others by this web of rules and regulations, it was easy for people to become suspicious, to resent the clannishness, even to dislike them. Anti-Jewish sentiment, widespread but not universal, was especially the case in areas where the Jews were concentrated.[1]

This seemingly natural response to a people who not only appear different but also clannish was a continuing reaction throughout the history of the West. The specifically Christian contribution built upon this foundation, making its claims all the more plausible.

What was the specific Christian contribution? This is a very delicate question, since the answer comes close to the heart of what the Christian faith is all about. The resources that church people drew upon to build up their anti-Jewish arguments were close at hand in the New Testament. Included are the controversies that Jesus had with Jewish leaders in his day, the denunciations that were made against these leaders, the involvement of the Jewish leaders and populace in the crucifixion of Jesus, the belief that Jesus was the rejected Messiah, that the Jewish law or Torah had been fulfilled and was no longer valid as a required rule for life, the belief that the church was a new Israel, chosen and called by God.

None of these items in themselves argued for an anti-Jewish attitude. Nevertheless, for whatever reasons, already in the early centuries of the Church, from at least 200 to 600, a one-sided interpretation of the Gospel in not a few cases led to a powerful anti-Jewish polemic. Why was this so? It is hard to say. Was it resentment at the growing strength of Rabbinic Judaism that refused to die away even after the terrible destruction of Jerusalem? Was it anger at Jewish contradiction of, if not polemic against, Christian teachings? Was it gentile arrogance over against a perceived Jewish clannishness? Was it fear that Christians might be too friendly with the Jews and be tempted away from faithfulness to the Church? Was it an unthinking inheritance of pagan anti-Jewish stereotypes? Whatever the case, there developed a strict we/they, black-and-white attitude with respect to the Christian and the Jew on the part of many. The history of the Jews was depicted as a perpetual decline from Abraham on, with an absolute and decisive break in the rejection of Jesus the Messiah.

The first clearly anti-Jewish writing in the Greek language was the "Dialogue with Trypho" of Justin Martyr, who died in 165. In this document he imagines a dialogue with a Jew whom he soundly refutes. The first anti-Jewish writing in Latin was by Tertullian, his *Against the Jews* in 200. The most significant influence on the attitude of the church toward the Jews, however, was the writings of Augustine (354–430).

Augustine made four major points. First, he continues the tradition that the Old Testament prefigured Christ and that the Jews in rejecting Christ in fact also rejected their own scriptures. Therefore, Christians are the true heirs of the faith of Israel. Second, he wants to account for the reason God in God's providence allows the continued existence of the Jews. The reason, he suggests, is that the homeless exiles, the Jews, with their Temple destroyed, are a continual witness that the church is now the true Israel and, in fact, their very existence furnished proof of the truth of Christianity. Without the Jews, pagans could argue that Christians had just invented the Old Testament prophecies, but now the Jews were witnesses to its veracity.[2] Third, he accused the Jews not just of unbelief, but of deicide—God- or Christ-killers. And this was a guilt not only carried by the Jews in Jesus' day but by all Jews down to the present. "In your ancestors, you killed Christ."[3] Fourth, despite this anti-Jewish viewpoint, he does not personalize it. He urged Christians to treat Jews with kindness and compassion, since salvation is unmerited, and one should not gloat over the fall of others.

These ideas of Augustine became very important in the formation of future attitudes of church leaders. On the one hand, the Jews were put in their place. Their homelessness and suffering were deemed their due reward. On the other hand, it was not fit to exterminate the Jews, since their very presence was testimony to the truth of Christian doctrine and, moreover, the gospel mandates kindness. Thus both disadvantage and tolerance were the facts of the case, and it was up to each generation to work out the proper mixture of the two. For some tolerance was forgotten and active persecution advocated. For others fair treatment was deemed the appropriate response.

His contemporary, Jerome, famous for translating the Bible into Latin, studied for ten years under rabbis and had continual contact and good personal relations with the Jews. Nevertheless, he could still refer to the prayers and hymns of the Jew as the "grunting of a pig and the bellowing of an ass."[4] John Chrysostom (344–407), perhaps the greatest preacher of the early church, was the most extreme. He wrote the most famous anti-Jewish book of all the church fathers. As he graphically puts it:

> Where Christ-killers gather, the cross is ridiculed, God blasphemed, the Father unacknowledged, the Son insulted, the grace of the Spirit rejected. . . . If the Jewish rites are holy and venerable, our way of life must be false. But if our way is true, as indeed it is, theirs is fraudulent. . . . I am speaking of their present impiety and madness.[5]

Fortunately these sermons of his were not translated into Latin and so were not widely accessible, until the fifteenth century, so they could not work as much mischief as they might have otherwise.

By 400 the basic elements of the Church's attitude towards the Jews had taken root. It was not long before Rome would be sacked (410) and then fall to barbarian hordes (476),[6] and although the Roman Empire retained some control in the eastern part of Europe with Constantinople as its center, the western part was divided and in general political disarray.

In the east, laws were put on the books, but because of a weakened government were not always effective. But the direction intended is clear:

> Jews were excluded from holding civil offices that would entail exercising power over Christians. They were also forbidden to own Christian slaves. Mixed marriages were outlawed, and conversion to Judaism was defined as apostasy and made punishable by death. . . . Jews were forbidden to seek converts from paganism as well as among Christians, [and] building or repairing a synagogue became a crime. Roman law even attempted to censor the Talmud, thus providing an imperial precedent for similar efforts by thirteenth century popes.[7]

In the West, these provisions in any case did not hold.[8] One of the great popes of this era, Gregory the Great (590–604) put forward the influential formula: "Just as the Jews ought not be allowed to do more in their synagogues than the law allows them, so too they should suffer no reduction in the privileges previously granted them."[9] This did not stop him from speaking ill of the Jews as blind, stubborn, arrogant, and "carnal," that is, without insight into the true meaning of scripture.

After the fall of Rome, local rulers throughout Europe were more interested in running their territories as they felt best and took little instruction from the popes. In any case, there were few Jews in their territories, whether Italy or northern Europe, so they posed a minor irritation at worst. There is little evidence of severe action taken against Jews by rulers or people in the following centuries.[10] Except for Spain where the Visigoths ruled, Jews and Christians lived more or less peaceably together.[11]

They lived together more peaceably, it seemed, than the church liked. Numerous local church councils were called to deal with the Jewish issue,[12] and not a few books and tracts regarding the Jews were written. But these things had little more than short-term local effects, and the decisions of the councils were mostly ignored. In any case the church had no power to compel rulers to heed them during this period. Meanwhile, in the seventh century, Islam arose and took over large swaths of land once under Christian domination. Now the Jews lived under either Muslims or Christians. In fact, 90 percent of the Jewish population now lived under Muslim rule.[13] Under Muslim rule they fared better.

By the eleventh century things began to change in Europe. Before the tenth and eleventh centuries, there were very few Jews in the northern parts of Europe. For centuries conditions had been more or less unsettled. Accustomed to a Mediterranean climate, there was little in northern Europe to attract them. This changed, beginning in the late tenth century. Political and economic conditions began to stabilize, and commercial expansion commenced, together with the rise of urban centers. These things began to attract some Jews to seek their fortunes farther north. Their presence brought great economic advantage to places they settled since usually coming as traders they brought a wide network of international connections with them. Local rulers saw the advantage of this and began to invite Jewish traders to come, and placed them under their protection. Thus it was, that a significant new immigrant community appeared in some of the cities of northern Europe. One place of concentration was in cities along both sides of the Rhine River.[14] This was the birth of the so-called Ashkenazi Jew, referring to the Jew of northern, and later eastern, Europe and the associated culture.[15]

This new immigration of Jews and their settlement began peacefully enough. But over the years various factors were to lead to their eventual expulsion from these same communities. This is much too complex a tale to tell here, but we can refer to some of the important factors in this development.

The First Crusade of 1096 was the first major explosion of violence against Jews. Many reasons account for this. One was the religious renewal that was taking place in France at the time. This brought a sense of Christian identity to the populace, both to the nobles with their armies of knights as well as to the peasantry, however superficial that identity might be. As it turned out, when Pope Urban II in 1095 called for an armed pilgrimage to Jerusalem to free the Holy Sepulchre from the control of infidels

(Muslims), the call fell on fertile soil. The nobles and knights were ready to show their ardor for the Lord. And so they mobilized.

At the same time there developed a parallel mobilization of peasants in what came to be called the Peasants' Crusade. This movement apparently developed from the bottom up, reflecting the religious enthusiasms of peasants, probably whipped up by bombastic preachers. Moreover, the autumn of 1095 had yielded a poor harvest and food prices were high. The idea of a great expedition caught on. Cattle and belongings were sold to get cash for the journey. Common folk loaded what was left of their things on oxcarts, gathered their family, and started on the journey. Ignorant and illiterate, they imagined Jerusalem was just over the next rise.[16] Meanwhile, irresponsible preachers had called to their attention that infidels (in this case, Jews) were closer at hand than in far off Jerusalem. One might as well take care of them before setting out.

And so it was that latent hostility to new immigrants, a long history of church teaching about the deliberate unbelief of the Jews,[17] religious enthusiasm, and the dynamics of popular mob violence[18] without effective control of nobles and knights who had not yet set out on the journey, resulted in the mayhem wrecked upon the Jews of Worms, Mainz, and Cologne along the Rhine in Germany. Perhaps some three thousand Jews were massacred.[19]

Such disasters were episodic, feeding on popular imaginations and hostility to the stranger. But over time the Jew became more than the odd foreigner. As the economy developed, many others besides the Jews got involved in trade and commerce. Slowly the economic involvement of the Jews changed towards that of usury. There were many reasons for this. One was that according to Church teaching it was not permissible for Christians, at least not faithful Christians, to lend money at interest. Thus, lending at interest was left to bad Christians and Jews.

But the usury system in which the Jews were caught up served the interests of the rulers perfectly. There were several components to the system of usury that in effect used the Jew to serve as tax collector for the rulers. This is how it worked in England. People from all levels of society borrowed money from the Jews, and the rate of interest was directly or indirectly set by the prince or ruler, not the Jew. The princes or rulers also required the Jews to pay a fee for princely or royal protection, which could be raised or lowered as the ruler liked; the only way the Jews could pay was to collect on the debts that were owed to them. If the ruler needed more funds, he would charge the Jews a higher fee, and they in turn would have to increase interest rates and step up their collection efforts. The net effect was that the worse the conditions the heavier the burdens upon the people, with the Jew in the middle. Doing the dirty work for the ruling class, the Jews became an object of hostility on the part of the often debt-ridden populace.[20] Quite naturally, the Jews often despised those who despised them and took advantage when and where they could.

As hostility developed, the popular imagination fed it further. By the twelfth and thirteenth centuries unfounded charges of ritual murder by Jews, of desecration of the wafer used in the Sacrament of the Lord's Supper, of poisoning wells and streams (especially at the time of the Black Death in 1349), and the like circulated. Not surprisingly, this was also the time of the witch hunts in Europe.

The idea that Jews practiced ritual murder, for instance, first came to the fore in 1144. Then, as today, children occasionally disappeared in mysterious ways. In this case, the body of a young boy named William, a tanner's apprentice, was discovered in a wood. The word got around that the murder had happened on Wednesday of Holy Week. That year this day happened to coincide with the second day of the solemn Jewish Passover festivities. The conclusion drawn was that it must have been done by a Jew to reenact, and thus mock, the passion of Christ. It was not long before the young boy became not only a martyr but a saint in the popular mind and eventually affirmed by the Church as well. Thus, child saints such as St. William of Norwich, St. Andreas of Rinn, St. Hugh of Lincoln, St. Simon of Trent and El Santo Nino de la Guardia came into popular tradition.[21]

We have already mentioned the actions of church councils and of the pope with respect to regulations concerning the Jews, the ideas of theologians such as Augustine, and the popular preaching and writing of many over time. Even Bernard of Clairvoux, who vigorously preached support of the First Crusade, played his part. Though forbidding doing physical harm to the Jews, who "are not to be persecuted, killed, or even put to flight," he does not hesitate to describe them "in accordance with the common proverb: 'like the mouse in a pocket, like the snake around one's loins, like the fire in one's bosom.'"[22] Other popular preachers had fewer scruples.

The highest church officials were usually more circumspect. Over the years papal bulls (instructions from the pope) forbade mistreatment of the Jews, granting them the privilege to worship in their synagogues, forbidding any Christian use of violence upon them, and denouncing false and ridiculous charges of ritual murder and the like. Nevertheless, they also made clear that "we properly scorn the Jewish perversion of the faith, because they, persisting in their stubbornness, refuse to understand . . . their own scriptures and so accept the Christian faith."[23] Sometimes a bull would prohibit preaching of hostile sermons that would stir up the crowds, but at other times, the bull might itself stir up hostility and impose restrictions. At times a bull would go so far as to condemn the Talmud itself and forbid its use, something that was at the very heart of the faith of Rabbinic Judaism. Pope Gregory IX wrote in 1239 that he was deeply saddened to discover the following:

> To the archbishops throughout the Kingdom of France, whom these letters may reach. . . . If what is said about the Jews of France and of the other lands is true, no punishment would be sufficiently great or sufficiently worthy of their crime. For they, so we have heard, are not content with the old Law which God gave to Moses in writing: they even ignore it completely, and affirm that God gave another law which is called "Talmud." . . . [24]

Thus, he initiated the confiscation and burning of the Talmud, the oral Torah of the Jew, a policy continued by Pope Innocent IV and others as well. Thus it was that in Paris alone in 1242 "twenty-four cart-loads of Talmudic literature were destroyed in the public squares."[25] These and other judgments and prejudices regarding the Jews were also pervasive among the works of intellectuals and scholars of the day,[26] including Thomas Aquinas.[27]

Not surprisingly, mythologies about the Jew made their way into the art and literature of the day. In many cities and towns, there were annual presentations of passion plays by locals, which would run several days at a time. These gave many opportunities to depict the hook-nosed Jew with his devious eyes in dramatic fashion and to enlarge upon the enormity of their sin in crucifying Christ. One myth that made its rounds was that of the Wandering Jew. He might appear in the most unlikely times and places, much as Bigfoot or UFOs. Who was this person? An old tradition holds that on the way to Golgotha, this Jew had belittled Jesus, who turned to him and told him he would be a wanderer until his Return. And so, like Cain, marked as an outcast forever, this eternal wanderer would appear here and there, and so would continue until the last day. Many of us are familiar from our television programs of such eternal wanderers, modern renditions of the Wandering Jew theme.

Of course, not everything was equally grim. For the most part, Jews and Christians could relate to each other normally and could even enjoy one another. Even the supposed debates that were from time to time staged between Christian and Jew (the Christian would always win) could be a time for fun. One account records a dispute between a Christian and a Jew in which the Christian bet a jug of wine on the outcome, and the Jew his finger. The Christian won, of course, but he then informed the Jew he could retain his finger so long as he, the Christian, was not in need of it.

Yet the long-term outcome was not pleasant. There had been many minor or short-term expulsions from this or that town over the years. Finally, in England, they were fully expelled in 1290, some sixteen thousand persons. Jews were not to return to live in England until the seventeenth century. In 1306 Jews were expelled almost totally from France. In 1348 there were expulsions from Germany, but because it was politically disorganized, these were only partial. Many of these Jews fled to the less developed regions of Poland and Lithuania. Even there life did not always prove stable, and eventually many Jews moved into western parts of Russia. All of these were Ashkenazi Jews. In 1492 in Spain, after a long period of turbulent existence and exacerbated by the Inquisition, all Jews who would not convert to Christianity were expelled. In 1496 they were expelled from Portugal. These, some 300,000, formed the basis of Sephardi (Spanish) Judaism, which settled in North Africa, parts of southern Italy, in large numbers in Turkey, and in the Holy Land and nearby regions. The converted Jews who remained in Spain and Portugal were designated "Marranos," that is, swine.[28]

These expulsions, of course, were not the end of matters. Wherever Jews went in Europe, they were confined to Jewish Quarters, often called ghettos. Actually the Jewish Quarter began from Jewish initiative itself, since they voluntarily congregated on a particular street in order to be close together and free to live life in a way consistent with the Torah. They could thus observe its precepts, they would always have a quorum for the saying of prayers (ten adult males were required)[29] and organizing a synagogue, they could have their own cemetery, their own ritual bath (*mikveh*), and could provide mutual assistance and protection from attack by strangers and enemies. In some cases these became walled communities, with one or more gates. In Venice, in 1516, some Jews sought refuge in the city. The condition was that they live in the *geto nuovo* quarter, an isolated island among the canals of Venice that could easily be cut off by walls, gates and drawbridges. Soon the walls and gates were to become a permanent and required feature of the ghettos throughout much of Europe. Christians were appointed to guard the gates, with the Jews paying their wages; Jews had to wear distinctive badges; from time to time there was compulsory attendance at preaching services to convert them; the professions they could engage in were restricted. Usually ghettos could not be enlarged, and so as population grew they became extremely overcrowded.

Beyond this, in place after place, not least in Russia, pogroms[30] were carried out, in which numberless Jews were slaughtered. In 1648 Bogdan Chmielnicki, a Cossack chieftain, led a revolt against the ruling Poles. The Jews were caught in the middle of this revolt and became a special target, since they were in the employ of the Polish lords. The slaughter that resulted for several years resulted in a minimum of 100,000 Jewish deaths. And the slaughter was cruel. "Their infants were slit like fishes, their women were ripped open, live cats were let into their bowels, and they were then sewn up again."[31] Such events are not unlike those we have seen in our own days. This, says Parkes, "brought the whole period of medieval Jewry to a close."[32]

Unfortunately, the Reformation, while it renewed the church, did not bring any benefit to the Jew. In fact, Luther had been an indirect beneficiary of one of Ashkenazi Judaism's greatest scholars, Rashi (1040–1105). Rashi wrote a lucid commentary to both Bible and Talmud, and his massive commentary on the Talmud is now printed with every edition of the Talmud. Nicholas de Lyra (ca. 1270–1340), a Franciscan professor of theology, studied Rashi's biblical interpretation extensively and himself wrote a fifty-volume running commentary to all the books of the Old and New Testaments. His work became Luther's guide in his translation of Scripture.[33] Indeed, Rashi, in contrast to the allegorical interpretation of the Bible so common throughout the Middle Ages, offered a very different, literal interpretation of the text, a procedure that was to affect Luther profoundly.

In his early years, Luther, who lived from 1483 to 1546, thought kindly of the Jews. He felt that the Christian attitude towards the Jew should be one of persuasion, not force. He had high hopes they would be attracted to the Reformation movement. But that was not to be. In his later life Luther wrote some of the worst diatribes regarding the Jews of all history, including his *Concerning the Jews and Their Lies* of 1543. Read and weep:

> Let me give you my honest advice.
>
> First, their synagogues or churches should be set on fire, and whatever does not burn up should be covered or spread over with dirt so that no one may ever be able to see a cinder or stone of it. And this ought to be done for the honor of God and of Christianity in order that God may see that we are Christians, and that we have not wit-

tingly tolerated or approved of such public lying, cursing, and blaspheming of His Son and His Christians. . . .

Secondly, their homes should likewise be broken down and destroyed. For they perpetrate the same things there that they do in their synagogues. For this reason they ought to be put under one roof or in a stable, like Gypsies, in order that they may realize that they are not masters in our land, as they boast, but miserable captives, as they complain of us incessantly before God with bitter wailing.

Thirdly, they should be deprived of their prayer books and Talmuds in which such idolatry, lies, cursing, and blasphemy are taught.
Fourthly, their rabbis must be forbidden, under threat of death, to teach any more. . . .

Fifthly, passport and traveling privileges should be absolutely forbidden to the Jews. For they have no business in the rural districts since they are not nobles, nor officials, nor merchants, nor the like. Let them stay at home.

Sixthly, they ought to be stopped from usury. All their cash and valuables of silver and gold ought to be taken from them and put aside for safekeeping. For this reason, as we said before, everything that they possess they stole and robbed from us through their usury, for they have no other means of support. . . .

Seventhly, let the young and strong Jews and Jewesses be given the flail, the ax, the hoe, the spade, the distaff, and spindle, and let them earn their bread by the sweat of their noses as is enjoined upon Adam's children. For it is not proper that they should want us cursed *Goyyim* to work in the sweat of our brow and that they, pious crew, idle away their days at the fireside in laziness, feasting, and display. . . . We ought to drive the rascally lazy bones out of our system.

If, however, we are afraid that they might harm us personally, or our wives, children, servants, cattle, etc., when they serve us or work for us . . . then let us apply the same cleverness [expulsion] as the other nations . . . and . . . drive them out of the country for all time. . . .
To sum up, dear princes and nobles who have Jews in your domains, if this advice of mine does not suit you, then find a better one so that you and we may all be free of this insufferable devilish burden—the Jews.[34]

The *Encyclopedia of Judaism* comments on Luther's words thus: "Short of the Auschwitz oven and extermination, the whole Nazi Holocaust is pre-outlined here."[35] The Reformation unleashed attitudes that in some cases worked towards better treatment, and in others increased enmity.

I 2

INTO THE MODERN WORLD

$\sim$

Expulsions, pogroms, and ghettos, however, are not the end of the story. The expulsions helped to create a new situation for the Jews. Scattered once again to the four winds, they ended up giving a new economic and cultural vigor to Jews in the Muslim countries, including Palestine. Here, one of the expelled, Joseph Karo, was to produce the definitive code of Jewish law that was to be accepted by all of Judaism. They brought new Jewish communities into Protestant Netherlands, into northwestern Germany and England and, as part of a widespread Jewish commercial network, helped the development of capitalism there. They crossed the oceans into the New World, first finding safe haven under Dutch rule. Ironically, Columbus is said to have chosen the very day the Jews were forced from Spain as the day for his departure. In his journals he "wrote movingly" on the mad scramble of Jews in their rickety ships.[1]

The expulsions from western Europe drove Ashkenazi Jews ever farther eastwards, into Poland, Lithuania, Russia. They became the nucleus of the largest Jewish population in the world. Eventually from there they were to spread above all to North America.

Of course, other forces were at work as well. The Reformation had sundered once and for all any monolithic Christianity. With old-style Christian uniformity gone, the possibility of tolerance for religious dissenters entered the picture. Jews were to benefit also. Gradually strong, centralized nation-states developed. On the one hand, these were a threat to dissenting groups, for the rulers wanted direct and unhindered rule of the people. But, on the other hand, it put forward a universal requirement that all people were to be treated on the same basis. When this political reality combined with the liberating ideas of the Enlightenment, a new possibility was born.

Emancipation

Emancipation refers to a process in which the Jewish people in western countries won their rights as citizens and the enjoyment of political equality.

It was a long, slow and uneven process, which required gentiles to think differently about Jews, and Jews about themselves.

Several things led to this change in the ways of thinking. Nothing was more important than the Enlightenment, that intellectual tradition that came into Western thinking in the early part of the eighteenth century. It emphasized the use of reason, not reliance upon external authority, in understanding life and in the making of decisions. Reason was universal; reason stood on its own two feet; it was something everyone properly educated possessed. It opposed creeds and doctrines which, undergirded by the authority of popes and churches, were not universal. Powerful political consequences followed. Governments, however centralized, were to be endowed with reason and run by the will of the people, not by princes, kings, rulers, and emperors who had their positions based on birth and heredity. Radical new ideas were afoot.

If gentiles needed to have their thinking changed, they had an abundance of their own philosophers to help them—Lessing, Kant, Hegel, Montesqieu, Rousseau, Locke, and many others. But the Jews too would have to change their thinking. The ghetto not only helped produce but also expressed their limited horizons. They had to begin to see themselves not only as different from others but also like others.

One great thinker who helped lay the groundwork for the Jews in this regard was Moses Mendelssohn (1729–1786). A small, brilliant, hunchbacked Jew, he became something of a sensation in Berlin society. As a fourteen-year-old Yiddish-speaking boy, he first got to Berlin by hook or by crook, despite the fact that Jews were normally excluded from the city. He mastered the German language. In his twenties he met Gotthold Lessing, one of the most liberal spirits of the day, who took him under his wing. Mendelssohn came to public attention when he competed in an essay contest put on by the Berlin Academy. It was on a complicated intellectual topic, and he won first prize, even beating out Kant, who was soon to become one of the most renowned philosophers of all time.

As the result of an encounter with a Christian who would have converted him, he reaffirmed his Jewish identity: "I hereby witness before the God of truth . . . that I shall abide by these my convictions as long as my soul shall not change its nature."[2] Two activities of his might be mentioned. He translated the Pentateuch into German, hoping thereby to usher his own Jewish people into the wider culture of his day through the learning and use of German. It was not done without considerable opposition by fellow Jews who considered vulgar German an insult to the Bible and feared contamination by gentile culture. But he persisted and, having given the manuscript to the printer, said, "I placed my soul in my hands, raised my eyes to the mountains, and gave my back to the smiters."[3] He also published a small volume called *Jerusalem*. Expressing thoughts similar to those of Lessing, he argued for freedom of conscience, that no religion could claim all truth, and that the test of the truth of a religion rested in the moral conduct of its followers. He urged, "let everyone who does not disturb public happiness, who is obedient to the civil government, who acts righteously towards his fellow man, be allowed to speak as he thinks, to pray to God after his own fashion, or after the fashion of his fathers, and to seek eternal salvation where he thinks he may find it."[4]

But this was only one of many voices at the time calling for the same thing. Nevertheless, in Europe things first came to a head with the French Revolution. With its "reign of terror," it was for many a terrible time— certainly for Louis XVI, the soon-to-be-executed emperor. The Declaration of the Rights of Man (August 27, 1789) found its practical fulfillment for the Jews when the National Assembly also granted them full equality on September 27, 1791.

For the Jews what did this mean? One speaker in the National Assembly in 1789 explained the principle well: "The Jews should be denied everything as a nation, but granted everything as individuals."[5] That is to say, the Jews could not form a nation within a nation, running themselves by their own religious laws (as had been done in the ghettos, for instance), or imagining themselves to be a unique nation that is temporarily exiled from their native land, Israel. Like all other religions, they were to be disestablished. But as persons, they were to have equal freedoms to everybody else, without regard to religion. As we shall see, this principle had profound implications for what Judaism was to become. Jews too had to accept the distinction between one's political and one's religious identity.

As it turned out, a simple declaration was hardly enough. While the new Republic led unexpectedly to a new ruler—Napoleon was crowned emperor in 1804—after 1796, the story of Europe was essentially the story of Napoleon. "Soldier, statesman, despot, adventurer, the most spectacular personality in modern history," his armies ranged through Europe and brought the ideals of the French Revolution with them. While his own personal views on the Jews seemed to shift somewhat uncertainly, everywhere the French revolutionary armies went ghettos fell and Jewish equality was proclaimed: Belgium, the Netherlands, Italy, southern Germany, Prussia, even Spain. But with his defeat at Waterloo in 1815, things in most of these places began to unravel. It was not until around 1879, and only after many struggles, that the Jews in western Europe were made equal and free citizens. It was to take some decades yet before the same was the case farther to the east.

In fact, even before the French Revolution, a different, and less violent process, was taking place across the Atlantic Ocean. It was in the United States of America that the Jews first received the full rights of citizenship. We will touch on that happy story below.

However, over the horizon lurked an unforeseen danger. A new form of anti-Jewish sentiment was to arise, a form to be called anti-Semitism. No longer founded on religious principles, a racist doctrine was to arise and to be given a human incarnation in Adolf Hitler and the Nazi movement. From 1933 to 1945 the Jews of Central Europe were hounded to death. In the end some six million were gassed, burned, buried alive. There was no darker day in Jewish history. We will not recount that horror here. The churches were ambivalent, and so complicit. Other nations, including the United States, were ambivalent, refused to receive not-yet-murdered exiles, and so were also complicit. But again we see the pattern of the Jewish experience of exile. They are a people whose existence is always at risk. Emancipation cannot be taken for granted. Though today citizens of many nations, all Jews, even those dwelling in the land of Israel, still live a double existence: an emancipated people and a people in exile or at risk of exile.

From One Judaism to Many Judaisms

Among other things, emancipation introduced entirely new dynamics into the life of the Jewish community. Released from a ghetto existence, what did it mean to be free and equal citizens? There was promise here, but also a danger. Would they lose their identity and simply assimilate with the larger gentile crowd? For many Jews this did happen. Could they retain their identity and still be patriotic citizens without a dual allegiance? If so, what would that identity be? These were only two of the many questions that had to be asked. The many Judaisms of our modern world give the answer.

Already the foundation for many of the changes had been and continued to be laid by the Jewish intellectual aspect of the emancipation. It was called the *haskalah* ("enlightenment") movement,[6] and Moses Mendelssohn was an early leader. What were its goals and what did it do?

Haskalah aimed at the assimilation of the Jewish people into the particular nations and cultures within which they lived. Only if the Jews became like the others, in language, in dress, in manners, in education, in employment, would they really be able to benefit from their emancipation.

One extreme response of the Jewish people to emancipation was complete assimilation into the surrounding culture, leading to the loss of Jewish identity. Less extreme was a secular reinterpretation of Judaism that dropped all the religious paraphernalia. Thus, for instance, the rules and prescriptions for ritually proper Jewish lives as laid out in the Talmud, like eating habits, Sabbath habits, and so forth, were simply set aside. In place of the future hope of a messiah, identity with the Jewish people expressed itself in a Jewish nationalism that was anti-messianic. Whatever hope there was for a Jewish homeland would have to be done by human action without divine assistance. Again, rather than an interpretation of Jewish history based on notions of revelation to Moses, the history of the Jewish people was to be studied in a scientific way, like all other history. It was a history of human actions, triumphs, and foibles. This became the soil out of which Zionism and Reform Judaism arose.

As for Reform Judaism, with emancipation came a radical new orientation for the Jews—no longer could religion and national identity be seen as one. Judaism was now only a particular religious persuasion, nothing more. In one fell swoop, the foundations of Rabbinic Judaism as they stood in the Talmud were undercut. In that massive, centuries-old restatement of what it was to be a Jew, all facets of life had been covered by Torah. Now that unity was broken.

It did not take long for this realization to begin to reshape the nature of Judaism itself. Since all religion, as the enlightenment thinking had it, was to be based on reason, not on the authority of tradition, much less on the authority of divine revelation, the peculiar Jewish eating and worship habits were up for grabs. Innovations in the early nineteenth century in Germany tried to make Jewish worship look more like Protestant worship. A new liturgy, hymn singing and a sermon, all in German, were introduced, as well as organ and choir music. A rite of confirmation was installed and included both boys and girls. Men and women sat together in worship, and so on.[7] These actions were, obviously, a direct affront to historic Rabbinic Judaism, for whom strict observance of the Torah commands (*mitzvodt*) was essential. In one happy change, the morning blessing that thanked God for "not making me a woman" was abolished.[8]

The underlying idea behind these alterations was simple. As with everything else, religion is in a continual process of change. The permanent elements in Judaism, it was said, were a belief in God and the moral law. All ceremonies and rules were its changing elements.[9] These latter only expressed the inner meaning of the first two for a particular age. If the Jewish people were once a nation, they are so no more. If there used to be hope for a messiah in the future, the hope was now only for a moral society which would in fact be the messianic age. Some thought it already existed in modern society. If the Jews once had their own land, now the whole world was their land. And so it was that every generation has the right to decide its own practices and rethink those of the past. One of the more radical reformers put it in simple language: "In the talmudic age, the Talmud was right. In my age, I am right."[10]

In the early stages Reform Judaism tended toward a generic religiosity.[11] In America it was for a time to become the dominant form of Judaism. Conservative, Reconstructionist, and Orthodox Judaism are all the result of varying responses to the challenge that Reform ideas and innovations brought.

The American Experience

The Jewish Coming

Today the United States has the largest Jewish population in the world. It is also the freest environment Jews have ever known within the gentile world. Indeed, while the long political struggle for emancipation in Europe was going on, a parallel and earlier process of a much more peaceful nature was taking place in North America. Here the Jews were to attain their first permanent status as full citizens in a gentile nation.

Actually, the story of the Jews in America is as old as the story of Columbus, who may himself have come from a Jewish background. In fact, the leader of the first European party to set foot on American soil was Luis de Torres, a Jew who had been baptized the day before the expedition sailed out of Spain.[12] Soon the New World became a place of refuge for many Marranos fleeing from the watchful eye of the Inquisition.

For a short while the Dutch took control of much of Brazil from the Portuguese, only to lose it to the Portuguese again. From 1631 to 1654 there was an open and well-organized Jewish community in the area of Recife, the capital of Dutch Brazil. Fleeing Portuguese reconquest in 1654, a small group of Jews (some twenty-four of them) took refuge in New Amsterdam, also under Dutch rule. Despite some prejudice against them, they were granted full citizenship in the colony because they were

Dutch citizens. In 1664 the colony came under British control and New Amsterdam was renamed New York. Thus begins the story of Jews in America.

There are three periods of Jewish immigration to North America. The first had its small beginnings as indicated and was largely of Sephardi Jews exiled from Spain and Portugal. They were soon joined by Ashkenazi from Amsterdam and London. At the time of the war of independence there were some two thousand Jews in the colonies.[13] They lived with much the same freedom as others enjoyed. With the Virginia Bill for Establishing Religious Freedom, 1785, full citizenship was granted without respect to religion. The same was granted with the United States Constitution in 1789. "Jewish emancipation was formally established for the first time in history."[14] Many had fought in the Revolutionary war, and not a few leaders gave them strong support. Benjamin Franklin, for example, was first on the list of subscribers to the synagogue in Philadelphia. George Washington, in a letter to the Jewish synagogue in Newport, Rhode Island, wrote, "Happily the government of the United States, which gives to bigotry no sanction, to persecution no assistance, requires only that they who live under its protection shall demean themselves as good citizens in giving it at all occasions their effectual support."[15] So also the Jews intended.

The second group of Jews to come to North America were German Jews, attracted both by opportunity and by religious freedom. They arrived during the middle third of the nineteenth century. Largely merchants and itinerant traders, they spread across the country, even becoming a part of the Gold Rush of 1849. By the time of the Civil War there were 150,000. In 1875 there were 250,000. Mostly coming from Germany and surrounding areas, they had been heavily influenced by the *Haskalah* ("enlightenment") movement and Reform thinking, so that by 1880 almost all synagogues in the country were Reform synagogues.

In the 1880s, persecution intensified in Russia, leading to a new and third immigration. Again the Jews were drawn by the twin desire of escape and opportunity. The face of Judaism in North America was completely changed as a result. Between 1881 and 1929 more than 2.3 million immigrants from Eastern Europe came to America, 73 percent of them from the Russian empire.[16] At the same time, a lesser number of Sephardim from the Mediterranean region began to arrive. By the mid-twentieth century American Jews numbered more than 5 million. More than 2 million lived in New York, making it the largest urban Jewish center in all of Jewish history.[17]

Between Exile and Redemption

The history of Judaism has been a history lived forever between exile and redemption. To be exiled means to be some place one does not finally belong. Yet at the same time, it means one retains an identity, an identity despite one's circumstances. Redemption means that one has been liberated from a fate one has not chosen and cannot change oneself.

In Israel's ancient history, redemption came first and exile second. Israel experienced exodus from Egypt, only later, after centuries of possession of the land, to experience exile and scattering again. Return from exile was a second redemption. But then exile happened again. Today exile comes first and then redemption.

Redemption can mean the coming of the Messiah and the full and complete coming of the Messianic age. But it can be something less as well, a redemption in history that may not yet be total. That is our concern here. Two forms of such redemption are being experienced today. The first is redemption while still in exile, the emancipation, and so the integration of the Jewish people as a worthy and worthwhile element in the lives of the nations in which they live. Exiled still, but somehow not in exile. The second is the restoration of the land, Eretz Israel. The Jews have returned, and exile is over. But not quite over, for the final outcome is still in the balance, land and temple are not fully theirs, and renewed exile, partial or full, always looms as a future possibility. The American experience represents the first kind of redemption; the State of Israel the second. Yet the pain of exile remains embedded in both forms of redemption.

When the Jewish immigrants came to the shores of America, whatever their persuasion, all brought a passion for doing what is proper to God's will. Some came deeply convinced that obedience to the ritual prescriptions (*mitzvot*) embodied in the Torah and Talmud was of first importance. Some came deeply convinced that conformity to the prophetic demand for righteousness, charity, and social justice (*tsedakah*) was primary. Some came with a deep sense of the need to establish a healed and healing community that would exemplify in life and implement in society a mending of the broken social fabric (*tikn olam*). All came with an ethical demand.

America offered the Jews redemption. How were they to live their dual experience of exile and redemption in the American context such that it was faithful to who they were? The answers varied. To one extreme it was full and complete assimilation. This was the radical secular solution. American society offered the redemption Jewish people had always striven for. Any notion of exile was lost. Many such persons simply became lost to a specific Jewish identity. For another extreme it was a perpetuation of isolation. Extreme Hasidic, Jewish pietist groups responded this way. Freedom was still only the freedom to be different. This radical religious response turned freedom into an opportunity for perpetual exile.

Reform, Conservative, and Orthodox responses attempted to keep a hold on both the experience of a partial redemption and a continued exile that spoke of one's identity. Their responses are complex and still ongoing. The key issue was always what to do with Jewish identity.

The Reform tendency was to believe that Judaism was always undergoing transformation. Jews were not bound to eternal, unchanging forms but could adapt in any way that served the genuine Jewish commitment to universal justice. The Orthodox tendency was to stress the already given Jewish identity of Torah and Talmud and to give continued expression to these in new circumstances. They were, in effect, traditional Judaism that had become conscious of itself. No longer could Jewish practices be taken for granted. They had to be consciously chosen; they are observant Jews. The Conservatives walked a middle pathway as they tried to keep identity and transformation together.[18]

Reform Judaism, as we saw, shortened the synagogue religious service, dropped Hebrew for German, got rid of prayer shawls and skullcaps, sat women and men together without a partition, and so on. This is the Reform religion that reigned at the height of the German immigration in 1880. All of the two hundred synagogues in the United States, save for some eighteen to twenty, were Reform. But they were unable to minister to the new wave of immigration from Eastern Europe. For instance, they showed a premature self-confidence when, to celebrate the tenth anniversary of the Union of American Hebrew Congregations, they held a non-kosher banquet. The first course was shellfish, forbidden by Jewish law. The devout, especially of the new immigrants, were scandalized. This effort to transform Judaism revolted the observant for whom identity was foremost. By 1890 the majority were Orthodox, and by 1910 of the two thousand synagogues 90 percent were Orthodox. But this situation did not hold either.

The Orthodox, strict in practice, found that it did not appeal to their children. As one Jewish paper reporter describes it, he:

> would pass a synagogue where a score or more of boys were sitting
> hatless in their old clothes, smoking cigarettes on the steps outside,
> and their fathers, all dressed in black, with their high hats, uncut

> beards, and side curls, were going in . . . tearing their hair and rending
> their garments. . . . Two, three thousand years of devotion, courage,
> and suffering for a cause [were] lost in a generation.[19]

It is clear that simply clinging to a particular Jewish identity lacked enough
transformation to be appealing.

The Conservatives tried to fill the gap between these two extremes. They
too were disturbed, as were the Orthodox, by the Pittsburgh Platform of
1885 of Reform Judaism.[20] Some therefore formed the Jewish Theological
Seminary of America and dedicated it to "the preservation in America of the
knowledge and practice of historical Judaism as ordained in the law of
Moses expounded by the prophets and sages in Israel in Biblical and Talmudic writings." Yet, they could not apply the full load of past tradition without
discrimination. Not only was there a reverence for the past, but change was
possible where it was accepted by and benefited the community as a whole.
But who were they really? Some of their synagogues were traditional. Others introduced some of the Reform innovations. Was it simply anything any
congregation chose to be? So the quarrels that existed between Reform and
Orthodox became internal quarrels for the Conservative. Nevertheless,
trying to hang onto both ends of the quarrel appealed to some so that by
1945 the Conservatives were the largest of the three, and by 1970 the
Reform were 30 percent, the Conservative 40 percent, and the Orthodox
10 percent.[21] The struggle for self-definition continues in all three groups.[22]

One area of consensus has become the attitude towards Zionism and the
land of Israel. Originally Reform Judaism rejected the aims of Zionism. It
was, they believed, a wrong emphasis upon a particular place. One could
not, for instance, be a good citizen of one country and then lay claim to yet
another. It was the time for Jews to find their home in the world. Orthodox
Judaism also rejected it, but because they believed such things should be left
in God's hands and not taken over by humans. The Conservatives, in contrast, supported the goals of Zionism, a Jewish nation. Eventually all three
came to this position but without finding any need themselves to move to
Israel and become its citizens. Choosing to remain in exile, as it were, they
found one form of redemption while also becoming deeply attached to the
redemption that was Jewish nationhood.

Some Characteristics

What kind of Jewish community then lives in America today? First of all, it
is a small minority, despite the fact that over half of the world's Jews live in

America. In the 1990s they were 2.5 percent of the population. Secondly, they are achievers, overrepresented in certain categories: "college graduates, doctors, lawyers, university professors, publishers, editors, television producers, advertising executives, investment bankers, computer scientists, Nobel Prize winners, and millionaires."[23] They also reflect, third, a certain ethos. As one writer puts it: "The Jews are . . . too well-educated, too liberal, too secular, too metropolitan, too wealthy, too egalitarian, too civic-minded to be normal Americans when compared to the overall U.S. population."[24] Fourth, even though there is a strong attachment to Jewish identity, they are not particularly religiously observant except at certain points, and many if not most synagogues are quite empty on regular Sabbaths. "Twenty percent or more of Jewish Americans (just less than half of them Orthodox) remain religiously observant. . . . Seventy percent fast on Yom Kippur and place *mezzuzot* [small scrolls containing scripture portions] on their doorposts; more than 80 percent light Hanukkah candles, and more than 90 percent attend Passover seders."[25]

There has been a steady growth of the Jewish population in the United States up to 1980. At that point a slight drop has taken place, perhaps in large part due to intermarriage and the fact that only 25 percent of these children are raised as Jews,[26] as well as to a relatively low birth rate of 2.1 for Jewish families.[27]

JEWISH POPULATION IN THE U.S.				
	U.S. POP.	JEWISH POP IN U.S.	% OF U.S. POP.	% OF WORLD JEWRY
Sephardi Jews 1790—	3,930,000	1,350	0.03	
German Jewish immigration 1820—	9,340,000	2,700	0.03	
East European immigration (Ashkenazi) 1880—	50,156,000	250,000	0.50	3.27
Restrictive immigration laws (Ashkenazi) 1920—	105,710,630	3,600,000	3.41	22.86
After Holocaust (1933–45) 1950—	150,698,000	5,000,000	3.32	43.48
1980	243,801,650	5,900,000	2.42	40.75
1990	252,174,910	5,800,000	2.30	45.00

The pattern of settlement in America has been that of "concentrated dis-persion."[28] While there has always been a wide scattering, there has also been a heavy concentration in the Northeast. That is becoming less so.

"Practically all East European Jewish immigrants after 1870," we read, "initially found their way to the Lower East Side [of New York], and . . . remained within its nucleus, a twenty-square-block area south of Houston Street and east of the Bowery."[29] This pattern is still present more than one hundred years later as reflected in these 1990 statistics of the ten cities with the largest Jewish population.

TEN CITIES WITH LARGEST JEWISH CONCENTRATIONS

CITY	JEWISH POP.	PERCENTAGE OF TOTAL POP.
New York	1,450,000	25.0%
Los Angeles	500,870	8.6%
Miami/Ft. Lauderdale	330,000	5.7%
Chicago	261,008	4.5%
Philadelphia	250,008	4.3%
Boston	228,000	3.9%
San Francisco	210,000	3.6%
Washington, D.C.	165,000	2.8%
Bergen/Essex, N.J.	160,008	2.7%
Baltimore	94,500	1.6%

In recent decades Jewish population centers have been shifting west-wards and south. In the late 1940s 67 percent lived in the East and North-east. By the 1990s this was only 40 percent. An example is San Francisco, which in 1977 had only 77,000 Jews, or the Miami and Ft. Lauderdale area, which in 1948 was not on this list.[30] But whatever the shift in population, the pattern of concentrated settlement remains. Perhaps this helps to give a critical mass for the continued development of Jewish identity and Jewish institutions in widely scattered areas. Not surprisingly, close to 95 percent of Jews live in cities or their immediate suburbs.[31]

It is clear that the Jews represent a small minority. But they are nonethe-less a significant one. Compared to the rest they are overachievers. One author documents their achievements in areas such as culture, humor, lib-eralism, radicalism, journalism, and filmmaking, noting that Jews earn 72 percent above the national average.[32] To take one area, Jews are known for their social activism. This activism began in Europe during the years of the emancipation. Suppressed so long, they were now free to look to their wider social interests and apply the ethos they had brought with them when they immigrated. In 1897 many local workers groups formed the first Jewish social democratic party, the Bund, which spread throughout Russia and Poland.[33] In New York, where they concentrated in the garment industries, it was not long before labor activism took hold. As the union advocates tried to mobilize the Jewish workers, they appealed to biblical injunctions about justice as well as to apt sayings in the Talmud.[34] In the 1920s they formed 15 percent of the Communist Party in America.[35] Of course, there were also many political minds among the Jews. In the early part of the twentieth century they tended to vote Republican nationally and Democratic locally. That tendency has now shifted to an across-the-board preference for the Democrats, with large concentrations supporting left-wing Democrats.[36] Later, Jewish names would read as a Who's Who list of radicals in the 1960s and 1970s.[37] One other measure of Jewish political activism is that they are twice as likely to vote as are other Americans.[38]

Being strong advocates of justice, including affirmative action, one wonders about the charge by many African Americans of Jewish racism. The charge has been made that the Jews were early on involved in the slave trade. But to claim that they dominated the trade is unfounded. For example, "The slave sales of all Jewish traders taken together did not equal that of the one gentile firm dominant in the business."[39] Perhaps Henry Ford contributed to black mistrust of Jews with his vociferous anti-Jewish propaganda. In his newspaper, the *Dearborn Independent,* he published the fraudulent *Protocols of the Elders of Zion.* The idea of this forgery was based on an 1868 novel which had a rabbi give a speech in which he informs his coconspirators that the Jews "must become the editors of all daily newspapers in all countries." This, together with Jewish control of money, "will make us the arbiters of public opinion and enable us to dominate the masses." Ford's paper ran this and numerous anti-Semitic columns from 1920 to 1927.[40] To what degree these ideas filtered down to the working black masses in Detroit may be significant.

In any case, Jews and blacks lived often in the same neighborhoods in the Northeast and the industrialized Midwest. Both shared a history of oppression. Thus, Jews have almost always heavily favored policies that favor blacks. But where they lived they did not meet as equals. Blacks had Jewish landlords; they bought supplies in Jewish shops; they got work under Jewish employers; blacks provided domestic help for Jewish housewives; they were taught in school by Jewish teachers; they came to Jewish social workers to

apply for social benefits; blacks were the rank and file, following the directions of Jewish labor leaders; they often were the entertainers in Jewish
clubs.[41]

The question of Zionism also became a sore point. The war of 1967 in
particular raised black anger. Many blacks, even if not Muslim themselves,
have a deep sympathy for the Palestinian, and so Muslim, side in the Middle
East. They see in Israel a "white, Western, racist, imperialist, Zionist entity"
victimizing a "people of color."[42] There are other factors complicating the
relationship as well. For example, they saw teachers' strikes involving many
Jews as a demonstration of greed and bad faith towards black schoolchild-
ren. While Jews vigorously supported affirmative action measures, when it
came to quotas they took a different stance. Thus, "they said yes to an affirmative action that encouraged the use of race as a criterion in admissions,
but no to numerical quotas." Blacks felt that "unless quotas are used, [they]
and other minorities just won't get a fair shake."[43] A severe split that defined
justice in terms of self-interest resulted.

The Other Redemption—Eretz Israel?

The Jewish people have long lived between the fact of Exile and the hope of
Return. Traditionally return was seen as a redemption, an act to be brought
about by God. Thus, those Jews in whom the hope still lived waited patiently
and passively for the coming of the Messiah to bring this about.

Things began to change during the first half of the nineteenth century with
the movement towards emancipation. Before the Jewish people were
accepted into their societies on the basis of political equality any talk of a separate Jewish nation would have been risky, to say the least. But once
accepted, they too became influenced by the ideas of nationalism that were so
powerful in Europe at the time. Many Jews, as we saw above, were also influenced by the climate of thought that emphasized reason over religious beliefs.
Gradually the hope began to take shape that the Jewish people could have
once again their own land and that this hope could come about not by simply
waiting for some supernatural event to happen but by active human effort.
These concerns were strengthened when some began to advocate removal of
references to Zion in Jewish prayer books and total assimilation into the gentile cultures surrounding them. By the 1860s several streams of thinking
among the Jews began to converge, and the Zionist movement was born.[44]

Some of the early enthusiasm proved to be unrealistic. Rabbi Kalischer,
impressed by the economic rise and influence of the Rothschilds, appealed

to them to buy the land of Israel outright from Muhammad Ali, or at least Jerusalem and the Temple mount. This plan, of course, came to nothing.[45]

Nevertheless, the assassination of the Russian Czar in 1881, in which a young Jewish woman was involved, led to an outbreak of violence or pogroms against Jews. Jews began in small numbers to emigrate to Israel from there and elsewhere. Rothschild was in fact a supporter of such small groups. Some 2.6 million, however, went to the United States from 1881 to 1914. Under the inspired leadership of Theodor Herzl (1860–1904), a journalist turned advocate of Zionism, the first Zionist Congress was held in 1897. In his mind there was one purpose for Zionism, to place "a people without a land" where there is "land without a people."[46] There were many obstacles to overcome, however, before a homeland was to be established.

A big stride forward in this regard came with World War 1. Turkey, which controlled Palestine, joined with the Axis powers. In 1917 England made the Balfour Declaration, stating its support of a homeland for the Jews in Palestine. This was followed by the League of Nations Mandate over Palestine, which had been removed from Turkish rule, and the British took responsibility for that mandate beginning in 1919.

In succeeding years Jewish immigration to Palestine increased significantly. But because Britain did not want to offend the largely Arab population, which was profoundly opposed to Jewish immigration, much of the influx was illegal. The Jewish population increased tenfold from 60,000 to 600,000 between 1919 and 1940. With the rise of anti-Semitism proper and the advent of the Holocaust, tremendous pressures arose for further Jewish immigration. Violence on both Jewish and Arab sides was the order of the day. Despite these obstacles, the State of Israel was proclaimed May 14, 1948, as the British mandate over Palestine expired.

The Six-Day War in 1967, which Israel won in a swift and complete victory, had a decisive impact upon world Jewry. From now on it was widely accepted that central to twentieth century Jewish identity was the existence of the State of Israel. The resolution of relations between Arabs and Jews in Palestine is a tortured process, involving enormous international effort that continues still today. There is hope that a resolution is in sight.

The return to the Land of Israel is a remarkable fact of the twentieth century. Few Jews today, whatever their motives, whether religious or otherwise, and whether they live in Israel or among the Diaspora, are willing to compromise on its existence. Questions that will be pressing for the foreseeable future include the relations between Arabs and Jews both within

Israel and between Israel and Palestine, the relation of secular Jews to religious Jews within Israel, and the relation of the Jews in Israel with Jews in
the Diaspora. But whatever the case, an earthly redemption as Jews see it,
engineered by human ingenuity and effort, is represented by the land of
Israel. Will it be a permanent solution? Will it end in another exile? The last
question is one no Jew wants to contemplate, but the bitter history of Exile
offers little other choice. Jews in Diaspora have now a dual identity, that of
their place of exile whether chosen or endured and that of their commitment to Israel.

13

THE CONTINUING CONVERSATION

Introduction

Believing Jews and Christians share one thing in common. They accept the Hebrew scriptures as God's revelation. For Jews this scripture is their own story. For gentile Christians it too becomes their story, but by adoption only, not by right of original heritage.

Yet the two differ greatly, indeed fundamentally. Claiming the same Hebrew scripture they come out with very different understandings. For Jews the oral torah, the Talmud, is the key to the scriptures. For Christians Jesus Christ, the embodied Word, is the key. The New Testament records this interpretation, and the controversy between the two.

At least two questions meet the Christian. The first is, what shall we as Christians make of this difference in our sameness? The second is, what might Judaism have to say to us out of this difference?

How Shall We Proceed?

This is a vexing question. How could the history between Jews and Christians have gone so badly that Holocaust could become a twentieth-century event? On the side of Christians, does the fault lie with the gospel that is believed, in the faith in Jesus Christ? Or does the fault lie with Christians themselves, and more specifically European Christians, who acted contrary to their faith? Is the New Testament itself the seedbed of anti-Semitism?

Christian answers to these questions tend to move in one of two directions.[1] For some it is the faith that Christians have held over the centuries that started this whole process, and it is this faith itself that has to undergo a more or less radical change. For many this means that the minimum requirement is that Christians reject the belief that Jesus was the Messiah for Israel and that the church replaces Israel. In short, Christians have to reject supercessionism, to use the theological term. Christians have behaved wrongly, says this group, because they believed wrongly.[2]

For others it is Christians who have acted contrary to their faith. They acknowledge that there are many hard sayings in the New Testament. In

Matthew the crowd clamors, "His blood be on us and on our children!"[3]
Paul, speaking of the people of Israel, says, "whenever Moses is read, a veil
lies over their minds."[4] Peter, commenting on the disbelief of the people of
Israel says, "They stumble because they disobey the word, as they were des-
tined to do," and then speaks of Christians as though they are a New Israel:
"But you are a chosen race, a royal priesthood, a holy nation, God's own
people."[5] In Revelation, John the seer refers to Jews as "a synagogue of
Satan,"[6] reflecting the words attributed to Jesus in the Gospel of John that
his Jewish opponents "are from your father the devil."[7] The Gospels are
filled with controversy, and on numerous occasions Jesus denounces the
Pharisees, who represent the best that is in Judaism, as hypocrites and
whitewashed tombs.[8] There are many others.

But then one could also cite another set of very different words. Jesus
upbraided those who would point the finger at others and ignore one's own
even graver faults.[9] Enemies were to be loved, not hated.[10] "Father, forgive
them for they do not know what they are doing," Jesus cries out on the
cross.[11] "Lord, do not hold this sin against them," Stephen cries out as he lies
dying.[12] "Salvation is from the Jews," Jesus says to the Samaritan woman in
John.[13] Paul refers to himself as the worst of sinners.[14] "They are Israelites,
and to them belong the adoption, the glory, the covenants, the giving of the
law, the worship, and the promises; to them belong the patriarchs, and from
them, according to the flesh, comes the Messiah," Paul writes.[15] Yet, recog-
nizing their rejection of Jesus he speaks of his "great sorrow and unceasing
anguish. . . . For I could wish that I myself were accursed and cut off from
Christ for the sake of my own people, my kindred according to the flesh."
Again, in Paul's words it was always "the Jew first, and also the Greek."[16]
There are many such references.

Neither of the above lists can stand alone. Each implies the other. To any
reader of the prophetic texts of the Hebrew scripture it is no surprise that
every word of God is double-edged. Indeed, the virulence of Old Testament
denunciations of Israel easily match those of the New Testament. Neither
Jew nor Christian escapes the reality of the double-edged word. This is no tea
party. Real issues are at stake, matters that the writers of the New Testament
believed to entail life and death. The history of Christianity is to a large
degree, certainly in relation to the Jew, an abuse of the very scripture that it
affirms. What has to be denounced is Christian abuse of both worldly and
religious power.

So there are these two broad tendencies: correction of the faith received,
as the first group says, or recovery of the faith handed down, as the second

group says; placement of original blame upon Jesus[17] and the early witnesses to him or placement of original blame upon those who inherited and
abused the gospel. I find the latter course the only viable way forward for
Christians.

Taking this position has several implications. First, Christians meet Jews as
their elder brothers and sisters to whom they owe a debt of great gratitude.
It is because of what the Jewish people have given to us that we can share so
much in common. The Jewish people are, moreover, our neighbors. Thus
Luther's rule on the freedom of the gospel holds here: Christians believe
themselves to be the freest of all people, subject to none; yet, Christians are
at the same time the most dutiful servants of all, subject to all.[18] Luther, let it
be noted, violated his own affirmation in his diatribes against the Jews.

Second, we acknowledge and make plain our differences without rancor
or pretense. We bear witness each to our own faith. "In the past," Jacob
Neusner and Bruce Chilton remind us, Christians and Jews

> were uncomprehending and expressed contempt for each other's
> absurdities. . . . Now, for the first time in the United States and the
> English-speaking world in general, differences between those two
> complex sets of religious traditions come under discussion free of ran-
> cor and recrimination. Consequently, outlining the points of concur-
> rence and conflict may take place in a spirit of enlightenment and
> friendship. There arises no need to negotiate, or even place limits upon
> difference, but only to understand the other more fully and more
> accurately.[19]

Commenting on this approach, Martin Marty writes:

> If they [Jews and Christians] keep making up soft versions of their own
> traditions, they will produce mush or hypocrisy. They will waste
> everyone's time and create nothing but illusions.[20]

Third, we attend to and heed each other's voices where appropriate. Why
should it be impossible to learn from one another and experience changes
even while remaining faithful to our separate witnesses? For the Christian
this will mean paying attention to some of the things that Jewish people out
of their own faith want to tell us.

Fulfillment

For many Christians this has become a bad word to use in speaking of our
faith. It offends Jews if we say that Jesus fulfills the prophecies of the
Hebrew Scripture or that the church fulfills Israel's destiny. On this much
we can agree upon at the outset. It is clear that neither the Roman Catholic

Church, Orthodoxy, or the Protestant denominations, whether squabbling or uniting, fulfill Israel's destiny. There has got to be something better than these after all. But is there fulfillment of something essential in Jesus Christ and his Body, the church? Of that the New Testament seems very certain.

What does fulfillment mean? It means that something partial is made complete, that something begun is finished. It means that the end and purpose of something is realized. It does not mean that the expected happens. It is not like drawing up a house plan so as to be able to predict how the house will actually turn out. Instead, when the New Testament speaks about fulfillment it means that something unexpected connects with something already known or experienced. The unexpected is not just something odd, or strange, or puzzling, but fits with something else without being the same as that something else. The fulfillment is always different from and more astonishing than the expected.

How is it that the idea of fulfillment came to be used by the earliest Christians to make sense out of Jesus? Most likely it was something like this.[21]

Jesus came preaching the Kingdom of God. He picked up this language not so much directly from the Hebrew Scripture itself, but from Aramaic paraphrases of the Old Testament that he used in his day. One thing astonishing was that he simply announced its coming. The kingdom was not an idea to be explained but a fact of present day life to be experienced. But, secondly, Jesus didn't just announce the coming of the kingdom, he enacted the realities of the kingdom in his teaching and in his life. By parables he drove straight to the heart and conscience of the people of his day. Not just nice stories, the parables called people to account before God or brought actual comfort and assurance to the despised and oppressed. His acts of healing and works of compassion demonstrated actual instances of God's working. God's kingdom does not leave the world the way it was. It brings continual change and transformation.

No doubt, by this time the followers of Jesus had begun to recognize certain things in their Bible, the Hebrew scriptures, that suggested things that might help them understand what Jesus was doing. Jesus himself spoke of fulfilling. One time in Nazareth Jesus read some words from Isaiah before the synagogue. They spoke of one sent to bring good news to the poor, proclaim release to captives, and other things. Having read the text he then said: "Today this scripture has been fulfilled in your hearing."[22] What might Jesus have meant by fulfilled? Jesus hadn't released any captives from prison. John the Baptist had been arrested, and Jesus had left him to die in prison. What Jesus clearly meant was that the kinds of things that happen when God is around are now happening in your midst in his very ministry.

But fulfillment was always a surprise. In the area of Ceasarea Philippi, Jesus asked his disciples whom people said he was, what analogies, what terms did they use to try to make sense of him. The answer was John the Baptist or Elijah or another prophet. When Jesus asked the disciples what analogies they came up with, Peter said, "You are the Messiah." Jesus does not reject that. But he also says that he will experience things that no Messiah was expected to experience—"undergo great suffering . . . be rejected by the elders . . . be killed . . . rise again." Was the Messiah model the right one for understanding Jesus? Did Jesus fulfill Israel's messianic hope? If he did it surely was in a completely unexpected way.

Not only was Jesus the herald of the kingdom as well as one who enacted the kingdom in word and deed, but his own fate became tied up with the kingdom. It was only when the preacher and doer himself became the victim, only to be raised from the dead, that the disciples finally began to identify Jesus' presence itself with the kingdom. It was from the viewpoint of the resurrection that the Gospels, as well as all the books of the New Testament, were written. From this point of view Jesus fulfilled the witness of the Hebrew scriptures in a fresh and surprising way, a way that gave new meaning to its promises.

Christian faith cannot do without some such understanding of fulfillment. It means that the Hebrew scripture is necessary for Christian faith. Without it, there is no adequate way to begin to understand Jesus. Jesus' link with the Old Testament is not just an accident of history—that he happened to be born in a place where it was the accepted scripture—but an integral and real part of understanding who Jesus is. To deny that Jesus fulfills the scripture in some real sense in fact makes the Hebrew scripture unnecessary to the Christian. But it is necessary. To understand who Jesus is requires a link with the Old Testament, as we call it. Yet, the Hebrew scripture is not sufficient. The Kingdom that Jesus preached, enacted, and himself ultimately was, reached beyond the confines of a single scripture, giving it a new interpretation, a new content. This is why the relationship of the Christian community to Jewish people is such a complicated and absolutely important matter.

The Fruit of Spontaneous Goodness (Zekhut)?

If the risen Christ is the lens, so to speak, through which the Christian reads the Hebrew scripture, the believing Jew reads Hebrew scripture through the lens of the oral Torah.

Scholars talk about a Pharisaic revolution during and after Jesus' days. Doubtless Jesus' own thinking and ministry was profoundly shaped by Pharisaism. Because of their closeness in many ways, the differences they had became all the more important. Thus Jesus had many controversies with the Pharisees.

However, we are not fair to the Pharisees if we equate them with hypocrisy. They were the ones who began to develop the oral Torah. Their concerns were for the ordinary Jew. They wanted to combine the rich insights of the prophets with the guidance for life given in the Torah. They were not satisfied to have religious life reduced to occasional sacrifices in the Temple, rituals controlled by an elite class of priests. They wanted to bring the faith of Israel into the life of the people. For this to happen it was necessary that the commandments (traditionally 613) become applicable to daily life and not remain an antique curiosity. All of life belonged to God. They argued that an oral tradition accompanied the giving of the law at Sinai. This was a living tradition that was continually being shaped and reshaped under the demands of contemporary life. For them what became most important was not just the rules and regulations in themselves, but a way of thinking that turned all of life into a praise and worship of God. This could only be done by making the commandments livable in every new situation of daily life.

But Judaism has also been quick to realize that devotion to Torah and its continual study and application in life does not limit righteousness to those, like the rabbis, who have the time and intelligence to do this. Side by side with the emphasis upon the study and practice of Torah is the recognition of the value of spontaneous acts of goodwill (*zekhut*), acts that may themselves violate the Torah. These acts are open to all, the humble folk, women who traditionally were not allowed to study Torah, and all others.

These spontaneous acts of good will and the value, or *zekhut,* that they bring show what truly is at the heart of the concern for Torah. In the Talmud there is the story, in the form of a dream, concerning a certain ass driver. He appeared before the rabbis and prayed, and rain came. The rabbis themselves lacked this power, and they were astonished.[23] "What is your trade?" they asked him. "I am an ass-driver," he replied. Still puzzled, they asked:

"And how do you conduct your business?" He then told this story:

> One time I rented my ass to a certain woman, and she was weeping on the way, and I said to her, "What's with you?" and she said to me, "The husband of that woman [i.e., me] is in prison [for debt], and I wanted to see what I can do to free him." So I sold my ass and I gave her the proceeds, and I said to her, "Here is your money, free your husband, but do not sin [by becoming a prostitute to raise the necessary funds]." At this the rabbis said, "You are worthy of praying and having your prayers answered."[24]

Here an ass-driver attains a degree of righteousness or favor with God that rabbis who have spent a lifetime in study of the Torah have not been able to attain. We don't hear about the woman. But it was her willingness to prostitute herself to aid her husband that gave the energy to the ass-driver's less dramatic but spontaneous act of rescue.

These spontaneous acts of goodness—and perhaps it can be granted that even the woman's intended act was of such a kind—speak of an original goodness in persons which when activated brings, perhaps even compels, a response from God. Such acts can pass down blessing to future generations and can be replenished by further acts of a similar kind. Thus, Abraham's act of being willing to sacrifice Isaac (not unlike the willingness of the woman to sacrifice her body) created power for future generations. This logic is expressed in Exodus 20:6 where it speaks of God "showing steadfast love to the thousandth generation of those who love me and keep my commandments." It was this same logic that led the Jews in the Gospel of John to appeal to their forebear saying, "Abraham is our father."

In this notion of *zekhut*, involving the spontaneous doing of good even when it might seem to violate the commands of God, we see into the inner intention of the Torah—the bringing of God's will into the midst of daily life in such a compelling way that even God takes notice.

Might this give a hint of what the cross means for the Christian, or the contrast between faith and works in Paul? Perhaps.[25]

Zekhut and Cross

There are indeed a number of references in the New Testament to a way of thinking that reflects this notion of the power of spontaneous acts of goodness to effect great results. Think of the faith of the gentile woman whom Jesus initially rebuffed with the words, "It is not fair to take the children's food and throw it to the dogs [gentiles]." She then replied, "Yes, Lord, yet even the dogs eat the crumbs that fall from the masters' table." With that Jesus marvels, "Woman, great is your faith! Let it be done for you as you wish."[26] Or, again, the woman who was a sinner washing Jesus' feet with her tears and wiping them with her hair. In response to this, as he sits at table with disgruntled and offended Pharisees, Jesus rebukes his hosts saying, "Do you see this woman? I entered your house; you gave me no water for my feet, but she has bathed my feet with her tears and dried them with her hair. You gave me no kiss, but from the time I came in she has not stopped kissing my feet. You did not anoint my head with oil, but she has anointed my feet with ointment. Therefore, I tell you, her sins, which were many, have been forgiven."[27] Or, yet again, the woman insistent in pleading to the judge who in exasperation granted her request.[28] James writes, "The prayer of the righteous is powerful and effective."[29] There are many such stories and sayings.

This same logic might seem to apply to the cross. It is true that for the Christian, Jesus' dying on the cross performed an act of spontaneous goodness which had the power to bring incalculable blessing to humankind. "While we still were sinners, Christ died for us," Paul writes. We see the extraordinariness of the moment in these words of Jesus: "My God, My God, why have you forsaken me?"[30] "Christ redeemed us from the curse of the law by becoming a curse for us," Paul writes.[31] Or, as Paul puts it even more strongly, "For our sake he made him to be sin who knew no sin, so that in him we might become the righteousness of God."[32]

Is this not the logic of *zekhut*—an act of self-sacrifice that wins a power that even God must acknowledge? Perhaps in part. Neusner recognizes this. He writes:

> Christianity's conceptions of the crucified Messiah, the power of weakness, and the glory of surrender find a counterpart in the concept of zekhut. Here we find the ultimate reversal, which the moves from the legitimacy of power to the legitimacy of weakness, in perspective, merely adumbrate. "Make God's wishes yours, so that God will make your wishes his."[33]

But there is a difference. This difference lies in the reversal of direction. It is not God who is compelled by these acts of excess. Rather, it is God who goes to the act of excess God-self. As John puts it, "For God so loved the world that he gave his only Son, so that everyone who believes in him may not perish but may have eternal life."[34] Clearly, it is the divine act of excess in self-giving that is the basis for the claim and power of the gospel to save. The logic and orientation of the New Testament witness is that God is the

Subject, the Subject of excessive love, the Subject of humiliation, the Subject of giving, the Subject of pain and loss. The logic of reversal is not only that in which power is upstaged by weakness, but in which the glory of God becomes the shame of the cross. In this divine degradation is life. This is the "happy exchange" or the great reversal in which we give God our worst and God gives us his best—life. God has become not only the recipient but the agent of *zekhut*.

Torah and Grace

Christians have often spoken of Judaism as a religion of law and the Christian faith as a religion of grace. Jewish believers find this offensive, and rightly so. What is the relationship between law and grace in Judaism?

A Jewish philosopher, Emil Fackenheim, speaks of it this way. He asks, is the command a burden or a joy? He answers that it is a joy. In contrast he sees that for Paul it is a burden. And because God's commandments, the law, had become for him such a burden, he finds release from this burden by his faith in Christ. But why does Fackenheim find the Torah as joy, and how do we understand Paul?

The second century Rabban (Rabbi) Gamaliel used to say this:

> Do God's will as if it were thy will, that God may do thy will as if it were His will. Nullify thy will before God's will, that He may nullify the will of others before thy will. [35]

Fackenheim asks, "How is such a thing possible for people of flesh and blood, to make their will like unto that of the God of heaven and earth?" Didn't Gamaliel think about that? Don't the Jews think about it? Isn't Paul more profound?

Fackenheim then cites a longer passage which he says he has pondered repeatedly since coming across it in the Midrash (Jewish Bible commentary) years ago. In this passage a rabbi says that at Mount Sinai, when the Israelites hear God say the word "I" (as in "I am the Lord your God") "their souls left them as if they were going to die.[36] Then this Voice that spoke returned to the Holy One and said, 'Lord of the world. You are life, and your Torah is life. Yet when I speak people are as dead. What is going on?' God, then, the passage says, softened his Word for the people. As another Rabbi added, 'The Torah which God gave to Israel restored their souls to them,' as it says, 'The Torah of the Lord is perfect, restoring the soul.'"[37]

What do we find here? As the Bible tells us, when God descended to give the Law, thunder rolled, lightening flashed, Sinai shook. The people were terrified to death and asked Moses to represent them on the mountain. They couldn't take any more of it. The Voice of God was too terrifying. But in this story we learn another side to God's commandment. And if we understand this we also understand the Jew's love for the Torah. If one understands this, Fackenheim says, then "one understands what Judaism is."[38]

One side of the Torah (Law) is its absolute demand, its terrifying reality. How can humans possibly keep it? Doesn't the law kill? The other side of the Torah, however, is that the law itself, when it is given, at the same time brings life with it. The law is both grace as well as demand. Only because of this are we able to bear the law and, indeed, find our joy in God's commandments. For the Jew, therefore, grace came into the world through Abraham, through Moses, and especially in the gift of the Torah with its commandments. Paul, Fackenheim suggests, only knew the overpowering demand of the law but not the grace of the law. We "must conclude," he says, "that Paul's study with the rabbi was either not long enough or not deep enough."[39]

At this point Jew and Christian seem so close, yet so far apart. It seems that when Paul, the pious Jew, the Pharisee, became a disciple of the crucified and risen rabbi Jesus, his whole worldview was turned inside out.

Before coming to faith in Jesus, the question that troubled Paul was hardly the question about whether he could keep the law or not. He tells us of his devotion to the Law, his confidence,[40] and we can assume his joy as well, a joy that any authentic Pharisee of his day would share. It was not a burden. No, his question, from all we can tell, was not an inside question— about himself and the Law—but an outside question—about a crucified religious renegade whom his followers were peddling off as the messiah. This claim he considered blasphemous in the extreme. Therefore it was that he violently persecuted the church.[41] Blasphemy of this nature deserved the most extreme measures.

The decisive event in Paul's life he puts very simply: "But when God . . . was pleased to reveal his Son to me . . . "[42] What a startling fact! Paul encountered the crucified blasphemer as risen Lord.[43] This experience threw his interpretation of the Torah into complete disarray. What he had considered to be the proper curse of God upon a false messiah—the crucifixion[44]—he now discovered to be the basis for Jesus' exaltation and lordship.[45] The curse of death became the gift of life. The Torah becomes no longer itself the guarantee and source of life, but an interim law awaiting an unexpected fulfillment.

In this process Paul discovers first his failure to live by Torah and second the inescapable consequences of sin. He didn't begin with this insight. He first met Jesus and only then discovered the depth of sin. In good conscience he had kept the law. In good conscience he persecuted the church. But he discovers, in his encounter with the risen Jesus, that the good that he in good conscience had intended—obedience to the Torah—became in fact disobedience to God. In his Torah faithfulness he had in fact been unfaithful because he had been rejecting Jesus as Lord.

Doubtless this deepened exponentially his understanding of the consequences of sin. His language is very dramatic. "Christ . . . became a curse."[46] "God made him to be sin."[47] It is as if something strikes at Jesus that is completely undeserved.

Sin, by its very nature, is something that is unforgivable. An unkind word is spoken. Can it ever be taken back? A gesture of help to a needy person is overlooked. Once overlooked it in effect is forever overlooked. The wrongs we do are forever irreversible. Perhaps it is true that God can make the best out of the mess that we have made. Perhaps it is true that the sinner can be forgiven, but can the sin? Can forgiveness reverse the evil that has been let loose in life? Will it raise the dead who have been wrongfully killed? The most extreme case of evil that we know hitherto in history is the Holocaust. Indeed, it is evidence of the unremitting consequences of sin. It is the collective fruit of centuries of human wrongdoing. Is it a forgivable evil? What good would forgiveness do? Would it raise the dead? Would it heal the families long ago broken and destroyed? Will it restore what is lost forever? No. Evil, in its very nature, is inherently unforgivable, for its consequences are irreversible.

Perhaps it is something of this that Paul is hinting at with his dramatic words about "curse" and "sin" applied to Jesus. The only basis for a real forgiveness that will bring life by overcoming evil itself is if the consequences of sin find an end point. If that end point is in history, then may God save us from history. The only end point that offers any possibility of hope is in God's own life. Christians believe that in Jesus these consequences impacted the very life of God and only thus do they come to an end—to an end for us if not for God, whose pain may be unto eternity. Only the eternal can bear the eternal. The eternal consequences of evil meet the eternal endurance of God. This is pain. This is suffering. This is a pathos without end, for it is in God. This end point is made concrete and real in Jesus Christ, God's Son. Moreover, in seeing Jesus as present in every victim, all human evil finds its final destination in God. Only a God who bears the consequences of sin is worthy of forgiving sin. And only such a God can turn death into life.

These things will mean very little to our Jewish neighbor. But for us as Christians it means everything.

Judaism Still Speaks

Is Christianity the end of Judaism? Obviously not. We can leave open the questions that Paul raises in Romans 9–11. The least we can say is that in scripture it seems that there is no salvation for the Jews apart from the gentiles, and that there is no salvation for Christians apart from the Jews. But how that final resolution works out, we cannot pronounce today.

Paul's resolution is no resolution. I doubt we can do any better than Paul from the Christian side. Every effort will simply be one more rationalization. Paul's resolution is stark. "As regards the gospel they are enemies of God for your sake; but as regards election they are beloved, for the sake of their ancestors. . . . For God has imprisoned all in disobedience so that he may be merciful to all."[48]

The only interim resolution is for Jew and Christian to live by their faith and bring their witness to bear upon each other. Paul writes Romans 9–11 as a missionary. "But how are they to call on one in whom they have not believed? And how are they to believe in one of whom they have never heard? And how are they to hear without someone to proclaim him? And how are they to proclaim him unless they are sent? . . . So faith comes from what is heard, and what is heard comes through the word of Christ."[49] It is in the context of the ongoing witness that he can say: "So too at the present time there is a remnant, chosen by grace."[50] This refers to those Jews believing in Jesus, Paul among them. But the majority of Jews believe otherwise. Such a Jew has his or her reasons, and the Christian theirs, for their respective beliefs and for their mutual, but divergent, ongoing witness.

As the Jewish people witness to us, what might be some of the things that we Christians need to hear? First, Jews bring a charge against Christians. If it is said in scripture of the Jews by the Jews that "His blood be on us and on our children!"[51] then it is no less true that the Jews rightly remind us that the blood of Jews is on Christian hands. The history of Judaism is an everlasting testimony to the sin of Christians.

But this is a negative message. What positive witness do Jews have to offer Christians?[52] Second, then, one must mention the Jewish sense of peo-

plehood. This sense of belonging to an unbroken community, however fragmented in time, is central to Judaism. Christians are not born Christians, as
Jews are normally born Jews, but become Christians through baptism. If
the Jewish tendency is to overstress their difference as a people from the
rest of humanity, the tendency for Christians, at least Western Christians, is
to stress overmuch our individuality, and thus our independence from all
community. Judaism reminds us of the centrality of peoplehood both in
their faith and in ours.

Third, the Jewish emphasis upon Torah can contribute to a richer and
fuller Christian understanding of the gift and place of law in our lives. The
instinctive Christian emphasis upon freedom needs always to be supplemented by a Christian emphasis upon social responsibility. The Torah places
human responsibility for society at the center of the religious life. It cannot
be less so for the Christian. As Luther put it, "We are servants of all, subject
to all." Judaism reminds us of the deep-going ethical dimension to all of life.

Related to this, fourth, is the Jewish emphasis upon the positive place
that human action has in life. We are made in God's image. We are divine
representatives of God on earth. We are co-creators with God, not as equals
with God, but as necessary partners with God. It is not enough to harp continually on human sin and ignore the human possibility given to us by God
in creation. God's image may well be distorted, but it is not lost or absent.
We remain God's good creation even in our sin.

Fifth, there are many continuing issues of controversy between Jew and
Christian. From the Jewish side one of the more important of these has to
do with the Land. Christians may take diverse views on the specific issue of
Eretz Israel, the land of Israel. But in all cases, the particularly of land, of
location, of being rooted, of belonging in a world in which there is the continual displacement of peoples, and widespread homelessness, can never be
forgotten. Human beings need a place. They cannot exist otherwise. Even
while we realize that in the end we are wayfarers on Earth, always threatened by new forms of exile, this reality of "landedness" cannot be set aside.

Finally, Christians can never forget that Jewish convictions, grounded in
the covenant testified to in the Hebrew Scriptures, have entered into the
very substance of the Christian faith. The Jewish people are a continual
reminder of and witness to this substance, which will remain a continuing
factor that shapes Christians' convictions.

Because the Jew Jesus is our Lord, the Jewish people are our elder brothers and sisters. Let us honor them, even in our witness to Jesus.

Part IV
What Then?

This is the section in which we have to do some very hard thinking. The questions we want to deal with, having met our neighbors with their many convictions, are important for us who are Christians. What sort of God do we really have after all? Does that help us in our understanding of our neighbors? What does it mean for a Christian to be a witness? Should we be nice to people but hide what we believe? Certainly we don't want to harass people with our beliefs, but what if others do not believe in the gospel? Does it make any difference? What sort of difference? Do any of the ideas we have considered here affect our own understanding of God?

These are some of the heavy questions we want to address. At the very least, our discussion will help us be honest and open in our relations with others. In the last chapter of this section we want to think about what some of the beliefs that others have might mean for the way we believe in God. Can we get a deeper understanding of God through considering what others believe? This does not mean we end up agreeing with whatever others might believe or say, but their convictions might help us understand our own convictions in a fresh way.

14

GOD IS LIKE THIS!

"No one has ever seen God."[1] That's about as true a statement as was ever made. We have looked at many different ways of viewing our world, God, and ourselves. With so many ideas about God isn't it a bit arrogant for Christians to think that they have the truth and that others are mistaken? Since God is unknown and unknowable anyway, isn't it much better to agree that there are many ways of knowing God and that each is just as valid as the other? Maybe the world would be better off if Christians weren't so sure of themselves.

The Greeks in Paul's day asked a very similar question. Greeks believed in many different kinds of gods. Of course, they were wise enough to realize that they didn't really know what God was like. And so, as we read in Acts, they had an altar dedicated "To an unknown god."[2] Perhaps that is the God we all should really worship. Perhaps we should be more honest about the fact that we don't know God. God is too great to cram into our puny minds. God is invisible. God is beyond our ability to touch, feel, or see. God is really unknowable. To think less of God is to demean God and make God like us. Let us worship this inscrutable, unknowable, invisible reality in a way that befits its mystery. Yes, let's erect our own altar to "the unknown God." But before we do, let us try to make clearer what we are really talking about.

Different Kinds of Knowing

The first thing we might do to make things clearer is to remember that there are different kinds of knowing. Let me talk about two kinds here.[3] There is first the knowledge that comes from our sense experience. We touch, see, feel, hear, taste, smell something and come to some understanding of it. We get to know things this way. It is also basic for other kinds of knowing as well. Without this kind of knowing we would in fact know nothing. Still, this sensory kind is not the only kind of knowing.

Another kind of knowing I will call personal knowing. This of course depends upon the first kind of knowing but includes something more. In personal knowing we know something we cannot see, we cannot feel, we cannot touch, even though seeing, feeling, and touching may all help. What do we know in personal knowing? Not something, but someone. Who is this someone? When my father died, I saw his body there on the bed. But was that body still my father? Who and what was my father? Clearly he was more than the body I saw, even when it was alive. But neither was he just a soul stuck into a body, for the body was part of who he was. Visible, yet invisible. I still don't have answers to these questions. So, what sort of things do we know when we know someone—mannerisms, behaviors, of course. Someone talks a certain way, walks a certain way, thinks a certain way, behaves a certain way. But that is only the beginning of personal knowledge. What is it we really come to know? Friendship? Perhaps. Love? Generosity? Kindness? Tenderness? Intelligence? Patience? Perhaps. Hate? Resentment? Secrecy? Perhaps. These are things we can't see with our eyes or touch with our hands. We can only know them in our heart. None of these can be proved in some scientific laboratory, no matter how sophisticated the equipment or the methods. Can love be proven? No, it can only be experienced. The experience of love is its proof. Since this is so, sometimes someone can be deceived. You cannot know what is in someone's heart unless they reveal what is there. Personal knowledge comes only through revelation.

While there are different kinds of knowing, there are also different degrees of knowing. Is it possible for sensory or personal knowing to exhaust the subject of its knowing? Or is it, rather, that one can keep knowing something more and more and more and never exhaust its richness and meaning? The knowledge that we gain through our senses might be like this. Some think that the world is somehow infinite. Certainly Buddhists and Hindus think that. If so then our knowledge, which is always finite, will never exhaust what can be known of the world. Even those who believe in God will think the world is somehow infinite, because its source is outside itself and so one will never exhaust the knowing of this world without also coming to know its source. So even our knowledge of the physical world, the subject of science, is somehow inexhaustible. Certainly, in that regard we barely have a toehold on knowing our world, marvelous though the knowledge we already have might be.

Even more than sensory knowledge, personal knowledge is inexhaustible. Can knowledge of love ever be exhausted? One can keep knowing it more deeply and more deeply, but if it is love one is knowing, one will never exhaust it. If it were exhausted, then it would cease to be love. All personal knowledge is like this, because you or I can never hold the other person in our mind or heart completely, as if there were nothing more to that person than what I have taken hold of. Personal knowledge is inexhaustible. It depends upon continual personal revelation.

I think these distinctions are not only helpful but also essential if we are to understand the concern of this chapter—knowledge of what God is like. Let us apply these kinds of knowing to our knowledge of God.

The mistake many make when they say that God is unknowable is to treat God like an object, a thing. But things, objects, can only be known through our senses. "No one has seen God." That means God is not available to our senses. To say that God is unknowable, and mean no more than this, is not of much importance. If this is what one means, then it simply means that God is irrelevant to life. In fact, it is no different from saying that we don't even know whether there is a God or not. If God is simply unknowable, then one can't even know that God is. If God *were* knowable in this way, then God would be a thing, an object. But God is not a thing. People are things—you are, I am—but not God. God is the maker of the world. The world is just the collective term for the inexhaustible multitude of things. So this way of speaking about God as unknowable does not strike me as particularly wise.

When we come to personal knowledge, however, it is very different. In this way we do know God. Let us remember these things about personal knowledge. Knowledge of persons, for one thing, is knowledge of something that is more than can be seen. It is knowledge of the invisible. Knowledge of persons, again, only comes about through revelation. I can only know as much of you as you reveal, whether on purpose or inadvertently, and you can only know so much of me as my words and actions reveal. Knowledge of persons, once more, involves a knowing that can never be exhausted. Of course, knowledge of persons does come to an end when, for instance, we become separated, or a person dies, or for some other reason is no longer able to communicate in any way. But even then, memory continues to keep the knowledge alive and growing.

Knowledge of God is most like personal knowledge. "No one has seen God." If it is true that no one can see into who you really are, even if they can see your activity as a physical person, it is more so the case with God. God is not a physical being, even if he is a person in the sense we are speaking about. So it is no surprise that God is not visible. As with all persons, again, knowledge of God comes only through revelation. One cannot see God, but one can read and interpret God's actions. That is what the Bible is about, an interpretation of God's actions in and through creation, history, and the experience of individuals. It is no more odd that God should be known only through revelation than that you and I can be known only through revelation, free self-disclosure.

Knowledge of God, once more, is inexhaustible. This is obvious at the physical level of things. God is greater than our minds, even the best scientific minds, can figure out. In fact, God is not accessible to science. God isn't contained or available in our senses, much less in the neurons in our brain, or even in the neurons of all our brains put together. God isn't contained by the physical world. Though unknowable in any direct way, still through creation God is knowable. This knowledge too is inexhaustible, as we have already indicated. Even more important is the fact that knowledge of God at the personal level is even more inexhaustible. No one can plumb the depths of God, not least the depths of God's love. It is this reality that mystics often talk about. Some might call it the unknowing knowing. That is, the knowing that can't ever be fully known, for the more one knows the greater one's awareness of ignorance. It is like the shore of a lake. The larger the lake, the larger the shoreline. The more our knowledge of God, the greater we find is our ignorance, the vaster the boundaries of the unknown God.

A Second Habit of the Mind

In chapter 3 we talked about a habit of the mind, a habit by which our minds always seek to connect many things together into one. That is a necessary and important part of the way our minds work, but we observed that it can also lead us astray if we try to reduce the many into the one too quickly.

There is another habit of the mind that is also important for how we live our lives but which can also lead us astray if we depend too much upon it. This second habit consists of our habit or tendency to treat what we see or think about as an object. It becomes something out there, separate from me. This often happens when we give names to things. When we give a name to something it seems like it becomes definite and clear. So we have names for hammers and nails, and bugs and screens. Without these names we couldn't be definite about things. Names are necessary. We need to turn things into definite objects if we are going to use them. We can't just use the word "thing-a-ma-jig" to refer to everything from boots to children and get anywhere. One of the first tasks God gave to Adam was to name things.[4] By doing this Adam had a world now full of many identifiable things, and he now knew how to relate to them and use them.

Does this habit of the mind work in our relationship to God? It won't, but we try it all the time. Even by our using the word *God*, God becomes an idea in our minds, a mental object, and as soon as that happens we no longer know God in the only way that God can be known. If we persist in trying to know God as an object, then, as with hammers and nails, we begin to think we can use this idea for something. The idea "God" becomes something that serves our needs—emotional, political, intellectual, and even religious. One result of this is what the Bible calls idolatry.

Philosophers, of course, have long ago begun to think about these things. One philosopher, for instance, said that the ideas and names that we have in our head aren't really the things themselves. We should not mistake our ideas for them. His name was Kant, and he lived in the eighteenth century. There is, of course, a lot of truth to this and we need not argue about it overmuch here. But there is a problem.

If all we can ever know is our own ideas, not things themselves, then truth is only something in our minds. Your ideas, and so your truth, are yours, and my ideas and my truth are mine. Truth becomes my private opinion. You see it that way, I see it this way. We then begin to ask why one person sees things this way and another that way. Philosophers have come up with many different explanations for this. Freud told us that how we think and act is largely because of our childhood upbringing and the way we have learned to control our sexual drives. Marx tells us that the way we think is controlled by our relationship to the way we make things, our relation to the economy. Am I a CEO? That will shape what ideas become important to me. Am I an out-of-work laborer? That too will shape what ideas become important to me. Today we have many social and political movements that emphasize in one way or another the way in which our environment has made us think the way we do. So we have race issues, class issues, gender issues, sexuality issues, and on and on.

All of these things reflect a habit of our minds. We tend to turn things into objects. We categorize. But then we discover that the object is only an idea in the head. And then we wonder where the idea came from and figure that it came from the environment in some way. Perhaps, we tell ourselves, it came from our upbringing, our genes, our economic status, our gender, or whatever.

My suggestion is not that we should quit naming things. What would our world be like if we had no names for anything? But we should be aware that naming things has its problems. One problem is that we tend to turn everything around us into objects, put them into categories, and then treat them like things, and manipulate them as we please. The other problem, which is just the opposite, like the other side of a coin, is that we turn everything

into private opinion, a projection of our minds, which is caused, supposedly, by social or cultural or genetic factors. The only way for someone's
private opinion to win out is by power. If enough people share the same private opinion, then they will win out in the end. Power is what makes truth.

It is not necessary to get tied up into knots about these problems. The
point I want to make here is very simple. All those problems depend on one
thing: the habit of mind that turns the world into a realm of objects. It is
because of this habit that many people naturally think that no religion can
possibly have a more valid truth than any other. They are all just different
perspectives, equally valid, each with equal merit. This way of looking at the
question of God begins by turning God into an object, like the single mountaintop to which all paths supposedly lead, an object that religions try to
describe.[5] But, as philosophers inform us, the idea we have of God in our
mind is no more than a private opinion, whether it be that of an individual
or a group of individuals. Frankly, if we begin thinking about God the way
we do about things, then the philosopher is right. But that way of thinking
is precisely what is wrong. The first way of knowing I talked about above, the
way we come to know through our senses and intellect, is not the way we
will come to know God. Only when we enter into the personal way of
knowing will that occur.

I think the Bible makes this clear. In Exodus, Moses encounters what
seems to be a fiery bush in the middle of the desert. It turns out to be an
encounter with God, who is sending Moses to deliver the people of Israel
from Egypt. But Moses isn't so sure he wants the job, so, looking for an
excuse to turn it down, he asks for God's name: "If I come to the Israelites
and say to them, 'The God of your ancestors has sent me to you,' and they
ask me, 'What is his name?' what shall I say to them?"[6] Moses gets an answer
that refuses to turn God into an object, a tribal God of their ancestors
whom Israel can use for its own purposes. Instead, God insists on defining
himself. The answer is that unsettling disclosure of a name that is no name:
God said to Moses, "I AM WHO I AM."[7]

Scholars have been arguing about what this means ever since.[8] Whatever
scholars might decide is the best translation—and that may never be
decided—it is clear that God's answer is first of all a refusal to become an
object that can be named. God will always elude being turned into an
object. When we deal with God we are not dealing with the realm of things.
Rather, we are in the realm of personal relations. While it is true that we
give names to our children, it isn't the same with God. By giving names to
our children—John, Mary, Rebecca—we make our relationship with them

concrete. The purpose of naming them is not simply to make them into objects, though by naming them that does happen, but to make our relationship with them special and concrete. But God is no child of ours. God cannot be made concrete by us in any way that we choose. God needs neither our guidance nor our discipline. Neither will God give us a name by which we can then use God for our own purposes, or make God obey our wishes. God is self-naming. God refuses to become an object to us. That also means God will never consent to become merely an idea in our minds, a private opinion which we can push over onto others if only we have the power to do it. God's relation with us is nothing like what we have with other things—we name them.

God's relation with us is radically personal—from God's side. Perhaps the best translation of that verse above is "I will be who I am," or "I am who I will be."[9] God will be the kind of God, God in fact is. This means we will find out who God is in the story of God's relations with God's people. And so, through the story of Israel we see a God who is always the subject of the sentence, a God who calls, addresses, promises, confronts, rules, acts with faithfulness and loving kindness. One can only respond to God in God's self-naming, never rename God or turn God into an object. If we slip out of the personal way of knowing and begin to treat God as an object of thought, then all the intellectual problems that we have already hinted at will take over. To be sure, thinking about God has its place, but that place is always secondary to the personal way of knowing. We must get that straight first. Centuries ago a theologian put it just right: theology is always "faith seeking understanding." It is not understanding that produces faith. Turning God into an intellectual object will never foster faith. Faith seeking understanding is the order that begins from personal knowledge, not objectifying knowledge.

God Is like What?

Personal knowledge we suggested earlier is knowledge about that which cannot be seen, it is knowledge that only comes by revelation, and it is naturally inexhaustible. It is this middle point that we will consider here.

We have already spoken about the fact that God reveals himself to all people. We also talked of the universal work of the Spirit. Let us not forget that. But here we want to speak specifically about the Christian experience of God. As we have made clear before, there is no Christian experience of God that is not at the same time rooted in faith in Jesus.

"No one has ever seen God." We have repeated that several times. The one who wrote these words immediately goes on to say: "It is God the only Son, who is close to the Father's heart, who has made him known."[10] Everything the Christian faith is about is contained right here. The believer in Jesus knows who God is from God's heart out. For to know God's heart is to know God. Whoever knows a God with a different heart does not know the Father of Jesus Christ or does not know this God well enough. Jesus gives us the most intimate personal knowledge of God possible.

Above we just finished saying that God's relation to us is not like our relation to any other thing. But now we have to correct this statement. God refuses to become an object to us; yet, God chooses to become subject to us. That is to say, God chooses to become personal for us in the most intimate and vulnerable way possible. For to be a person is ultimately to be vulnerable. That which has no name takes a name; that which forever eludes our grasp submits to our grasp; that which is no object risks becoming one more object. God becomes knowable for us like any other person. Just as is the case with any other person, the only way we can come to know God is if God reveals God's self to us. There are many other modes of divine revelation of God, but only one revelation of the very heart of God. "For God so loved the world that he gave his only Son."[11] This is what the story of Jesus is all about.

God is like what? All-powerful, all-knowing, everywhere present? Others might say that, but that is not a particularly Christian answer. Shall we recite God's actions? A God who creates, a God who makes promises, a God who is faithful? That is getting closer. The Jewish people say that. Shall we point to a real person? That is what the Christian does. The Christian points to Jesus and says, "God is like that!" In his teaching Jesus said, "The Kingdom of heaven is like . . ." and then spoke a parable. Jesus acted as though what he said and did were the equivalent of God speaking, God acting. "Your sins are forgiven."[12] "Take your mat and go."[13] "You have heard that it was said, but I say to you. . . ."[14] "If it is by the Spirit of God that I cast out demons, then the kingdom of God has come to you."[15] "All things have been handed over to me by my Father, . . . and no one knows the Father except the Son. . . ."[16]

All of the above has to do with Jesus teaching and healing. What about his miserable death? Do we see what God is like there? Is God weak? Does God submit to abuse? Is God vulnerable? Does God undergo pain and loss? Is Jesus a shadow play about God, or is Jesus the real thing? If he is a shadow play, we learn little about God we didn't already know. If he is the real thing, then let us wake up and pay heed!

Is God like this, the crucified, rejected Jesus? That one, all messed up and ugly, is the "Who" of God? The mind, the body, the presence, the heart of

God? To discover this is to know God in a way that one has never known God before. No other knowledge of God can supersede this, for this is personal knowledge, specific and concrete—a man hanging on a cross and dying. "My Lord and my God!" stammered Thomas when he touched Jesus' nail-scarred hands.[17] How right he was. As Paul puts it:

> who, though he was in the form of God . . .
>   became obedient to the point of death—
>   even death on a cross.
> Therefore God also highly exalted him
>   and gave him the name that is above every name,
> so that at the name of Jesus
>   every knee should bend,
> and every tongue should confess
>   that Jesus Christ is Lord. . . . [18]

And what is the "name . . . above every name?" It is none other than that name given in Exodus 2:14, "I AM WHO I AM," the name which is no name, and which is usually expressed by the word *Lord*. There you have it. God is like this!

Thomas, who first doubted but then believed, knew this only because of one thing: the resurrection of Jesus. Without that resurrection in which God confirmed that Jesus was indeed God's personal presence in the world, no disciple would have become an apostle, proclaiming the good news of Jesus. Jesus would have been one more name in the list of martyrs—a noble and stunning martyr, but deluded and self-made for all that.

One Knowing and Many Knowings

So then, what about all those other ways of knowing God? Are they to be discarded? Are they to be embraced?

Remember that we are talking about personal knowledge. That is to say, our knowledge of God is not like knowledge of things, which can become objects in our minds so that we can handle and use them. It is rather like coming to know a person. You may come to know him or her very well, but others will know him or her in a different way. Who is right and who is wrong?

I recall that my wife, Ida Marie, always felt some fear and apprehension in the presence of my father. My father was quiet, he was serious, and he was firm in his convictions. He had a quiet dignity. (That she has little fear of me might be because I don't measure up to that standard!) At the end of his life, Ida Marie came to understand him in a different way. Near death from the ravages of cancer, he turned to my wife, who is a nurse, and said, "I would like to go home." Wow! How human that was! He wanted to be home, not in some well-furnished institution. And it was to her that he spoke these words. So she arranged for him to come to our small summer cabin and spend his last days with the family. During those days she lost her fear of my father and came to know him more like we, his children, knew him. What do you think? Was her knowledge of Dad when she feared him right or wrong? Did she gain a better knowledge of him during the days she cared for him as he was dying? Which was the real Dad? Which knowing was the best? Were we children better because we knew Dad differently? That would be a foolish conclusion.

Should we treat the many different accounts of God that we have in the religions in the same way? If we are talking about personal knowledge, I think the answer is definitely yes. To be sure, there are some ways God is believed in that those who know Jesus will clearly have to say are not right. There are other ways that those who know Jesus will clearly have to say are right. There are yet other ways that one who knows Jesus will have to say seem partly right and partly not right. But making decisions on those matters is not the most important thing. The most important thing for the believer in Jesus is to share what we know to be the very heart of God with all whom God loves—and who is not included? Can we do less? Would we want to do less?

It is often wished that Christians would be less sure of themselves. I think that this is doubtless a very healthy counsel for Christians. To be less sure of ourselves might well be a virtue. But to be less sure of God would hardly count as a virtue. Instead, to be sure of God who has made God-self known and present in the face of Jesus Christ will open us up to all people.[19] Isn't that the way Jesus was?

We mentioned earlier different degrees of knowing rather than a kind of knowing. There is a knowing that is inexhaustible. Can we ever exhaust our knowing of God's love given to us abundantly in Jesus Christ?[20] Should not that very inexhaustibility render us humble? We are just at the very beginning stages of knowing God. Bon voyage in your eternal journey.

15

SHOULD WE EVANGELIZE EVERYONE

OR DIALOGUE?

You Are Witnesses

Jesus was God's presence in the world for us. We are linked to this Jesus in our baptism. As Paul says: "As many of you as were baptized into Christ have clothed yourselves with Christ."[1] We then are the presence of Jesus in the world for the sake of the world. This is the sum and substance of what life means for the Christian. That is to say, whatever we do, wherever we go, we are witnesses. The question is not whether we are witnesses, but what manner of witnesses.

Of course there are many modes of being a Christian presence or witness in the world. Some Christians have the gift to speak directly to people about the love of God in Jesus Christ. Others are most effective pointers to God and to Christ by the way they carry out their particular vocation in life. Paul, for instance, is very clear about this. He compares our link to Jesus in baptism with the image of a body. We are the body of Christ, and as a body has members, so also do we have many roles to play on behalf of the world for God's sake. As Paul again puts it: "and God has appointed . . . first apostles, second prophets, third teachers, then workers of miracles, then healers, helpers, administrators, speakers in various kinds of tongues."[2] We could probably add many more job categories, yours included.

Witness on behalf of God for the sake of the world is the whole of a Christian's life. This can take place in many ways. Here we will be discussing just two: evangelism and dialogue.

Some people are a bit nervous about the word *evangelism*. For them it brings to mind the picture of someone badgering others, applying all kinds of pressure to make someone become a disciple of Jesus. Other people are a bit nervous about the word *dialogue*. For them it smacks of a wishy-washy Christianity that substitutes talk about values, or concern for social or economic behavior or even political agendas of one kind or another, for clear verbal witness to Jesus Christ. Neither of these may be a problem for you.

Even so, it may be helpful to think about what relationship evangelism and dialogue have with each other, and where we and our discussion of religions fit in relation to them.

Consider the following diagram:

```
        WITNESS
        E
        V    D
        A    I
        N    A
        G    L
        E    O
        L    G
        I    U
        S    E
        M
      CONVERSION
```

Witness is at the top because it is the whole of the Christian life. Evangelism and dialogue are below, indicating that they are two distinct but related activities through which we carry out a Christian witness. Of course, we could add many things alongside them as we have already said. Vocation, for instance, would be one useful addition, charity might be another, or service. But we are limiting our discussion to the first two. Conversion comes at the bottom, indicating that it is a consequence of these activities. For many people *conversion* too is a bad word. Because of this we will have to spend some time to clarify what is meant by the word.

The Nature of Dialogue and Evangelism

Evangelism is a public offer; dialogue is a public reasoning. It is as simple as that.

What do I mean when I say evangelism is a public offer? I mean simply that in one way or another some person who does not know the gospel becomes acquainted with the gospel and its invitation to share in God's love in Jesus Christ. This too can happen in many ways. For evangelism to take place, however, it is necessary that words be spoken. Without a verbal witness a public offer of the gospel is not possible. The story of Jesus becomes known. The opportunity to come to faith in Jesus Christ now becomes a real and concrete opportunity. With no verbal witness that opportunity is not there. Without knowing the story of Jesus no one can come to faith in

Jesus Christ and enjoy the gifts of that faith. Evangelism creates a new situation of previously unavailable opportunities.

What do I mean when I say that dialogue is a public reasoning? I mean simply that clarification or exchange of thoughts, understandings, perspectives is required. I will expand on these issues more elaborately under several headings.

The Origin of Dialogue

If dialogue is a public reasoning, how does this come about? What are its origins? Again the answer is simple and straightforward. Dialogue arises because of a question asked. If there is no question there is no dialogue. An illustration might help.

Back in 1981, not many years after the Cultural Revolution in China, I led a group of lay Lutherans and a few clergy on a visit to China. Only in 1979 were religions again permitted to be publicly practiced. We visited several major cities. We were also the first foreign group to visit some of the churches in these cities that had just reopened after a decade and a half of closure. It was a moving experience for all of us.

In every city we visited it was my duty as the group leader to negotiate with the local guide to work out our schedule for the two or three days that we were in that place. We came to the city of Xian, site of the ancient capital of China, where some of the most striking archaeological digs have been made. A vast array of slightly larger-than-life-size terra-cotta figures of soldiers, horses, and chariots stand guard on the perimeters of the tomb of the First Emperor of the Qin (Chin) dynasty, Qin Shihuang (third century B.C.E.). The word "China" derives from his name. For me the most striking feature was the fact that each face of these hundreds (and perhaps many thousands have yet to be excavated) of soldiers was unique. They weren't a vast horde of puppets, but each was an individual.

After getting off the plane, I sat down in the front of the bus with the local guide. He knew no English. We introduced ourselves. As soon as he heard that I had something to do with religion he asked, "Can you tell me the story of Jesus?" It caught me by surprise.

What was I to say? I hadn't told the story of Jesus in Chinese for many years. He had been brought up an atheist and obviously knew only that some people talked about a certain Jesus, but had no idea what this was all about. How does one tell the story of Jesus at such a raw and unformed level? I quickly ran through the Gospels in my mind and decided that the Gospel of Luke had some themes I would like to bring out. This Gospel places special emphasis upon the gospel being brought to the poor, and pronounces God's judgment against oppression. The story of the prodigal son might also be easy to grasp. I thought some of these things might be readily understandable to a young man brought up as a Communist. So I did my best to tell the story of Jesus, and he listened. As we conversed briefly, I found out that he was a young schoolteacher, that he loved literature, and that his favorite author was Mao Dun, a famous twentieth-century Chinese author who had been drummed out of the Communist Party for not toeing the line but had just been reinstated into the Communist Party posthumously.

We didn't have any chance to talk more about these things, since we had to get the schedule worked out. The next morning, as we traveled to our next destination, we talked more. He began by sharing his discovery of an essay Mao Dun had written back in the 1930s about the life of Jesus. I asked which book this was in and later found a copy in Beijing. The essay was a very sensitive portrayal of Jesus by an atheist, who presented virtually the whole of the gospel story except for the resurrection.

Having shared this, he then asked me, "What do you mean by 'God'?" Of course I had used the word *God* in telling the story of Jesus, so he wondered what to do about that word. How would you answer this or the previous question? Not easy?

You may have noticed that with this second question an important turn was taken in our conversation. The first question asked me to tell the story of Jesus. I did so. That telling was evangelism. It was making a public offer of the gospel. I wanted to tell that story to someone who had never heard it before in a way that would be attractive and meaningful. Whether I was successful or not is another question, but I certainly wanted to do that. When, however, he asked the second question about God, the situation was very different. We moved suddenly from the public offer of the gospel to a public reasoning. I had to give reasons for why I used the word *God*. I couldn't just tell stories, much less jokes. I had to state reasons. Thus dialogue began. It arose from a question.

So I stated some of my reasons. After a while he interrupted; "Oh, I understand. A person is either a materialist or an idealist," using Marxist vocabulary to process what I was saying. This was not quite what I intended, but I could only make a few more comments before we were interrupted. This was about as far as our conversation could go that day.

The third day, on our way to the airport, I began by asking him to share what he understood about life. I did so because he had indicated that over his years, brief though they were, he had changed his mind about things. So he began talking about his childhood and early youth, when during the Cultural Revolution he had believed implicitly in Chairman Mao, and then how what he saw happening disillusioned him, and the changes that began to take place in his thinking. He and some of his friends were interested in literature. They would get together privately and talk about these things. They weren't free to write and express their ideas now, but someday they hoped they would be. We got to the airport before he could finish.

In this way, a process of sharing began. Unfortunately, it was interrupted by my departure from China. But one sees here the critical beginning steps in the process of dialogue. It presupposes that some kind of public witness, intentional or not, has already been made. A question presupposes that some new information has been communicated. Dialogue proper arises, then, out of the question. The exchange is, moreover, mutual in that both partners are free to share and question on an equal basis.

The Goal of Dialogue

The goal of dialogue can be simply stated. It is to make a convincing witness and to heed a convincing witness. Anything less than this would not be honest.

The key words in these two phrases are *make* and *heed*. This means there must be genuine exchange. On the part of the one who seeks to make a convincing witness, any lesser goal would be unworthy of the witness. When, for instance, I was asked the question, "Can you tell me the story of Jesus?" I wanted to tell that story in a way that was meaningful, conveyed the gentle love of God, and evoked a desire to know more about the gospel. If I had thought, "Well, this isn't such a big deal," and then just tossed off a few light comments—what sort of disrespect would that have been on my part both for his question and for the gospel itself? When the question about God came up, I wanted that to be as simple and clear as possible, that he might feel the subject of God worth some pondering. If the goal of a Christian in dialogue is anything less than evoking a genuine interest in what God has to offer in Jesus Christ, I say forget it. Where such costly love is involved, could such a level of disinterest qualify as a worthy representation of it?

But what about the heeding part of dialogue? This is fully as important as the making. If it is the case that the Christian wishes to speak well for the gospel, it is no less the case that the Muslim wants to speak well for the message of the Qur'an and the Buddhist wishes to speak well for the enlightenment he or she points to. Can you imagine a Muslim being embarrassed about the message of the Qur'an and still giving a good representation of it? Or a Buddhist ashamed of the Buddha's teaching and still make an engaging case for the Buddhist experience? Moreover, if we expect others to listen with respect to us, others too have an equal right to expect that we listen with respect to them. Neither Christian nor Hindu wants to make folly of their faith.

But there is more to dialogue than simply presenting our side in a compelling way. Christians are eager that others listen attentively to what we have to offer and are delighted if they take a genuine interest in the gospel. So too, others are eager that we listen attentively to what they have to offer and are delighted if we take a genuine interest. If others ought to heed the gospel if it has convincing power, so ought also we to heed what others have to say when and where it comes with convincing power. This is what makes the engagement genuinely dynamic. Making and heeding belong as a pair together for Christians as well as for others. It is the importance of the component of heeding that requires that at some point we talk about change or, as I have put it to be a bit provocative, conversion.

Modes of Dialogue

We have been commenting above as though dialogue were a strictly verbal enterprise. In the narrow sense it of course is. However, it is much better to have a broader understanding of what interreligious relations might mean than simply talking. In this broader sense dialogue is the whole range of ways in which persons of different religious commitments intentionally and actively engage each other in their commitments. Moreover, it is not necessary to think of dialogue as an exclusive academic enterprise reserved only for those who specialize in it—the illustration I gave above certainly wasn't. Dialogue in its most real form is part of what takes place in ordinary life. The whole Christian community, where it lives in, with, and among people of other commitments—and where is that not the case?—is rightly engaged in dialogue. Where it is not, it has isolated itself. This it does either by accepting a ghetto existence where it is a minority or where it is a majority by assuming a domineering position that in effect ignores the other. Neither way is worthy of Christian witness.

Assuming, then, that dialogue most properly occurs in the midst of the give-and-take of ordinary life, let me suggest four modes or levels. There is first what I would call low level dialogue. By this I mean the very basic activity of simply coming to know something about each other. This may occur in many ways. It may occur during the conversation with a neighbor, per-haps my Muslim neighbor down the street whom I meet in the grocery store or in my place of work. Once strangers, we become acquainted with each other, learn about each other's families, our backgrounds, and our interests. Maybe we even have each other into our homes, or our children play with each other. It is simply the activity of getting to know each other for what we are. It may occur in other ways as well, such as in an academic setting. Here our daughters and sons take classes from scholars of religion, entering into that conversation and so come to know more about the wider world. It happens in other ways as well.

There is next what I would call "midlevel dialogue." This too takes place in many ways. I would include such things as coming to genuine under-standing of each other and engaging in cooperative efforts.

Such understanding is no easy matter. We are so busy with our own pre-conception of things that we can hardly hear what the other is trying to say to us. This is a constant difficulty in daily life. How much more so when cul-tural and linguistic differences as well as differences in fundamental beliefs are involved. To understand comes about only by patience and attentiveness. Understanding is not the same as agreement, but it does involve empathy. This is the willingness to see and experience as much as possible from the other person's point of view, setting aside my own point of view in the meantime. Some call this a crossing over into the world of the "other." Of course it is not the same as becoming something other than I am; rather, it is extending myself to stand in the place of another and see and hear as far as possible with that person's eyes and ears. It involves an effort of the imag-ination. Then one begins to comprehend how the other feels about things, what reasons are important for the other, and what concerns motivate the other. As I get to understand the other I will also see how the other looks at me and so contribute to my own self-understanding as well.

To engage in cooperative efforts assumes that although we have so many differences we can only understand with considerable effort, we still have a great many common concerns. These matters affect our lives. Maybe there are community projects that need to get done. Maybe there are issues of local education that need to be addressed. Maybe we share concerns for a healthy environment for our families. Maybe some needy people could ben-efit from our joint effort. These things can happen at the local, national, and international levels. Many of these things will be more adequately carried out if we work together. The assumption should not be that religious people have better ideas about things because they are religious and so should band together against secular society. The assumption is simply that Christians should work together with all people, religious and irreligious, for the welfare of all.

Finally, there is what I shall call high level dialogue. This is the most difficult of all and a rare commodity indeed. By this I mean the deepest sharing that is possible between different persons. To share with another what are one's deepest commitments and to be open to another's deepest commitments is not easy. Only where there is mutual trust, a basis of deep friendship, can such sharing be achieved. In my opinion, dialogue is only partially fulfilled until this deeper exchange takes place.

Yet, let us not say "finally" too quickly. For beyond all of these is the fullest and most complete form of relationship with people of other faiths. It is the kind of relationship Jesus had. It is a relationship defined on the Christian side by self-expenditure for the sake of the other, a self-giving for the other's sake, regardless of how we might agree or disagree. If this were to truly permeate all levels of dialogue, who knows what might happen? Yet, is there any other way that is truly Christian?

The Result of Dialogue

Genuine encounter with a person or community of another commitment than mine always leads to change of some kind. The external dialogue, whatever its form, will be followed by internal dialogue of all concerned. How shall I deal with what has been experienced? Where do we go from here? What is required of me so that I respond in an honest way to what has taken place? What did that person mean? Am I looking at this in the wrong way? These and many other questions will foster an internal dialogue. Inevitably, an honest dealing with the internal dialogue will lead to some change. One theologian talks of "mutual transformation" as the natural result of such a process.[3] I have previously used the word *conversion*. Since we are here talking about significant change, perhaps we should look more carefully at that particular word.

Conversion

Some people don't like this word. Some like it for the wrong reasons. There is a popular conception about this word reflected in statements like this: "We don't go out to convert. . . . " It's a hard statement to respond to because it has so many built in assumptions. It's rather like being asked,

"When did you beat your wife last?" Perhaps some of these assumptions need to be exposed before we can go further.

One assumption a statement like this makes is that coercion is involved in conversion. I will call this the coercion fallacy. In fact, it is impossible to bring about a fundamental change in anybody's mind by coercion. Coercion can only foster outer changes, not a change from the inside out. But who wants to foster an outer change without a change that comes from the inside out? Authoritarian governments and authoritarian systems of every kind of course do this. When the gospel is involved, coercion of any kind is out of place. The gospel seeks to change us from the inside out, not the other way around. Coerced change is not conversion.

Another assumption implied in this statement is that conversion is something that is the result of human activity. I will call this the human fallacy. The word *conversion* comes from the Latin and is the word used to translate a Greek term in the New Testament for "repentance." This Greek word actually means "turning to" or "turning from" or "turning around."[4] *Conversio*, the Latin term, means a turning around. That is a fairly close way of saying the same thing. What does conversion mean in English? It means to change one's mind about something, whether an action, behavior, or conviction of the past. Biblically speaking one can no more say that we convert people than that we repent people. It makes no sense. As Christians we should use the term conversion in its proper biblical sense. If that is the case, then it is obviously not something that happens as the result of human activity. It is the proper work of the Spirit. That is the kind of change we are talking about.

Often there is a third hidden assumption in the above statement. Some say it because they are upset that Christianity has destroyed other cultures. The encounters between Christianity and American Indian, African, and pre-Christian European cultures are often cited. Without question, Christian people have been instrumental in destroying many cultures. There is hardly any need to deny that. What needs to be clear, however, is that their behavior was itself not Christian and stands under the judgment of the gospel. But this historical question is not the one we want to deal with here. Rather, it is the larger cultural question of change. All living cultures are in the process of change. Some want to preserve cultures, like one preserves wetlands or a forest. In fact, no culture can be preserved unchanged. A culture that ceases to change, whether from internal forces or in contact with other cultures, becomes closed in on itself and will eventually disappear in any case. The question is not whether cultures should change, but what kind of change will take place, and what are the factors leading to change. The longing to preserve a culture unchanged, like an antique, I will call the romantic fallacy. If there is anything that needs to be preserved unchanged, it is not the culture, but the free choice of those who live within a culture to set their own directions. As I write this I am in Hong Kong. Here, court judges follow the British legal system, including the practice of wearing wigs while they sit in judgment. They look like pictures of George Washington. The wigs are a relic of the past. If some want to preserve that relic—our culture is full of such things—that is fine. But we see how far our culture today has changed from that of the eighteenth century when our nation came into being. Has a culture been destroyed? One could say so. Is that good or bad? You be the judge.

So what is conversion? I would like to suggest two things essential for a proper understanding of conversion. First, it is an event that takes place within a person or a community in free response to a hearing of the gospel, and reflects a change of mind and action. That will include both the big and little conversions we talked about earlier. Second, conversion is the work of the Spirit alone, based on the Word. Wherever the gospel takes effect, there is conversion. Could we hope for anything less for ourselves? For others?

Let me give an illustration from the old mission days, in this case the 1920s in China. A group of elderly countrywomen met in the marketplace for a catechetical class. The teacher was leading a discussion about John 3:16. At one point the question was posed: "Who is included in this 'whosoever believes'?" This was a puzzle indeed. The old women simply shook their heads.

After a while one elderly woman, who was at least eighty-five years old, suggested an answer: "It's my father and my father's father and my great-great-grandfather, and my sons and my sons' sons." "But," came the next question, "does it really say whosoever son . . . father . . . great-grandfather?" She replied, "I don't know." They continued to think about that profound question, "Who is included?"

Finally, a spark seemed to ignite. "Can it be possible," she said, hesitating, "that God can love *me*, worn-out old woman that I am?" She of course was old and worn-out, a woman who had served her purpose, ready for discard, a great-grandmother with grandsons and great-grandsons. Could it be that she was included in this promise?[5]

Is this an example of conversion? Is the woman's realization that "whosoever" might include herself the work of the Spirit? Is this a change of mind, an entry into a whole new view of the world? Is this the kind of change the gospel seeks to bring?

This, of course, would be an example of a big conversion, one in which one's previous worldview is thrown into question and a radically new worldview becomes one's own. There are little conversions too, but this we have already talked about. Change, whether big or little, is the proper result of dialogue. We ourselves will be changed in a genuine dialogue, not just the other person.

Evangelize Everyone?

We have already described evangelism as making a public offer and dialogue as engaging in a public reasoning. It would seem that both are proper activities of a witnessing community. When should we engage in public reasoning? Whenever questions are asked; whenever the need for appropriate action is required. When should we make a public offer? Whenever and wherever such an offer is not available. Why not then? Who should be denied the opportunity to hear the gospel?

Evangelism and Dialogue: The Same but Different
When I say that evangelism and dialogue are the same but different I mean that they both have the same deep root in God's will and purpose and so are always interdependent, yet they have different functions and so have independent significance as well. That is to say, they are intertwined modes, two manners of speaking, two patterns of interaction, in which I am present to others as a Christian, not two separate ways. The two manners are interactive and cannot be sundered.

The common root that they share lies in God's will that the whole of creation be a realm of reconciled community, including all of humanity and all of nature, sharing each in ways appropriate to them in the life of God. Romans 8:19 is only one dramatic statement of this ultimate vision: "the creation itself will be set free from its bondage to decay and will obtain the freedom of the glory of the children of God." Both evangelism and dialogue are rooted in this deep conviction.

But their function, as we have already indicated, is different. This is worthy of further discussion. Dialogue has to do with us in so far as we are creatures; evangelism has to do with us in so far as we are sinners. As creatures, dialogue is essential to our experience of community together. As sinners, evangelism, that is the hearing of the good news of the gospel of Jesus

Christ, is essential for our community with God. Not only do we stand before our neighbor and so need to dialogue; we also stand before God and need repentance and faith. Dialogue has to do with our community together on a horizontal plane, and it necessarily includes our relations with all people and the entire world about us. This community is our destiny. Evangelism has to do with our community together in its relationship to God. This is community on a vertical plane. It too necessarily includes all, for nothing in all creation is outside of God's reconciling love. Divorce these two (dialogue and evangelism) and human community becomes simply secular and our relation with God an abstraction.

Since both are so deeply rooted in the love and will of God, we cannot dismiss either one or the other. Even though there is a deep interdependence between the two, for they both serve the same will of God, they cannot lose their own integrity and simply make one become a means to the other. Dialogue, for instance, cannot be made a subterfuge for evangelism. Neither can evangelism displace dialogue. By the same token, evangelism cannot be reduced to some bland words about human moral possibility. Neither can dialogue become preaching.

At the same time each requires the other. Dialogue, if it is Christian engagement in dialogue, presupposes that a public offer of the gospel has been made. It presupposes some awareness of Christian identity on the part of the neighbor. Similarly, evangelism is not sufficient unto itself. It needs dialogue for its completion. Dialogue without evangelism is devoid of Christian content. Evangelism without dialogue, that is evangelism that ignores the questions of people, is incoherent. It is impossible to evangelize without dialogue, and it is impossible to dialogue without evangelizing. To many who call themselves Christian this will be distasteful because they like to keep them separate and unrelated. But each without the other in fact does not exist. Of course if being a Christian (sharing the gospel) or being a human being (reasoning) is irrelevant to what one is doing, that is another matter. If the vertical line that indicates our relation to God never cuts across the horizontal line of our relations with the other and the world, then how can it be called a vertical? Our relationship with God and with the world is an inseparable relationship. There is no redemption without creation.

It is clear, then, that the public offer of the gospel is for all, just as the public reasoning and public action of the Christian is in the midst of and for the sake of the welfare of the whole human community. There can be no privatization or isolation of either of these.

Witness or Martyr?
The word in the New Testament for witness is the same as the word for martyr. At the heart of both evangelism and dialogue is the manner of the witness. If there is power with the witness, the power does not reside in the witness herself or himself but only in the content of the witness. The witness herself or himself can only be present in weakness. That means that one is exposed to the response of the neighbor.

If this is true of dialogue, it is even truer of evangelism. This must be said, because in the past there has been much abuse of evangelism. Great weight has been given to the power of the witness, the cleverness of the witness, the ability of the witness to define the terms of conversation. This is a major reason why so many have decided evangelism is a bad thing. The abuse of a good thing destroys the good thing.

Evangelize everyone? Yes, but how? The content of what is proclaimed must control the way it is proclaimed. We are servants of the message, not its masters. Does the message of the cross rule us? Only in the way of the cross can the evangel, the good news, be shared.

16

WHO WILL BE SAVED?

Who will be saved? Does it matter? Let us suppose that most people throughout history have never heard of Jesus Christ. Let us also suppose that most who have heard of Jesus have not believed in him. What is our conclusion based on these suppositions? That everyone who has not heard or not believed is automatically damned to hell? Are the religions no help here? This is the question we will probe in some detail in this chapter.

A Case In Point

Except perhaps for some shipwrecked sailors, Francis Xavier, one of the founders of the Catholic Jesuit Order, was the first Westerner to arrive on the shores of Japan. He arrived on August 15, 1549. He came for "the greater glory of God,"[1] by bringing the gospel of salvation in Jesus Christ.

On his way to Japan aboard a Chinese junk, he writes letters back to his friends in the Order. He has a strong faith:

> They say that all my friends and acquaintances wonder at me very much for trusting myself to so long and dangerous a voyage. I wonder much more at their little faith. Our Lord God has in His power the tempests of the Chinese and Japanese seas, which they say are as violent as any others anywhere in the world. To His power all the winds are subject. . . . He also holds in His sway all the pirates . . . who are exceedingly savage and are wont to put to death with exquisite tortures all whom they take prisoners, and especially all Portuguese. . . . I fear nothing from any of them. I only fear God Himself.

Then he continues, commenting on the last two and a half months of his voyage from Malacca (now Melaka, a town in western Malaysia) to Kagoshima in Japan:

> The captain and the sailors were always, against our will and in spite of all our efforts to prevent them, offering abominable worship to an idol which they had with them on the poop, and consulting the devil. . . . Our sailors offered many superstitious sacrifices to the idol, and fell again to casting lots, asking the devil whether we should have good

winds. . . . What do you imagine we thought and felt during that part
of the voyage, while the devil was being consulted by his own wor-
shippers as to our voyage to Japan, and the captain of the ship managed
the whole business just as the devil willed and chose?

What Xavier calls the devil was very likely the kindly and motherly goddess
Mazu, worshiped widely throughout the South China Sea by sailors even
today. She happens to be colored black, to indicate auspiciousness. In any
case, he continues:

> . . . there came another roll of the ship and the daughter of the cap-
> tain was cast overboard into the sea. The violence of the storm was so
> great that our efforts to help her were all in vain, and she sank in the
> waves in the sight of her father and of all of us, close to the ship. There
> was so much wailing and groaning all that day and the night which fol-
> lowed, that everything seemed very mournful and miserable, whether
> from the grief of the barbarians, or the danger in which we were.

As a man of God who has every confidence in God's control and providence, we wonder what comfort was he able to bring to this grief-stricken
father. Not much, it turns out. We find his attitude towards the fate of the
daughter in this later letter:

> One of the things that most of all pains and torments these Japanese is
> that we teach them that the prison of hell is irrevocably shut, so that
> there is no egress therefrom. For they grieve over the fate of their
> departed children, of their parents and relatives, and they often show
> their grief by their tears. So they ask us if there is any hope, any way to
> free them by prayer from that eternal misery, and I am obliged to
> answer that there is absolutely none. Their grief at this affects and tor-
> ments them wonderfully; they almost pine away with sorrow. But
> there is this good thing about their trouble—it makes one hope that
> they will all be the more laborious for their own salvation. . . . They
> often ask if God cannot take their fathers out of hell, and why their
> punishment must never have an end. We give them a satisfactory
> answer, but they did not cease to grieve over the misfortune of their
> relatives; and I can hardly restrain my tears sometimes at seeing men
> so dear to my heart suffer such intense pain about a thing which is
> already done with and can never be undone.[2]

One wonders, sometimes, who is closer to the kingdom of God. Is it those
who show their profound humanity in grief and lamentation or the cock-
sure theologian certain of God's implacable nature?

Xavier was an exclusivist. Was he right in his belief that all who had not
believed in, or even heard of, Jesus would be automatically damned to hell,

including the captain's daughter? Would it be better to think that other religions are also ways to salvation?

Readers may recall that we have already touched on this question in chapter 4. Some related questions were also touched on in chapter 14, especially on our different ways of knowing God. In chapter 4 we talked about a habit of the mind that wants to reduce the many into one as quickly as possible. Also in chapter 14 we talked about a second habit of the mind that tends to turn things that we name into objects, which then leaves us unsure whether we really know that thing out there or if we only know what is in our minds. Both habits of the mind tend to make us think about God and the religions in a way that leaves God ultimately unknowable and the religions as equally valid paths to a common goal.

Both habits are misleading. The second habit is misleading because God is not an unknowable object as we argued in chapter 14. The first habit is misleading because we cannot find some neutral place from which we can pass judgment on the religions. We can only work from within a commitment. We must listen to the religions themselves and not fit them into our own neat theories as we argued. If our thoughts are based on those habits, further discussion will not accomplish very much. It will be helpful to keep this in mind as we continue.

On Religious Aims

Religions themselves define the ends towards which they aim. In part 1, we have seen how different these can be. Let us remind ourselves of some of these different aims.

For example, for one kind of Buddhist the goal is enlightenment. That is, the aim is to achieve a new kind of consciousness, a consciousness no longer securely tied to a sense of personal identity, but to an expanded, universal identity. This expanded identity is with the whole network of interdependent things. Here personal identity is a brief moment in this network of things, like a cloud that appears for a short while and then again dissolves. Such a consciousness is experienced as a steady state of peace and quiet.

Again, for one kind of Hindu, such as a devotee of Krishna, the aim is to be in the presence of, to see and be seen by, the deity. Like is joined to like, as one's soul sets aside the passions of life and is joined in worship to the deity. For the Muslim the aim of life is simply to do the will of God, following God's guidance with a steady and humble heart. For the Confucian, it is to fulfill one's moral obligations to the fullest extent possible, and give a moral completion to the cosmos.

Each of the aims comes with its characteristic patterns of behavior. For the Buddhist described earlier, the pattern of life is one of a steady awareness fostered by various techniques of meditation and a quiet empathy with all things. This empathy shows itself as compassion, as a steady resolve, as patience and many other virtues. It will contrast sharply with a life of anxious turmoil, of conflict, of striving for endless new forms of pleasure. For the Hindu described above, the pattern of life will vary, depending upon how one understands the role of caste and one's relationship to it. But one thing will always be there. Whatever one does will not be done for personal gain but for the sake of the value of the doing itself.[3] For Arjuna this meant battle. For Gandhi this meant the demonstration of the truth through nonviolent action to bring about a new, just, and self-reliant political situation. For the Muslim that pattern of life is devout obedience to the guidance of God, exemplified at its most basic in the five pillars—confession, prayer, almsgiving, fasting, and pilgrimage. All of life is to be consistent with what takes place in these. For the Confucian that pattern of life shows itself as living one's varied social obligations properly, whether that be in the home, the community, or as a responsible person in the political sphere and with a serious-minded sense of Heaven's will. The Buddhist pattern that permits, even in some cases requires, leaving of home, wife, children, and family, is viewed with abhorrence by the Confucian. Thus, in many ways, these patterns will be inconsistent with each other.

There is a very important conclusion to draw from all of this: the religions do not aim at the same thing. In some cases the goal sought appears to be entirely different. In other cases there are some similarities and some real differences. If the religions and religious believers really mean what they say, then we cannot ignore this and try to make them all aim for the same thing. There is little point in trying to climb some Mt. Everest of philosophical abstraction or superior moral insight and from that high vantage point say, "Hey, all the religions mean the same thing in the end."

Each religion must be taken on its own terms. What salvation does each in fact intend?[4] Let us consider now what Christians mean by salvation.

Revelation Is Not Salvation

That the religions are responses to the revelation of God of which we have already spoken is not something that should be doubted. But revelation is not the same thing as salvation. There may be many revelations, but only one salvation, at least as Christians understand it. What do we mean?

Revelation has to do with knowledge. Salvation has to do with an event. An event can take place without one even knowing about it, and that event can reshape things drastically. But something we call revelation is always something that is known. I remember the story of the lost Japanese soldiers from World War II who hid in caves on a desolate island for decades after the war had ended. The soldiers didn't know that the war had ended way back in 1945 and that the political shape of the world had drastically changed. Instead, they remained in hiding, loyal to their emperor, doubtless hoping some day to be recovered by their own troops. The end of the war, an event, was not the same as the revelation that finally enabled them to enjoy the peace and return home. The event saved them, but it was the revelation that the war had ended that enabled them to enjoy what the event had obtained for them.

So revelation should not be confused with salvation. That is one of the most common things done today, even by sophisticated theologians. Revelation has to do with knowledge, salvation with an event. Knowledge itself does not save. Salvation is always an event.

Second, revelation can be repeated innumerable times. The same information can be conveyed at many different times in many different ways. A baseball game, a football game, a tennis match, these are events. An event happens once. It cannot be repeated. So the Red Sox won or the Twins lost. A team loses, and they demand to replay the game. Is that possible? These are events. They are unrepeatable. They are finished. Of course another game can be played, but that is a different event. Winning the World Series is a climactic event. We know, of course, that all of these individual, unrepeatable events can be reported in numerous ways. Every radio station reports them in their own way. They reveal the results of the event. Revelation is in principle repeatable; an event is once and for all.

Third, revelation does not serve its own end. Reporting the results of a football game is not done for the sake of reporting. It is done to inform about an event. An event, however, is its own end. A game is played for its own sake. Of course it may be part of a series. Then the series as a long event is played for its own sake. Why else do we play? So it can be reported? Ridiculous. To make a lot of money? No doubt that motivates some, but no World Series would last very long if that is all there was to it. Why do we pay to see? The game is its own reward. Revelation does not serve itself; it is for the sake of something else.

That too is how we should read our Bibles. When Israel was delivered from Egypt that was an event. A once and for all event. Having been delivered, could they be delivered again? Not unless they once more became slaves, and then it would be a new deliverance, a new event. Even the babies, including those still in the womb, were delivered however little they knew about it. The event saved them, not the revelation or the knowledge of the event. Of course, as they grew up they would be told about the event, and then they would enjoy its meaning in a richer and deeper way.[5] But that telling was not for its own sake. It was so that they might enter into the full inheritance of the deliverance that had happened and freed them from a life of slavery. The telling could and should be repeated and repeated.

This is the pattern of mind that can best inform us as we read the story of Jesus. This too was an event, a saving event. His life, death and resurrection are unrepeatable events which have their meaning in the events themselves. Of course, the events also reveal things. But that illumines the event so that we can enter into the full inheritance of that event.

Something else is at stake here. The life, death, and resurrection of Jesus is not only an event for us, something that happened in our history, but it is also an event in the life of God, an event in God's history. When, for instance, Jesus cries out on the cross, "My God, My God, why have you forsaken me?"[6] it is as if something tears within the very life and heart of God. The Son suffers dying, the Father suffers loss. A tear like this had never happened in God's life before. God can now no longer be as if this suffering and dying had not taken place. God was changed. As Paul puts it dramatically, Jesus was "made . . . to be sin."[7] Somehow, in this event, among other things, our human sin, our alienation from God affected the life of God, shaking God, one might say, to the very core. Our alienation from God brought alienation into the very life of God. That is what love does. It takes upon itself the impact and consequence of the wrong another does.

> Indeed, it is rare that anyone would die for the sake of anyone else. But God proves his love for us in that while we still were sinners Christ died for for our sins, for us.[8]

We are talking of Jesus as an event specifically for us. But it was for us because it was first an event for God. This double-sided event constitutes our salvation. Such a God, and such vulnerability!

Revelation cannot reach that deeply into God's or our reality. It can disclose it. It can inform us. But it cannot in itself do it. To talk about a death is not the same as dying the death. What happens is what saves. It is always easier to reduce the complex to the simple. An idea, a word, a telling is much simpler than the event itself. If salvation is reduced to revelation, becoming more like information, we lose the event itself.

Faith, Destiny, and a Third Habit of the Mind

What we have talked about above is salvation as an event that has happened for all people whether they are aware of it or not. The next question is whether it does anybody any good if they don't know about it. That is, if it is something that has happened for all, has it still really happened for me if I do not know about it? We are justified by faith, the Bible says. What is the nature of this faith?

Again we have to face a habit of the mind, a third habit. This habit is that we tend to think of ourselves first as individuals. We look at the world, so to speak, from the inside out. We each spontaneously take ourselves as a center around which everything else revolves. It doesn't necessarily mean we are selfish or mean, it just means that we naturally begin with our own experience as an individual. Our relations are second to our own individual experience. We feel we are individuals first, perhaps like an atom or a marble, and only second social creatures.

This habit of mind is more or less instinctive for us. Take for example the way we usually interpret the Golden Rule: Do to others as you would have them do to you. Doesn't this seem to say that I can't love others unless I first love myself? The way I want to be treated is the way I should treat others. So we conclude that the secret to loving others is to love ourselves first. I wonder if that is what Jesus meant. The alternative, of course, is not to hate ourselves, but this is something else.

This habit of the mind also complicates what we call democracy. An important early ingredient in the rise of western democracy was the demand of religious communities for the right to assemble. This was the demand to be free to have a certain kind of community life. Today, however, democracy has become much more a demand for individual self-expression. Democracy means that I should be free to do whatever I want to do so long as it doesn't do real harm to another. If it does harm, it is still okay if the person being harmed has knowingly and freely accepted that harm—like cigarette smoking for instance. This is democracy to many. To do as I wish. This is one bad result of this habit of the mind.

Jesus pointed to the worst result when this habit of the mind takes control of our lives. For example, one time the disciples of Jesus were criticized for eating with unwashed hands. The problem was not hygiene; it was ritual purity. Jesus responded to this criticism with these words:

> Do you not see that whatever goes into a person from outside cannot defile, since it enters, not the heart but the stomach, and goes out into the sewer? . . . It is what comes out of a person that defiles. For it is

from within, from the human heart, that evil intentions come: forni-
cation, theft, murder, adultery, avarice, wickedness, deceit, licentious-
ness, envy, slander, pride, folly. All these evil things come from within,
and they defile a person.[9]

When this habit of the mind takes over our lives, then these terrible
things erupt from our heart. The New Testament never tells us that love and
kindness emerge from our heart, does it? The above list Paul calls the "works
of the flesh."[10] Look at the list he gives. It is very much like the list Jesus
gave. They all begin with the individual as the center. No, when the New
Testament talks about good things coming from the heart it says that these
are the fruit of being led by the Spirit.[11] That points to the exact opposite
source, an alternative habit.

What is the alternative to this habit of the mind? It is to discover that my
relationships are more basic than my individuality, and that I am unique
because of the relationships that have enabled me to become what I am. My
most basic relationships are not external to me, something I choose or discard, like a suit of clothes. My most basic relationships are outside and
inside at the same time. Many of us have been fortunate to grow up in a loving family with devoted parents. For these it is often easier to understand
what this means. From the very beginning the parents interact with the
newborn child, holding it, making faces, touching, rocking, and on and on.
If you are a parent, you have done that. From the very beginning your relationship with the child will shape the child's identity. If, God forbid, the
relationship is one of abuse, then that too shapes us. We are now often told
that this process begins in the womb, even before birth. I don't doubt it.
When I cited Paul in the previous paragraph where he speaks of the Spirit,
it is just this to which he points. Our relationships make it possible for us to
be who we are.

Faith does not have to do with us in our sheer individuality; it has to do
with us in our relationships. The wrong habit of the mind I have been talking about tends to see faith as a personal disposition, an inner attitude,
something that arises from inside of me and finds expression outside. I
doubt very much that one can find the Bible suggesting this. Instead, faith is
about relationship, my concrete relationship with somebody other than me.

As a twelve-year-old boy, I studied for confirmation. We had to memorize not only Luther's small catechism—that was easy—but also a big book
with endless questions and answers and supporting Bible verses. Today even
seminary students find it hard to memorize the small catechism. In any case,

I learned then that faith involves three things: knowledge, assent, and trust. Of course one must know something or, rather, someone, before one can assent or agree. And of course one can agree or assent to something without being committed to it. Only faith as trust counts as biblical faith. Trust is reliance upon someone outside of me. Let us not introduce the second habit of the mind we talked about earlier and make trust refer to an external object, like a set of doctrines. Doctrines are of value only when they lead us to trust in a person—Jesus Christ, God the Father, the Holy Spirit. Trust is not trust in doctrines but trust in God. It has to do with a relationship. We already spoke about this when we talked about personal knowledge in chapter 14.

Faith, of the kind that we are talking about, has two sides to it. One side of faith is trust. Trust relates the person of faith to someone that is outside of one's self. It is nothing more than a relationship in which one's own security or life or meaning or hope is guaranteed by that which is outside of him- or herself, with another person for instance. It is confidence in another. It is committal to another. It is like the confidence a child has in the presence of its mother or father, or the sense of security and worth a man or woman finds in a relationship of commitment and love. This is one side of faith. Maybe we could call it the form faith takes—trust and commitment.

The other side of faith, of the kind that we are talking about, has to do with its content. In what does one trust? On our coins we have written, "In God we trust." Is God the real content of our trust as an American people? One might wonder about that. In any case, trust is always in something, it is not just trust for its own sake. It is not earnestness, sincerity, or piety. It is important to know the "in" in which one trusts.

Faith as trust is not uniquely Christian. Luther in the *Large Catechism* talks about exactly what we have been discussing. He writes:

> A god is that to which we look for all good and in which we find refuge in every time of need. To have a god is nothing else than to trust and believe him with our whole heart. As I have often said, the trust and faith of the heart alone make both God and an idol. If your faith and trust are right, then your God is the true God. On the other hand, if your trust is false and wrong, then you have not the true God. For these two belong together, faith and God. That to which your heart clings and entrusts itself is, I say, really your God.[12]

So faith is a trust, and that in which it trusts is its content. It is the content that determines whether the faith is right faith or not.

Will these things help us with our question? I think so. As we have already pointed out, God's revelation is not limited to Christians by any means. Not even to Jews and Christians. Not even to Jews, Christians, and Muslims. God's revelation is universal. Even the heavens declare the glory of God. This means that throughout all of history there has been response to God— as far as God has been known. All faith that rightly responds to God's revelation, whenever and wherever it occurs, is surely born of the Spirit. Faith, true faith, you may recall, is not a disposition we own or possess by nature. True faith is always born within a relationship. It is always the gift of the Spirit. Hebrews 11 lists several examples of faith, such as Abel, Enoch, and Noah. Who were these people? They were not Jews. They were just people, before there were Jews or gentiles. But they were people of faith. Doubtless in cultures and peoples everywhere there have been people who like these had a right response to God's revelation even though they didn't know God the way Abraham or Moses and later Christians do. In Abraham's time, the pagan priest-king of Salem, the city David was later to conquer and make the capital of Israel, was called Melchizedek. Hebrews talks about him too, proclaiming that he was even greater than Abraham, the patriarch of the Jews.[13] Though Hebrews does not use the word *faith* when speaking of Melchizedek it can hardly be doubted that the word would be fitting. There are many other instances in the Old Testament of the fact that people outside Israel had a true knowledge of God even though they didn't yet know God in the way that Israel did.

The case of Cornelius in the New Testament can aid our discussion here. Acts records Peter's vision of a sheet full of unclean creatures, and while he saw all these ritually unclean things he heard a voice from heaven say, "Rise, Peter, kill and eat." Peter, of course, as any self-respecting Jew of his day, refused to contaminate himself. This vision happened at the very time that some envoys were coming from a gentile, Cornelius, who had seen a vision urging him to send for a certain Simon Peter staying at the tanner's house in Joppa. Peter eventually visits Cornelius, preaches the gospel to him, they receive the Spirit publicly, and Peter doubtless eats unclean food with these first gentile Christians.[14]

There are two things I want to point out in this story. The first is that Cornelius was a devout gentile. He was an outsider as far as the Jews were concerned. He prayed to God in so far as he knew God, in so far as God had been revealed to him. When Peter arrives and is informed why they requested his presence, Peter responds: "I truly understand that God shows no partiality, but in every nation anyone who fears him and does what is right is acceptable to him."[15] That's quite a mouthful for a pious Jew like Peter. When he first arrived, Peter was characteristically blunt: "You yourselves know that it is unlawful for a Jew to associate with or to visit a gentile." But then he adds, "but God has shown me that I should not call anyone profane or unclean."[16] What we learn, then, from this story, is that even though Cornelius did not know God as the Jew did, nor even as the fledgling Christian community did (though this takes place before this community was called Christian), nevertheless he did have a true knowledge of God. The fact that the Spirit was poured out upon them when the gospel was preached and he and his household believed suggests that the Spirit in some way was behind all of this, behind what happened to both Peter and Cornelius in their separate visions, from the beginning. Thus, that there is true faith outside of Israel, or outside of the Christian community, is hardly to be doubted. The Bible has never claimed otherwise.

But there is a second point. The fact that Cornelius was already devout and worshiped God did not mean he did not need to hear the gospel. On the contrary, his worship of God meant that the gospel was in fact precisely for him. And so Peter preached, they believed, and the Spirit was poured out. Without the gospel this would never have happened.

The point I want to make is this: God's revelation is universal. Wherever there is a revelation an appropriate response, like Cornelius's, is a possibility. At the same time, a positive response to God's revelation does not make the gospel superfluous because all revelation has an interior connection to Jesus Christ as God's truly saving act. And so, all who respond positively to God's revelation apart from the knowledge of Jesus Christ are connected by that revelation to what God intends in Jesus Christ. It is not their faith that connects them; it is the revelation, of which God is the subject, that connects the two. Hebrews 11 refers to this when it says that "from a distance they saw."[17] In the book of the Acts we read that God "allowed"[18] the nations to follow their own ways of interpreting God's revelation or God "overlooked the times of human ignorance."[19] That is to say, in God's providence God has given space to many different interpretations of God's revelation. It is now in Jesus Christ that the key is given, so to speak, to unlock the inner meaning of God's revelation however and wherever it occurs.

No revelation of God is a substitute for God's saving act in Jesus Christ; rather, all revelation of God, if truly revelation, points to or connects with that salvation in some way. What is decisive for faith is that it is "faith in," that is, there is a right response in the given circumstances to God's revelation—a revelation that is a finger pointing finally to Christ. Faith in itself accomplishes nothing; it is faith in what God has given that counts. Who can have this faith? It is possible wherever there is God's revelation. Can we doubt that where there is such faith it is saving faith? I don't think so. Of course, it is not really faith that saves but God who is the subject, or actor, in both revelation and salvation that saves. Can we determine who has this right and proper faith? That is not our human prerogative. What we can do is perceive that in other contexts, including other religions, there are elements that seem to connect with what we know in and through Jesus Christ. This is part of the reason why it is important to be attentive to that which is common. There are real connections. One famous theologian, Karl Barth, described these connections as "parables of the faith."[20] We can see these elements in the whole range of religions we have considered.

Is There a Providential Role for the Religions?

We need to ponder briefly one final question here. In the previous section I tried to make the point that God's revelation is universal and that right and proper response born of the Spirit is possible wherever God reveals himself. What is believed in, though it is not Jesus Christ, in so far as it is revelation even so has an interior connection to Christ grounded in the revealing will of God. Because this revealing will finds its goal in the saving work of Jesus Christ, such faith outside the Christian community invites the sharing of the gospel. No religion, however exalted, is a substitute for the gospel or makes the gospel unnecessary.

There is one more question we should ask. What about the religions themselves, not just elements in them? What about what the religions themselves intend, which as we have said is not the salvation Christians speak of? Must we simply reject the religions in what they themselves intend, an intention that does not seek a Christian fulfillment?

I have a hunch that there is indeed a providential role for other religions. Here perhaps I am doing a bit of guessing, but guessing that I believe has its roots in the gospel. In answer to this question I will surmise three things.

First, we must recognize the reality of human sin. What do I mean by this? I mean that other religious communities stand as a permanent protest against Christian exclusiveness and arrogance and in doing so expose the dark underside of Christian history. Without the rejection of Christ by the vast majority of the Jewish people, for instance, the awful darkness of Christian history might not have been so fully exposed. Paul in his day wrestled with the question of Jewish rejection. He saw it to be the mission of the gentile church towards the Jewish people to so live out their faith in Christ that the Jewish people would become "jealous," seeing here something they had missed, and receiving Jesus as their Messiah. Alas, we know how little gentile Christianity has made the Jewish people jealous by our faith and life. The Holocaust, if not earlier anti-Jewish pogroms, put an end to that hope. The persistence of other religions that refuse the gospel always threatens to expose Christian darkness when and where Christians fail in love. By exposing our faults they become one more reminder that "every mouth" is to be silenced and "the whole world . . . held accountable to God,"[21] not least the Christian world.

Another reason I believe this to be the case is the reality of human finitude. The insistent claims of other religious communities, claims to which they are deeply committed, and in particular the aspects of that claim that we find impressive, are a reminder that perhaps in our perception of the gospel we have not yet taken account of all that we should. Perhaps the pervading work of the Spirit throughout history has been far richer than we have imagined and other cultures and religions have more to contribute than we have yet been able to see or understand. Why should God be stingy with God's gifts? The rains fall and enrich the just and the unjust alike. But to confuse such gifts as a substitute for the gospel would of course miss the point of the gifts.

There is yet another reason, and here I am really guessing. We should not discount the possibility that in God's final future for all things that even there the other religions have a role to play. We do not know now how multidimensional God's final rule shall be. Perhaps what others religions are insistent about cannot always be glibly dismissed as idolatry. Perhaps the Spirit has enabled certain people to grasp onto some dimension of God's rule that partially eludes us as Christians, even though in the light of Christ it may not yet be the complete reality God intends. Maybe the salvation the Buddhist wants, for instance, has some place in God's future. Nevertheless, as Christians we would still say that whatever the case might be, it is a reality embraced within the lordship of Christ. Perhaps, in a way we cannot now imagine, the Buddha will discern a deep inner connection between the insight that dawned upon him and the new life given by the crucified and risen Jesus. I don't think Jesus would speak to the Buddha the way he did to Sadducees and Pharisees. And I wonder what the Buddha might say to Jesus? We cannot say this is so. But we can with confidence leave it to God's embracing will. At the same time, I am convinced that some fundamental

assumptions of the Buddha lead to a faulty interpretation of the world and
our experience of it. We touch on this in the last chapter. But does that make
the Buddha an enemy of Jesus?

One reason we need to take these possibilities seriously is the element of
surprise in Jesus' parables about the final end of things. Jesus warns the Jewish people of his day that in the last day the evil people of Noah's day, the
inhabitants of Sodom and Gomorrah, of Nineveh, of Tyre and Sidon, and
others will rise in judgment against Israel. This completely reverses what
Israel expects. They saw themselves as judges of these evil peoples. In his
parables Jesus speaks of gentiles entering into the kingdom before or in
place of Israel. In the parable of the sheep and the goats, those who knew
the Lord are surprisingly rejected, and those who did not are to their aston-
ishment welcomed.[22] The parables of judgment and of surprise are always
directed towards those who thought they were on the inside. The supposed
insiders in Jesus' day were the people of Israel. Today we see ourselves as the
insiders. Will there be unexpected surprises for us too? It is because the
lordship belongs to Jesus Christ, the one who did the most surprising thing
of all in humbling himself unto death, even death on a cross, that the end
time will be a time full of surprise. How the Spirit is working today to prepare things for those surprises we cannot begin to imagine now?

So the question is asked, Who will be saved? The disciples already asked
that question: "Lord, will only a few be saved?" How did Jesus answer?
"Strive to enter through the narrow door; for many, I tell you, will try to
enter and will not be able."[23] How satisfactory is that answer? It is a refusal
to answer speculative questions and in effect calls the one who asks the
question to account. We would completely miss the point if we were to
react, "Aha! We squeezed in, but most of you people out there aren't going
to make it!"

I have suggested a number of hints as to why we should be open to surprise in the future. What I have refused to do in this chapter and throughout
this book is to follow particular habits of the mind that pretend to give
answers to these questions on some other basis than the gospel of Jesus
Christ itself. To that gospel we are committed. And the greatest surprise of
all happens when that gospel is proclaimed and someone comes to faith in
Jesus.

Let us now push our reflections one step further. How do other commitments by their difference force us to a deeper understanding of our own
faith?

17.

Faith Responds

— —

"What then are we to say about these things?" Paul answers, "If God is for us, who is against us?"[1] Building upon this faith, what we shall do in this chapter is briefly draw upon our meeting of the commitments of other people and see how this can help renew our understanding of God. We will take cases from each family—a Buddhist, a Confucian, a Hindu, and a Muslim.

The Vertical Is Not the Horizontal

During a stormy night, I imagine a pilot trying to land will pay close attention to her altitude indicator—the device that tells her how far the plane is on or off the vertical and horizontal. Similarly, if a scuba diver dives too deep or stays under too long, too much nitrogen may accumulate in his bloodstream and he risks becoming disoriented and confused. If he gets confused about which way is up, he will soon be in big trouble. In both cases, lives depend on being properly oriented to the horizontal and vertical.

Horizontal and vertical are also fundamental to the life of faith. We often use the cross to illustrate what the horizontal and vertical mean for faith. The arms reach out to embrace the entire world. That is the horizontal, care for neighbor and world. The vertical axis indicates the gift that comes down from above—God's relation to us. If those two don't intersect in our lives, there will be a big problem for faith.

We can learn something both in our agreement and in our disagreement with the Buddhist. One of the most profound things that a Christian holds in agreement with the Buddhist is the conviction that all is interdependent. Many call this the central teaching of Buddhism. It is the doctrine of *pratityasamutpada*, the interdependence of all things.

We used the illustration of the cloud a couple of times.[2] This ephemeral cloud illustrates the Zen idea of emptiness, which means to be empty of my own self-importance as well as to be empty of an independent, autonomous existence. Rather than being independent, we discover that we are the result of an infinite number of conditions. We are interconnected with everything else. As one Buddhist puts it, we "inter-are."[3] Of course, the concept of interdependence is not unique to Buddhism. But Buddhism has its own way of talking about it and draws its own conclusion, namely, that there is no substantial, permanent self. We are finite moments of appearance that come and go in the snap of a finger. Buddhism also draws important moral conclusions from this, such as infinite compassion. We saw that when we talked about engaged Buddhism.

What do I find myself, as a Christian, agreeing with here? The Buddhist says there is no eternal, unchanging, particular you. One might tremble at the thought, but doesn't it seem true? Even the Bible says "What is your life? For you are a mist that appears for a little while and then vanishes."[4] Was James a Buddhist? It almost sounds like it.

In other places the Bible tells us that we are like grass or flowers that flourish for a season and then vanish.[5] Sometimes we see beautifully manicured lawns—like at golf courses—and we might get the mistaken impression that the grass is always that green and tidy. But it really is poor grass, poor flowers, poor bugs, poor cows, poor us. What are those words at a funeral? "You are dust, and to dust you shall return."[6]

This is a central teaching of the Bible about who we are as a people. We are finite, limited. We don't last long. We are dependent on everything around us to be what we are. We didn't manufacture our selves.

Yes, we are conditioned beings the Buddhist says. Think about it. Did you choose your birth? A lot of conditions joined together to bring about what is you—physical, biological, and social factors, ultimately reaching back to the beginning. If someone had traveled back in time and altered history so that your parents never met, there would be no you. And today, are you really free and independent? Not at all. We breathe, for instance, because we can't help breathing. But some day it will just stop, and then it will be too late to awake to the fact that we are interdependent beings. We are conditioned, finite, interdependent. I don't possess anything of myself. Not even my memory. Sometimes that even fails me. . . . Is there a permanent soul you own and possess? Don't bet on it. "Man is like the beasts that perish."[7] You are mortal.

This doctrine of our interdependence on all is the other side of the idea that we are finite. This is the teaching, both from the Bible and from Buddhism, that I indicate by the term "horizontal." Our very finitude links us up not only with what's immediately around us, but the whole universe as well. We have reached across the oceans of earth and plumbed their depths. We peer out across the expanses of space. And we reach inside to the infinitesimal vistas of neutrons and quarks and mesons. Reach in, reach out. We are conditioned by it all, a minute product of this vastness, and so finite.

The Buddhist says, "The bigger the emptiness, the greater the fullness." We are empty, completely empty of a solid core. Indeed, our emptiness is so vast that each of us contains the whole of the universe. I am right here and now the sum total of the universe. There is a vastness to this Buddhist idea of our horizontal interdependence with the total sum of things.

And this is where I turn to the other side, the difference. *Contingency*, a word theologians like to use, comes from Latin and means "to touch." This is the very idea we have been talking about. We are touching other things, we are connected and interdependent. But there are two kinds of contingency, two kinds of touching. The first is this horizontal dependence of everything in our world and universe. You are just as much dependent upon me as I am upon you. One quick illustration. Does a parent make a child or does a child make a parent? No one without a child is a parent. Your child makes you a parent. And no one without a parent is a child. So you are a child because you have parents. This is one kind of horizontal contingency. Everything cooperates in making everything else what it is. It is relative finitude, finitude of mutual dependence. This horizontal contingency is the realm of necessity. Things can't help being the way things are, because of the way other things are. We are part of the ecology of the universe.

But there is another kind of contingency, of touching, of which Buddhism does not speak. It is vertical contingency.

Here the relationship is not mutual or two way. It is a dependency that arises from one direction only. This is so because it arises only from the free will of another. This kind of contingency or dependence is one way, nonmutual, not necessary. Here I am thinking of creation as an example. God did not have to create this world. God freely acted to create it. God could have created something entirely different, or nothing at all. God's freedom to create was not dependent upon his checking out with us first. God is not dependent on us. We are dependent upon God. This is radical, vertical contingency.

This has profound consequence for how we understand what it is to be a person. In Buddhism the individual is only something that appears, based on conditions like a cloud, and then vanishes. For the ignorant that's all they know—birth and death. But the enlightened have seen through to the secret of emptiness. To give up self-clinging totally is to have the totality. True selfhood is not the passing, ephemeral self of time and space but that larger identity of the whole. True selfhood is gained by being so empty that

I expand to include the whole. True identity is attained not by attachment to ego, but by expansion through emptiness of ego.

What is it to be a person for the Christian? I understand it this way. I don't find the basis for my identity in horizontal contingency like the Buddhist. I find it instead in God's free will to create, in the vertical contingency from God who creates an other. To be a person is to be in relationship. To develop as a person is to develop through relationships. I develop not from the inside out (my inside whether ego or emptiness) but from the outside in. "I believe that God has created me and all that exists; that he has given me and still preserves my body and soul, all my limbs and senses, my reason and all the faculties of my mind. . . ."[8]

There I find my primal identity. Finding it there first I find it also deepened and enriched by all my horizontal dependencies—family, friends, and even enemies, not to speak of quarks and the rest of the physical world I depend on for my existence. True personhood is discovered not by expansion of the self to include all, but by a self identified by a relationship and the giving of that self for the sake of the other, all others, including God. That kind of identity in self-giving I will later suggest is what constitutes God's unique nature.

The Way Forward Is Behind

Now we shift to the Sinic family where the way we relate to the world is the most important thing, not how we understand and experience the self.

In Confucianism the idea of the Way, the Path one walks, is central. Here is one way that path is described:

> The person of character must be strong and resolute, for the burden is heavy and the road is far. Humanity (ren) is the burden. Is that not heavy? Only with death does the road come to an end. Is that not far?[9]

Everything depends upon the character of the one who walks the way. Confucianism has always had a deep confidence in the human possibility. Here again we can learn about ourselves from both our agreements and disagreements.

The Confucian is committed to the human possibility. We earlier got a sense of what that meant for Confucius. Once Confucius commented thus: "I have never seen anyone who was not able [to do the right]. There may be such, but I have not seen such."[10] He saw failure all about. Even his own life was not a great success, but he retained an unshaken human confidence.

The later successor of Confucius, Mencius, gave it classic form. We referred to that passage of Mencius in an earlier chapter where he talks about the four natural feelings of empathy, shame, modesty, and sense of right and wrong that lead naturally, if allowed to develop according to their own logic, into humanity (love), uprightness, respectful behavior, and wisdom.[11] Unless they are somehow snuffed out these traits will naturally blaze forth like a prairie fire.

Eventually this led to the doctrine that Heaven and Earth form a trinity with the human.[12] It is obvious that earth requires human activity to realize its full potential, at least as we understand it. In Genesis God places humans in a garden to tend it, and we are still tending it. The earth has untold possibilities humans can yet tease forth from our interaction with earth, unless we in foolishness and carelessness destroy her first. Let us hope that humans don't play the part of the asteroid that scientists think brought about the extinction of the dinosaurs. Without human interaction with earth would there be anyone to know, consciously enjoy, and express in art, music, architecture, and in many other ways the earth's powers and beauties and so bring it to fulfillment? Dinosaurs were unable to do that, and they roamed the earth for at least 150 million years. Nor is the capacity of primates very much advanced in this area. We humans bring a fulfillment to earth that would never have otherwise been realized.

It may not seem so obvious to us how that also applies in our relation to Heaven. For the Confucian, not only was earth dependent upon humans for its development, so also was Heaven.

Heaven on its own has no voice. Humans give voice to Heaven. Above all is the voice of the moral beauty of human justice and kindness. "Heaven is wordless," but it sees and hears with the eyes and ears of the people, for they are in effect the voice of Heaven.[13] If the ruler of Confucius' day wanted to know Heaven's will, then all the ruler had to do was look to the people. What do they need? What will bring health, wholeness, community, and well-being to all? Where must things be changed? Where is the wrong that needs righting? The ruler was not to look to himself, his councilors, or study the heavens, but to look to the people. And then act. For people gave voice to Heaven's will, and the king gave body to it.

This is a profoundly exalted view of human being, and profoundly right, I believe. "What are human beings?" the psalmist asks. They are "a little lower than God . . . [who has] crowned them with glory and honor."[14] Confucius would understand this. The psalmist goes on, and Confucius would give great assent:

> You have given them dominion over the works of your hands;
>   you have put all things under their feet,

all sheep and oxen,
    and also the beasts of the field,
the birds of the air, and the fish of the sea,
    whatever passes along the paths of the seas. . . .
O Lord, our Sovereign, how majestic is your name in all the earth![15]

Though later Confucians, who set aside Confucius' confidence in a personal Heaven, could not join in such praise, Confucius certainly could. And let us not trivialize the notion of having dominion by saying it means exploitation. It doesn't and never did. Kingly dominion in the Confucian view, just as in Israel, expressed itself by listening to Heaven's voice in the people *and* in nature, and heeding it.

And for the Confucian, Heaven would be at a loss apart from the human, for humans give voice to Heaven's will and bring into being a moral community. Thus the human forms a dynamic trinity with Heaven and earth.

Much rides on this for the Confucian. To belittle the human possibility is to put shackles on Heaven. This is the way one renowned contemporary Confucian scholar has described the Christian understanding of what it is to be human. He says: "It understands the object, not the subject; it obliterates the subject, and returns to the object."[16] The object here refers to God, and the subject refers to the human being. He is saying that Christians understand God, but in the process accuse themselves of original sin and make themselves totally dependent upon God. In this way they obliterate themselves and make God everything.

To belittle the human possibility robs Heaven of its voice and makes it impossible for the moral body of Heaven to take shape. We humans are the "completers" of Heaven. Let us once again affirm the human possibility and honor Heaven's will.

We come this far and again have to make a turn. From Genesis to Hebrews I see a biblical affirmation that humanity completes Heaven's will. Without that completion Heaven's will is frustrated. In the Old Testament we read: "In the image of God he created them, male and female he created them."[17] This is where things begin. In the New Testament we read: "He [Jesus] is the reflection of God's glory and the exact imprint of God's being."[18] Here Heaven's will finds its completion. And he continues, "Since, therefore, the children"—us, that is—"share flesh and blood, he himself likewise shared the same things, so that through death he might destroy the one who has the power of death."[19]

How far we have traveled from Adam and Eve to Jesus! But here faith sees a point that the Confucian does not yet see. To be human is to be created to trust in the One who alone gives life. The basis of the human possibility does not lie in the human possession of a capacity to fulfill the divine intent. The human possibility can only be achieved in a relationship of faith and trust, of receiving and giving. If the human possibility is transformed into human capacity, faith dies, the creative relationship is ruptured, and the human possibility denied its fulfillment. This is precisely where Jesus, the image of God comes in. "He learned obedience through what he suffered."[20] So also did Adam and Eve. So also do we. This was the obedience not of works but of trust. Jesus, unlike us, perfected the human possibility[21] for he did not rely upon his own human capacity. It was a perfection of faith.[22]

In this we agree with the Confucian—the perfection of the human possibility. But we take a different turn in the understanding of the human capacity. For the Christian, the possibility is achieved through faith; for the Confucian, through developing the human capacity. For the Confucian the sense of responsibility and obligation is deep and heavy and the way forward long. Christians have been called to take up the cross and follow. Here too there is a burden, but the "yoke is easy" and "the burden light,"[23] for the way forward is not the development of the human capacity through moral effort, but a discovery of our possibility by following behind in trust. Jesus alone walks ahead.[24]

Image Is Not Incarnation

Now back to the Indian family. Nothing is more characteristic of Indian religion than the worship of what the Bible calls idols. But exactly what is an idol?

It is true that the Bible does not have much good to say about them. Exodus 20:4 declares that "you shall not make for yourself an idol." It goes on: "whether in the form of anything that is in heaven above, or that is on the earth beneath, or that is in the water under the earth. You shall not bow down to them or worship them."[25] We read in Exodus that Israel soon forgot that command. They made for themselves a golden calf, bowing down to it, and when Aaron consecrated the golden calf he said, "These are your gods, O Israel, who brought you up out of the land of Egypt."[26] The books of the prophets frequently denounce idol worship. The words of Psalm 115 sum up these denunciations well:

> Their idols are silver and gold,
>   the work of human hands.
> They have mouths, but do not speak;
>   eyes, but do not see.

> They have ears, but do not hear;
>   noses, but do not smell.
> They have hands, but do not feel;
>   feet, but do not walk;
>   they make no sound in their throats.

It then concludes: "Those who make them are like them; so are all who trust in them." In contrast to the idols, "Our God is in the heavens; he does whatever he pleases."[27] Jeremiah finds idols to be a joke: "Their idols are like scarecrows in a cucumber field."[28] Elijah too found them an occasion for mirth and mockery: "Cry aloud! Surely he is a god; either he is meditating, or he has wandered away, or he is on a journey, or perhaps he is asleep and must be awakened."[29]

How different this attitude in the Bible is from the attitude of Hindus to their images. We have already referred to it as a dollhouse religion. Hindus bathe, feed, awaken, and put to sleep the image as if it were an honored living being. The image is not simply the symbol of a distant and powerful God but the very embodiment of that God. While God can be many places at once—God is in all the images—for them God is right here in this specific place. Here is immediate, direct, and palpable contact with God, who is both in and beyond the image.

This becomes an occasion for wonder and praise. How can it be that God, the all mighty, would reside in such a flimsy thing as an image, made by human hands? Is that not a marvel? Is that not a sign of divine graciousness? of divine accessibility? Let us quote once more those words of an Indian sage:

> Although omniscient, [Visnu in his image] appears unknowing;
> although pure spirit, he appears as a body; although himself the Lord
> he appears to be at the mercy of men; although all-powerful he
> appears to be without power; although perfectly free from wants, he
> seems to be in need; although the protector of all he seems helpless;
> although invisible, he becomes visibly manifest; although unfathomable, he seems tangible.[30]

It seems the Indian devotee is fully aware that the image is unable to do anything for itself, as the Bible describes it. Yet the Indian draws a different conclusion. Rather than mirth and mockery, the Indian experiences wonder. Who is right?

There are many kinds of symbols. Imagine that we are driving along a highway and see a sign that reads "Jackson 10 miles" and has an arrow pointing ahead. We of course immediately know that the sign is not talking about itself but about a town that is ten miles further down the road. If we were to stop, put the sign in the trunk of the car, and think thereby that we had Jackson, we would be silly indeed.

Or imagine we are hiking out in the mountains near Jackson Hole, Wyoming. We have a detailed topographical map. In the mountains we can see nothing but mountains. How shall we find our way to Jackson Hole? We examine the map, determine our location based on the landmarks noted on the map, and eventually find our way to where we want to go. Here the map shares in the reality of the location in a more important way than a mere sign. While the map is not the territory, it represents that territory in a different key, as it were. The topography is rugged, but the map is flat. Yet, it can depict that roughness in a way we can understand. It shares in the reality somewhat. If we happen to have a compass with us, which of course we should, the compass is even more deeply involved in the reality. It aligns itself with the magnetic poles so the reality in fact determines something about the compass. Nevertheless, we never mistake map or compass for the real thing. They are aids. But such aids are not trivial. In some situations they might in fact be life saving.

There are symbols with deeper meaning yet. Consider the notion of a designated representative. Let us say that the American secretary of state goes to some country to state our American policy with respect to something—war, peace, trade, or whatever—and negotiate an agreement. Is this secretary of state the president of the United States? Or is she the United States itself? Obviously not. But her presence has the force and authority of America's presence. To mistreat the secretary of state is to mistreat a whole country and its people. The office is more than an aid to something. Somehow, the real thing is there in the person of the secretary of state. There is an authority that counts for the real thing.

And there are other, more profound symbols. When, for instance, we get to what we call a sacrament, we find an even deeper relationship between symbol and reality. A sacrament does not just point to something else. It conveys what it points to. "This is my body given for you; this is my blood shed for you." Is the bread we eat the body of Jesus? Is the wine we drink the blood of Jesus? Yes? No? Yes and no. When we chew on the bread we do not masticate the literal flesh of Jesus. No chemical analysis would substantiate that. Does that mean then that Jesus is present only to our imaginations? God forbid! Jesus really is present in the bread and wine. Jesus' body and blood are the body and blood of the crucified and risen Jesus. Eating the bread and drinking the wine is connected with Jesus' word and promise, and in the eating and drinking of faith the destiny that belongs to Jesus' body and blood becomes a destiny that he shares with us. Destinies are joined. Here the reality, God's gift and promise, controls the symbol; the symbol does not control or limit the reality.

Finally, we come to incarnation. "The Word became flesh and lived among us," John writes.[31] The astonished Mary asks, "How can this be?" The answer comes, "The Holy Spirit will come upon you, and the power of the Most High will overshadow you; therefore the child to be born will be holy; he will be called Son of God."[32] And Matthew writes, "All this took place to fulfill what had been spoken by the Lord through the prophet: 'Look, the virgin shall conceive and bear a son, and they shall name him Emmanuel,' which means, 'God is with us.'"[33] Is Jesus a symbol of God, like a sign? Or is he more? Is Jesus a realistic picture of what God is like, a map of God? Or is he more? Was Jesus an emissary, a prophet, an authorized representative? Yes, but more. Was Jesus the sacramental presence of God? Perhaps one could say so. But he was more even than that. To cut his flesh with thorns, sword, and nails was to cut the flesh of the Son of God not symbolically but actually. For Jesus to be raised from the dead was for his flesh, not his ghost or his memory, to be raised from the dead. The tomb is empty. Here we have moved beyond symbol to irreversible event.

Where in this series are the images of the Hindus? Where are the idols of the Bible? In the Bible idols fall off the scale on the far end. They aren't even considered symbols, or at best negative symbols—of demons.[34] For the Hindus, in contrast, images are more like sacraments. God does not become an image as such but is present through the image.[35] And so Hindus go to the temple to see God and to be seen by God—*darsan*.[36]

Many Christians too use images. Where do they fit in this series? Eastern Orthodox Christians venerate images, but only in the form of icons.[37] Icons are pictures. They must always be flat, not three-dimensional. Roman Catholic Christians venerate icons as well as three-dimensional images. Lutherans don't venerate, but they often have pictures or three-dimensional images above their altars or in a prominent place in the worship space. Where do you suppose these fit in the series? In any case, none go so far with images as the Hindu. For Hindus who worship Visnu, images are an indispensable aspect of worship.

An image is not incarnation. Why do we say this? Why are idols forbidden in the Bible?[38] Images as idols are crafted. We the makers become the ones who determine when and where God is present. But that cannot be done to God. God is no more (or no less) present in a temple than in a nightclub. If there is a difference it is only whether and how that presence is acknowledged and honored. The difference between the Bible and Hindu image worship is not whether an image of God is important or not. Rather, it is what kind of image can truly be God's counterpart. To forbid the crafting of images is to protect the place where God's image is truly present: in the human.[39]

God is finally present for us not in thing or craft, not in a temple, but only in the Word, the Word become flesh. That the disciples could see, touch, and feel Jesus was important.[40] But that this Jesus was human, speaking to them and acting for them, as well as being hated and rejected, was even more important. It is that God is in a living relationship with us that matters. It is through words that we communicate and come to know one another. The deaf and dumb image is not God's counterpart. The human being is. Therefore, God created us in God's image. Therefore Jesus could be "the exact imprint of God's very being."[41]

The nature of God is at stake in the difference between image and incarnation. That is to say, God's relation with us is always personal, the relationship of one to another. Crafted images are not living and cannot speak or walk or cry.[42] They thus would necessarily misrepresent God. To worship a dumb god is to become dumb like that god. But Jesus was no dumb God. He cried, he prayed, he comforted, he condemned. He was not unconscious and immovable. He learned obedience through what he suffered.[43] He was crucified and buried. And he was raised.

When the Word became flesh, the true nature of God's transcendence was made plain. It is the transcendence of perfect freedom, including the freedom to become vulnerable to those who are loved. The true nature of God's accessibility was made plain. It is an accessibility that knows no personal limits. The true nature of God as God is made plain. God is only God as a personal presence, as a living God who is in relationship with those who are loved. And so, when God made us, we were made in God's image. We are God's counterpart, but disobedient and fallen. Jesus, Word became flesh, is God's counterpart, obedient to death and raised.[44]

Love Is Not Mercy

The Christian shares a deep affinity with the Muslim. We both affirm the mercy of God. How great and full of majesty is that mercy!

Recall the parable of the mean slave. A certain king wanted to settle accounts with his slaves. He discovered, to his dismay, that one slave owed him an impossibly large sum equivalent to ten thousand years of wages. Such a debt could only have been amassed through corruption. Incensed, the king ordered that he, his wife, and his children be sold and all his possessions seized in partial restitution. But the slave implored him for mercy, doubtless with copious tears and earnest promises. Moved to pity, the king forgave this huge debt.

It so happened that another slave owed the first slave a measly sum of one day's wages. He demanded immediate payment. When the second slave pleaded for mercy, the first angrily threw him into prison.

When the king heard of this, he summoned the first slave into his presence. "I forgave you all your debt because you pleaded with me," he said. "Should you not have had mercy on your fellow slave, as I had on you?"[45] So the king in anger handed him over to the torture chamber where he was to remain until he paid all that he owed.

Here we see mercy at work. God is a God of mercy; but God will not suffer fools who despise that mercy. Here Muslim and Christian are in complete agreement.

Nevertheless, mercy is not love. Wherein do they differ? The difference is simple but weighty. Mercy is always the prerogative of power. Love never is. The king in the parable is under no obligation, spoken or unspoken, to treat his corrupt slave kindly. As king he had every right, and all the power, to come good on his threat, but out of compassion he relented. When the servant failed to show mercy in return, the king withdrew his mercy. Again, the king was under no obligation to do so. In both cases the king simply carried out his good pleasure. Only the one who is in a position of power has the freedom to withhold or exercise mercy.

But this is not how love works. Love is never free. While one may freely choose to love, love itself is never free. It labors under an inner compulsion and obligation.

Consider the parent-child relationship. Parents freely choose to become parents. Yet, once a child comes into their lives they are no longer free to choose or not to choose to be parents to the child given them. It is intrinsic to parenthood to love their children. Parents who do not love violate not only the child's trust but also their very parenthood. Thus, the freedom to love has become, so to speak, bondage into love.

We may take another parable as a case in point, the prodigal son. This son rudely demands from his father his portion of the inheritance prematurely, an inheritance the father had labored to build up for him. With sadness the father gives it to him and the son departs for the excitement of the big city.

He spends recklessly in a dissolute and extravagant life, until he ends up on a pig farm slopping pigs. Destitute and desperate, he lived with the filthy beasts in the pigsty and fought with the pigs for the slop.

One day it suddenly dawned on him that he could return to his father. He compared his present state with that from before, and slowly a resolve took shape. At least he might be able to be a servant in his father's household. He would go back and confess, "Father, I have sinned against heaven and before you; I am no longer worthy to be called your son; treat me like one of your hired hands."[46]

We all recall the end of that episode. While the son was still far off, the waiting father got word of his return and rushed out to meet him. The son had hardly blurted out his well-rehearsed confession when the father swept him into his embrace, dressed him in the finest clothes, and began preparations for a festive banquet.

What do we see here? We see love. This is not the mercy of a king that the king could or could not choose to exercise. This was the love of a rejected father who was compelled by love, for this was his son. He didn't chose this love. This love, rather, chose him, compelled him.

Love is different from mercy because it is not free but bound; mercy is not. More than that, love is not the prerogative of power; mercy is. Love is always vulnerable. There is no love that is not vulnerable, present in weakness.

The father who received his son back with no questions asked made himself vulnerable. How does he know this is not a stratagem of the son to cheat off him again? But love does not make such calculations. It gives. To say, "I love you," is in fact to give up power and become vulnerable to the other. This is why betrayed love is so awful. It is to take advantage of another's vulnerability and weakness.

This is what the cross is all about: God bound in love to God's creation. God giving that love in a position of utter vulnerability. True love always risks a cross. Mercy never does. Mercy acts from a position of power and authority, not vulnerability.

This is what the Christian understanding of God is all about. When we read that "God is love,"[47] it means at least two things. First, in God's relation to the world God is love. Here is the law of love—love cannot choose not to love, for love creates its own obligation. In this free will to be bound, the law of love, lies God's holiness, God's singularity, God's uniqueness, God's sovereignty. To be bound like this is to be vulnerable.

Could God, having created a world, be as if God had not created a world? Not if God is love. God submits in a freely chosen, but now inescapable, tie

to the world—God will not forsake the world God created. What happens
to the world now also happens to God. Our desecration of the earth
becomes a desecration of God.

Could God, having promised himself to the people of Israel be as though
God had not so promised? God's holiness, which is God's faithfulness in
love, makes that impossible. "By myself I have sworn. . . ."[48] Henceforth the
story of the people of Israel becomes God's story. To practice holocaust
against the Jews is to attempt holocaust against God. God refuses such holocaust, even against a people caught in their wickedness:

> How can I give you up, Ephraim?
>   How can I hand you over, O Israel?
> How can I make you like Admah?
>   How can I treat you like Zeboiim?
> My heart recoils within me;
>   My compassion grows warm and tender.
> I will not execute my fierce anger;
>   I will not again destroy Ephraim;
> for I am God and no mortal,
>   the Holy One in your midst,
> and I will not come in wrath.[49]

Could the Word of God, having taken flesh in Jesus, be as if the Word had
not taken flesh? Impossible. To reject Jesus is to reject God. That is what the
story of Jesus is all about.

> who, though he was in the form of God,
>   did not regard equality with God
>   as something to be exploited,
> but emptied himself,
>   taking the form of a slave,
>   being born in human likeness.
> And being found in human form,
>   he humbled himself
>   and became obedient to the point of death—
>   even death on a cross.[50]

Second, God in God's self is love. The free will to be bound to love is
God's holiness. This is the kind of relation there is between the Father and
the Son. All things have been given over to the Son by the Father. That is the
vulnerability of love. That is almost as if the Father risks the Father's own
deity on the faithful working of the Son. All is given to the Son. Your destiny
is mine, God says to his son. Your deeds are mine. Had the Son become

prodigal, might not God's "Godness" have collapsed? But the Son is trusting and obedient and in response returns all to the Father. This relationship of giving and receiving between Father and Son is the absolutely unique relationship that faith has discerned. Again, the Spirit itself is the power of God to be a relationship. It is this Spirit that once again receives all from the Father and the Son, gives to us, gathering us up into this eternal relationship of Father and Son. When that has been done, "Then comes the end, when he [Jesus] hands over the kingdom to God the Father . . . so that God may be all in all."[51]

"What then are we to say about these things?" Paul asks. The answer faith has discerned is clear:

> He who did not withhold his own Son, but gave him up for all of us, will he not with him also give us everything else . . . ? Who will separate us from the love of Christ? . . . I am convinced that neither death, nor life, nor angels, nor rulers, nor things present, nor things to come, nor powers, nor height, nor depth, nor anything else in all creation, will be able to separate us from the love of God in Christ Jesus our Lord.[52]

This is the vision of faith, which has met this absolutely unique God of love in Jesus Christ.

Notes

1. Three Families

1. The words *India*, *Indic*, and *Hindu* derive from the ancient word for the Indus River, which is in present-day Pakistan.

2. This English word comes from the Latin *Sinae*, which has a connection with the word *China*. China, as *Sinae*, comes from Qin (pronounced "chin"), which was the empire founded in 221 B.C.E., uniting China after centuries of disunity.

3. Mark 12:28-30.

4. Qur'an 59:22-26. Citations from the Qur'an are taken from Arthur J. Arberry, *The Koran Interpreted: A Translation* (New York: Collier Books, 1986). Unfortunately, although the Arberry work may be the most stately of all the translations, its verse numbering system does not usually coincide with the standard in the version most widely used in North America by Muslims, 'Abdullah Yusuf 'Ali, *The Holy Qur'an: Text, Translation and Commentary* (Brentwood, Md.: Amana Corporation, 1989). I use the Arberry translation, but the 'Ali numbering.

5. For the most part, with Chinese words I will use the spelling current in China today. This is different from a common romanization used in the past, the Wade-Giles system. Many are familiar with the spelling "Taoism," which we here spell "Daoism." It should be pronounced with a *d*, not a *t* sound.

6. *Analects* (*Lunyu*) 1:2. *Lunyu* is the Chinese name for these writings.

7. *The Great Learning* (*Daxue*). See, for example, Wing-tsit Chan, *A Source Book in Chinese Philosophy* (Princeton: Princeton University Press, 1963), 86f.

8. *Zhuangzi 18*. See Burton Watson, *The Complete Works of Chuang-tzu* (New York: Columbia University Press, 1968), 193-194.

9. See N. J. Girardot, *Myth and Meaning in Early Taoism: The Theme of Chaos* (Berkeley, Calif.: University of California Press, 1983), 81.

10. Mark 12:31.

11. *Analects* 11:12.

12. *Analects* 3:12.

13. *Analects* 7:23.

2. And Then There Are More

1. This discussion is based on Sam Gill, "Whirling Longs and Colored Sands." *Native American Religious Action: A Performance Approach to Religion* (Columbia, S.C.: University of South Carolina Press, 1987), 47-57.

2. These stories come from the *Kojiki*. For a translated text, see Donald L. Philippi, *Kojiki* (Tokyo: University of Tokyo Press, 1968). *Shinto* technically means "the way of the gods" and was a term that arose after the Confucian, Daoist, and Buddhist traditions entered from China around the sixth century C.E. The word was used to differentiate the indigenous traditions as a collectivity against the new arrivals.

3. This study was conducted in the first half of 1981. It was funded by the National Science Council of Taiwan, Republic of China, and carried out by a team of faculty from the schools of nursing at the National Defense Medical Center and the National Taiwan University, both in Taipei. Prior to this, my wife, Ida Marie, completed a similar study in the United States, and since has conducted such studies in China, Korea, and Hong Kong as well as further studies in the United States.

4. This and the following pages draw considerable material, some of it verbatim, from Paul Varo Martinson and Ida M. Martinson, "The Religious Response of the Chinese Family to Childhood Cancer." *American Asian Review* 6(3) (Fall 1988):59-92.

3. All Religions Are the Same—Right?

1. After formulating these thoughts, as well as the other two habits of the mind later discussed, I was interested to read John Hick's treatment of these matters. He too is aware that the issues are more than historical and cultural in nature but go to the very roots of epistemology. We draw very different conclusions from the matter. What I call a habit of the mind, Hick terms "a product of . . . a religious insight." See John Hick, *A Christian Theology of Religions: The Rainbow of Faiths* (Louisville, Ky.: Westminster/John Knox Press, 1995), chapter 2 and especially 33f.

2. One version of this tale is cited in Christian Humphreys, *Buddhism* (Harmondsworth, Middlesex: Penguin Books, 1951), 11.

3. For a thorough analysis of these three, see, for example, Mark S. Heim, *Salvations: Truth and Difference in Religion* (Maryknoll, N.Y.: Orbis, 1995).

4. This is the point well made by J.A. Dinoia, *The Diversity of Religions: A Christian Perspective* (Washington, D.C.: The Catholic University of America Press, 1992).

4. What Can We Expect When We All Differ?

1. Genesis 1:26-27.
2. Psalm 19:1-4.
3. Amos 9:7.
4. Genesis 14:18-20.
5. Numbers 23.
6. 2 Kings 5.
7. Isaiah 45:1.
8. Malachi 3:11.
9. Genesis 1:2
10. Exodus 31:1-5.
11. 2 Corinthians 2:10-11.
12. Romans 8:19-23.
13. John 3:8.
14. Genesis 2:7.
15. 2 Corinthians 2:18.
16. 1 Corinthians 12:4ff.
17. Romans 8:26-27.
18. 1 Corinthians 12:3.
19. Acts 2:4.
20. 1 Corinthians 12:10.
21. George A. Lindbeck, *The Nature of Doctrine: Religion and Theology in a Postliberal Age* (Philadelphia: Westminster, 1984), 94.
22. For example, one of the earliest instances of this in the Bible is the Christ hymn of Philippians 2, especially verses 9-11.
23. John 1:14, and see also verses 1-3.
24. Martin Luther, *The Small Catechism*. In *The Book of Concord*, trans. and ed. Theodore G. Tappert (Philadelphia: Muhlenberg Press, 1959), 345.

5. Meeting Our Buddhist Neighbor

1. The date commonly accepted by scholars is circa 566–486 B.C.E. Theravado Buddhists generally place his birth in 624 and death in 544 B.C.E. Japanese scholars tend to place his birth and death dates at 448 and 368 B.C.E. See, for instance, Leo D. Lefebure, *The Buddha and the Christ: Explorations in Buddhist and Christian Dialogue* (Maryknoll: Orbis, 1993).

2. See Paul J. Griffiths, *On Being Buddha* (Albany, N.Y.: SUNY, 1994), 89. For the presentation of this legendary form of the Buddha's story we are more or less following his brief synopsis.

3. *Mahavagga* I.II.1. Cited from A. Foucher, *The Life of Buddha According to the Ancient Texts and Monuments of India* (Middletown, Conn.: Wesleyan University Press, 1963), 157.

4. Galatians 6:7.

5. James 4:14.

6. *Udana* 80-81. See, for example, David J. Kalupahana, *Buddhist Philosophy: A Historical Analysis* (Honolulu: The University Press of Hawaii, 1976).

7. *Time* 148, no. 6 (August 5, 1996): 63.

8. See Paul Griffiths, "Concentration or Insight: The Problematic of Theravada Buddhist Meditation Theory," *JAAR* 49 (1981): 606-624. Cf. Nathan Katz, *Buddhist Images of Human Perfection* (Delhi: Motilal Barnarsidass, 1982). Cf. also Paul Griffiths, *On Being Mindless* (La Salle, Ill.: Open Court, 1986), Nyanaponika, *The Heart of Buddhist Meditation* (London: Rider and Co., 1969); and Winston King, *Theravada Meditation: The Buddhist Transformation of Yoga* (University Park, Penn.: Pennsylvania State University, 1980).

9. For an example of this meditation see Nyanaponika, *The Heart of Buddhist Meditation*, 61–68, on various body meditations, including the decaying human corpse.

10. William Johnston, *Silent Music: The Science of Meditation* (New York: Harper and Row, 1974).

11. See, for example, Sallie B King, "Thich Nhat Hanh and the Unified Buddhist Church," in *Engaged Buddhism: Buddhist Liberation Movements in Asia,* ed. Christopher S. Queen and Sallie B King (Albany, N.Y.: SUNY, 1996). See pages 404 and 401 in relation to our comments.

12. On this last point see Queen and King's introduction to *Engaged Buddhism,* 14–33.

13. For brief and informative assessments of his life see Queen and King, *Engaged Buddhism,* 321–363, and Leo D. Lefebure, *The Buddha and the Christ: Explorations in Buddhist and Christian Dialogue* (Maryknoll, N.Y.: Orbis, 1993), 145–192.

14. Thich Nhat Hanh, *Peace Is Every Step: The Path of Mindfulness in Everyday Life*, ed. Arnold Kotler (New York: Bantam Books, 1991), 96–98.

15. King and Queen, *Engaged Buddhism.*

6. Meeting Our Muslim Neighbor

1. Qur'an 2:255.

2. Qur'an 112.

3. Qur'an 2:284.

4. Or "Messenger."

5. Qur'an 96:1-5.

6. Qur'an 5:4.

7. For one version of these events see Ibn Hisham, 'Abd Al-Malik, *The Life of Muhammad: A Translation of Ishaq's Sirat Rasul Allah*, trans. and intro. A. Guillaume (London: Oxford University Press, 1955), 104ff.

8. Ibn Hisham, *Life of Muhammad,* 683.

9. See Miller, *Muslim Friends,* 226f.

10. Another tradition says that the stone was given to Abraham by the angel Gabriel to build into this place of prayer.

11. Qur'an 25:4f.

12. Qur'an 42:51-52. The *We,* referring to God may most simply be taken as a *we* of majesty (signifying greatness) and not a *we* of number (signifying plurality).

13. Fazlur Rahman, *Major Themes of the Qur'an* (Minneapolis: Bibliotheca Islamica, 1980), 28.

14. Qur'an 33.72.

15. Qur'an 80:30.

7. Meeting Our Chinese Neighbor—As a Confucian

1. See the brief summary in Julia Ching, *Chinese Religions* (Maryknoll, N.Y.: Orbis Books, 1993), 54.

2. *The Analects* 7:1. I follow Julia Ching, *Chinese Religions*, 65.

3. *The Analects* 7:33. I follow Julia Ching, *Chinese Religions*, 54.

4. See *The Analects* 12:11 and 13:3.

5. See the brief reference to this in chapter 1, page 8.

6. See chapter 1, page 8.

7. See chapter 1, page 7.

8. *The Analects* 15:23. Cited from Ching, *Chinese Religions*, 57.

9. *The Analects* 4:15.

10. *The Analects* 6:28.

11. *The Analects* 1:2.

12. *The Analects* 2:4. Adapting Ching, *Chinese Religions*, 55.

13. *The Analects* 14:35.

14. *The Analects* 1:1.

15. *The Analects* 14:38.

16. *The Analects* 11:9, 10, 11.

17. *The Analects* 4:6.

18. *The Analects* 3:24.

19. Qin Shihuangdi called himself the First Emperor. After centuries of disunity, Qin ruthlessly united all of China and ruled from 221–208 B.C.E. Confucius would have been appalled at his methods. Some readers may have visited the terra-cotta diggings in Xian, associated with his tomb. He is also famous for the Great Wall construction.

20. Mencius lived from around 371 to 289 B.C.E.; Xunzi from about 298 to 238 B.C.E.

21. The first era includes the whole pre-Qin period, including Confucius, Mencius, and Xunzi, among others; the second is the Song (twelfth century) rethinking and after; the third is today. The Han period, which is deemed less intellectually respectable than these other periods, is ignored.

22. *Analects* 17:2.

23. *Mencius (Mengzi)* 7B:14. *Mencius* is the romanization of *Mengzi.*

8. Meeting Our Chinese Neighbor—As a Daoist

1. On this see especially Angus C. Graham, *Unreason within Reason: Essays on the Outskirts of Rationality* (LaSalle, Ill.: Open Court, 1992).

2. For a description of this movement see Daniel L.Overmyer, *Religions of China: The World as a Living System* (San Francisco, 1986), 34.

3. Quoted from Max Kaltenmark, *Lao Tzu and Taoism* (Stanford: Stanford University

Press, 1969), 9f. For my earlier discussion of Daoism upon which I draw here see Paul Varo Martinson, *A Theology of World Religions: Interpreting God, Self, and World in Semitic, Indian, and Chinese Thought* (Minneapolis, Minn.: Augsburg, 1987), 159–197.

4. See Max Kaltenmark, *Lao Tzu and Taoism*, 161.

5. On this idea see Herrlee G. Creel, *What Is Taoism?* (Chicago: University of Chicago Press, 1970), Creel, "The Great Clod," 25–36.

6. *Daodejing* 4 (6). A commonly used alternate chapter number for the *Daodejing* is provided in the parenthesis.

7. *Daodejing* 35 (42).

8. *Daodejing* 62 (76), my translation.

9. *Daodejing* 35 (42). I modified some of the spelling of Chinese terms to maintain consistency.

10. *Daodejing* 17 (21). This is a combination of the translations of N. J. Girardot, *Myth and Meaning*, 65, and Wing-tsit Chan, *The Way of Lao Tzu* (Indianapolis: Bobbs-Merrill, 1963), 137, with some spelling modifications.

11. John 1:14.

12. John 14:6.

13. *Daodejing* 19, cited from Joseph Needham, *Science and Civilization in China*, vol. 2, *History of Scientific Thought* (Cambridge: At the University Press, 1962), 87.

14. *Daodejing* 18, cited from Needham, *Science and Civilization in China*, 109.

15. The *Huainanzi*, opening of chapter 8. Cited from Needham, *Science and Civilization in China*, 109, who in turn cites E. Morgan, *Tao the Great Luminant: Essays from the "Huai Nan Tzu"* (Shanghai: Kelly and Walsh, 1933[?]), 82–83.

16. *Daodejing* 56, following interpretation of Hou Wai-Lu as cited in Needham, *Science and Civilization in China*, 112–113.

17. *Daodejing* 65, cited in Needham, *Science and Civilization in China*, 87, based on Chu Ta-Kao, tr., *Tao Te Ching, A New Translation* (London: Buddhist Lodge, 1937).

9. Meeting Our Hindu Neighbor

1. Mark Twain, *Following the Equator* (Hartford, Calif.: American, 1898), 504, as cited in Diana L Eck, *Darsan: Seeing the Divine Image in India* (Chambersburg, Penn.: Anima, 1981), 15.

2. *India* comes from the Greek word *indos* for the Indus River and also from the Persian *hindu* and is related to Sanskrit *sindhu* for river, specifically the Indus and its surrounding region.

3. Rig-Veda 2.1.3.

4. Brihad-aranyaka upanishad 3.1.3.

5. Brihad-aranyaka upanishad 3.2.13.

6. Brihad-aranyaka upanishad 4.4.5. Cited in Robert Ernest Hume, *The Thirteen Principal Upanishads Translated from the Sanskrit* (London: Oxford University Press, 1877), 140f.

7. Klaus K. Klostermaier, *A Survey of Hinduism* (Albany, N.Y.: SUNY, 1989), 75.

8. The word Brahman has several different meanings. The verbal root is BRH- which means "to grow." In the Vedas it means sacred speech through which the gods receive their greatness and power. Later it came to mean the sacrifice or ritual itself as well as the priest, which we here write as "brahmin." The Brahmanas are the texts of this phase. In the Upanishads the word means ultimate reality, that which is behind and in all things, the soul or energy of the universe.

9. Rig-Veda 10.90.

10. G. Buhler, *The Laws of Manu* (Oxford: Clarendon, 1886), 5:148.

11. See, for instance Niels C. Nielsen Jr., et al., *Religions of the World* (New York: St. Martin's Press, 1988), 146f.

12. This description taken from Nielson, *Religions*, 143. The scripture quotation is from *Regveda* 3.62.10.

13. Compare Klostermaier, *Survey of Hinduism*, 189f.

14. Cited by Nielsen, *Religions*, 175, quoting Dinesh Chandra Sen, *History of Bengali Language and Literature* (Calcutta, India: University of Calcutta, 1911), 714ff.

15. For clarification of the joining together of Krisna and Visnu, and thus making Krisna worship Vedic, see Nielsen, *Religions*, 176ff.

16. Bhagavadgita 4.6-8. Traditionally there are 7, 10, 22, or innumerable.

17. Bhagavadgita 2.22-23.

18. Bhagavadgita 11. Quoted from R. C. Zaehner, *The Bhagavadgita: With a Commentary Based on the Original Sources* (Oxford: Clarendon Press, 1969).

19. Isaiah 44:9-18.

20. The theologian referred to is Pillai Lokacarya of the Sri Vaisnava movement, whose approximate dates are variously 1205–1311 or 1264–1369. Cf. Bharatan Kumarappa, *The Hindu Conception of the Deity as Culminating in Ramanuja* (London: Luzac, 1934), 316–317, cited in Eck, *Darsan*, 15. For my earlier comments that I draw upon in this section, see Paul Varo Martinson, "World Religions: The Problem of Imaging Christ," in *Imaging Christ: Politics, Art, Spirituality*, ed. by Francis A.O.S. A Eigo (Villanova, Penn.: Theology Institute Publications, 1991), 128ff, and Paul Varo Martinson, "Imaging the Human Through Culture, Religions, Christ," in *Word and World* 10, no. 4 (1990): 336f. On the making and consecration of images see Klostermaier, *Survey of Hinduism*, 293–299.

21. See Klostermaier, *Survey of Hinduism*, 298, citing the *Arthapancaka*.

22. Klostermaier, *Survey of Hinduism*, 413–414.

10. The Faithfulness of Judaism

1. Romans 11:17ff.

2. Romans 1:16.

3. Jacob Neusner is adamant in arguing that "Judaism and Christianity are entirely autonomous of one another." He denies a shared "Judeo-Christian tradition." Again, "Judaism and Christianity do not intersect, even when they read the Bible," for "they bring different questions and reach different conclusions—no shared tradition there." See Jacob Neusner, *A Short History of Judaism: Three Meals, Three Epochs* (Minneapolis, Minn.: Fortress Press, 1992), xif. He, of course, has his reasons for arguing thus. Clearly his concern is to argue the autonomy of Judaism with respect to Christianity and that Judaism alone is the proper successor to Israel's faith. The question of Jesus as the Messiah has no relevance to the formation of Judaism. But on the other hand, it cannot be said that the question of the nature and status of the Torah has no relevance for the formation of Christianity. It has everything to do with it, even though the Christian has given a different answer to the meaning and significance of the Torah than Judaism. Already in this we see the controversy runs deep.

4. Genesis 32:28.

5. The first use of the term is actually among Greek-speaking Jews of the first century C.E. See, for example, 2 Maccabees 2:21; 8:1; 14:38. Cf. Galatians 1:13-14.

6. The word *ethnic* tends to be a bit complicated here. One is a Jew by right of birth. In this sense it is ethnic. However, it is not a racial term, for many races can be Jewish. An example of the complication of this term is Neusner's use when he describes Judaism as

not limited to "a single ethnic group," yet refers to adhesion as entering "an intensely ethnic community." See Neusner, *A Short History of Judaism*, 5.

7. Cited from Jacob Neusner, *The Way of Torah: An Introduction to Judaism* (Belmont, Calif.:
Dickenson, 1970), 87. See b. Shabbat, 31a; also Nahum N. Glazer, Hillel the Elder: The
Emergence of Classical Judaism (Washington, D.C.: Bnai Brith Hillel Foundations, 1959),
74f. One, of course, also recalls the similar saying of Jesus in Mark 12:31.

8. For example, Mark 7:1-13.

9. One will recall the controversy with Jesus and the Sadducees on this point. Jesus was
a close ally with the Pharisees here. See Mark 12:18-27. One also recalls Paul's identification with the Pharisees on this point. See Acts 23:6-10.

10. Psalm 137:1, 5-6 New English Bible (NEB).

11. Psalm 126:1-5 NEB.

12. Cited from Neusner, *A Short History of Judaism*,89–91. [No Neusner 1992 in Bib.]
Neusner in turn cites from Rabbinical Assembly of American Prayerbook Committee,
1962.

13. Ezra 9:2.

14. Ezra 9:3.

15. Ezra 9:6.

16. Ezra 10:1.

17. Ezra 10:44.

18. Hasmonian was a title applied to the Maccabees by Josephus. It derives from the
name of the great-grandfather of Mattathias, Asmonaios, and may be connected with the
village of Heshmon (cf. Joshua 15:23). They were a priestly family, the first of the twenty-
four priestly divisions that served in the First Temple (cf. 2 Chronicles 24:7). At the time
of the return from exile they probably were among those who opposed the reforms of
Ezra. Josephus came from this family. For further information see Cecil Roth, *Encyclopaedia Judaica* (Jerusalem: Keter Publishing House, Ltd., 1972), 7:1455; 9:1322; 12:89f.

19. It was only around this time that the word *Torah* came to designate these five books
specifically, the Pentateuch. In fact, they only became authoritative or canon by the fifth
century B.C.E. Prior to this the word *Torah* simply designated certain groups of laws as such
(see, for example, Leviticus 6:2, 7; 11:37, etc. and Numbers 5:29-30, etc.) or to teaching
or doctrine in general (Isaiah 2:3). Roth, *Encyclopaedia Judaica*, 10:389.

20. Exodus 19:5, 6.

21. Titus (under title of Flavius Vespasianus) was Emperor of Rome A.D. 79–81. He
destroyed the Second Temple in 70. His father, Vespasian, brought him to Judea when he
was appointed by Nero to suppress the uprising there in 66. In 69 he became Emperor and
appointed Titus to deal with the Jewish rebellion.

22. For the logic of these developments we are throughout following the interpretation
of Jacob Neusner. See, for instance, Neusner, *A Short History of Judaism*,and Jacob Neusner,
An Introduction to Judaism: A Textbook and Reader (Louisville, Ky.: Westminster/John Knox
Press, 1991).

23. Cited from Neusner, *Way of Torah*, 5. Yohanan is quoting Hosea 6:6.

24. Avot 1:1, cited in Leo Trepp, *Judaism: Development and Life* (Belmont, Calif.:
Wadsworth Publishing Company, 1982), 219. The "Great Assembly" was supposedly
founded by Ezra, and the members of this Assembly are regarded as the founders of the
rabbinic tradition.

25. Avot 1:17, 18.

26. Neusner, *Way of Torah*, 170.

27. The Talmud comes in two recensions. The earlier and shorter is the so-called Jerusalem Talmud, compiled in Palestine (not Jerusalem) and completed in unfinished form around c.e. 400, and the Babylonian Talmud, completed around c.e. 500 or later.

28. Trepp, *Judaism.*

11. The Fateful History of Judaism

1. See, for instance, Marcel Simon, "Christian Anti-Semitism." *Essential Papers on Judaism and Christianity in Conflict: From Late Antiquity to the Reformation.* ed. Jeremy Cohen (New York: New York University Press, 1991), 131–137. Note Cohen's comment here: "Simon . . . criticizes [some] Jewish historians . . . for underestimating the pagan roots of Christian anti-Judaism, and thus for exaggerating the hatred which Christological doctrine itself had spawned." Jeremy Cohen, "Scholarship and Intolerance in the Medieval Academy: The Study and Evaluation of Judaism in European Christendom," in *Essential Papers on Judaism and Christianity in Conflict: From Late Antiquity to the Reformation* (New York: New York University Press, 1991), 11.

2. He puts the argument this way: "But the Jews who killed him and refused to believe in him, to believe that he had to die and rise again, suffered a more wretched devastation at the hands of the Romans and were utterly uprooted from their kingdom, where they had already been under the dominion of foreigners. They were dispersed all over the world—for indeed there is no part of the earth where they are not to be found—and thus by the evidence of their own Scriptures they bear witness for us that we have not fabricated the prophecies about Christ . . . . We recognize that it is in order to give this testimony, which, in spite of themselves, they supply for our benefit by their possession and preservation of those books, that they themselves are dispersed among all nations, in whatever direction the Christian Church spreads. . . . This is the reason for his [God's] forbearing to slay them—that is for not putting an end to their existence as Jews, although they have been conquered and oppressed by the Romans; it is for fear that they should not forget the Law of God and thus fail to bear convincing witness." St. Augustine, Bishop of Hippo, *Concerning the City of God Against the Pagans,* ed. and trans. Henry Bettenson (Harmondsworth: Penguin Books, 1972), 827f.

3. John Y. B. Hood, *Aquinas and the Jews* (Philadelphia: University of Pennsylvania Press, 1995), 14. We follow him in the above discussion of Augustine.

4. Hood, *Aquinas,* 17.

5. John Chrysostom, "Against the Jews," Homily I, in Wayne A. Meeks and Robert L. Wilken, *Jews and Christians in Antioch in the First Four Centuries of the Common Era* (Missoula, Mont.: Scholars Press, 1978), 97.

6. In 410 the Visigoths sacked Rome. In 476 they completed Rome's destruction with complete control of the Italian peninsula.

7. Hood, *Aquinas,* 27. These things refer to the Roman Law codified in the Theodosian Code of 439 before the fall of Rome, and Justinian's Code of 534 after the fall.

8. In the West, Roman law survived in the form of the "Breviary" of Alaric. The anti-Jewish provisions were very much weakened, and because of a desire to equalize differences for the sake of holding territories together, such specialized laws fell into disuse.

9. Hood, *Aquinas,* 28f.

10. Hood, *Aquinas,* comments that between 481 and 850 "only a handful of monarchs issued so much as a single anti-Jewish decree," and that "During the long period of papal impotence in western Europe (roughly 400–1000), many rulers had instituted policies favorable to Jews. Some Jews served as royal officials and tax collectors; others were permitted to own Christian slaves. In both cases, infidel Jews exercised *dominium* over Chris-

tians. In addition, some rulers actually impeded missionary work by allowing Jewish communities to confiscate the property of converts. Medieval popes were scandalized by these situations." See pages 29 and 31. Langmuir also comments: "From the fall of Rome down to the eleventh century, the doctrine had almost no influence on how most Christians thought about or treated Jews." (Gavin I. Langmuir, "The Faith of Christians and Hostility to Jews." Christianity and Judaism. ed. Diana Wood (Oxford: Blackwell Publishers, 1992), 82.)

11. B. Blumenkranz sums up this period well: "In the history of relations between the Church and the Jews, the High Middle Ages in the West is an exceptional period. Generally speaking, at no other time were relations between the two communities so relatively smooth—and this without the Jews having to renounce any of their beliefs and practices, even the right to conduct missionary activities. It is true that the canons of Church Councils tended to accentuate the division between Jews and Christians, in order to save the latter from contacts which might have imperiled their faith. The Church also wished to see a further decline in the social status of the Jews, in the hope of facilitating missionary activities among them. It wanted its cause to be adopted in civil legislation, and canon law to become the law of the state. However, the Carolingian Princes particularly, and also the rulers of the Germanic Empire, gave effective protection to their Jewish subjects against such pretensions. Furthermore, the actions of the Councils had merely local reference, and were only rarely supported by the Papacy. What is more, the Papacy sometimes gave support to the Jews during local persecutions as was to be the case also in later periods." B. Blumenkranz, "The Roman Church and the Jews," in *Essential Papers on Judaism and Christianity in Conflict: From Late Antiquity to the Reformation*, ed. Jeremy Cohen (New York: New York University Press, 1991), 225.

12. Blumenkranz, "The Roman Church," 194–197, 201–204.

13. Roth, *Encyclopaedia Judaica*, 8:659.

14. For a defense of this thesis see Robert Chazan, *Medieval Stereotypes and Modern Anti-Semitism* (Berkeley: University of California Press, 1997), 142–144.

15. The term comes from the Bible and referred to the general region of Europe. It came to be referred particularly to Jews originally settling in the Germanic areas. See again Chazan, *Medieval Stereotypes*, 142–144.

16. H. Liebeschütz, "The Crusading Movement in Its Bearing on the Christian Attitude towards Jewry." *Essential Papers on Judaism and Christianity in Conflict: From Late Antiquity to the Reformation*. ed. Jeremy Cohen (New York: New York University Press, 1991), 260–275.

17. Cecil Roth, "The Medieval Conception of the Jew: A New Interpretation," in *Essential Papers on Judaism and Christianity in Conflict: From Late Antiquity to the Reformation*, ed. Jeremy Cohen (New York: New York University Press, 1991), 299f.

18. I use "popular" in the technical sense that R. I. Moore uses it. He restricts its use to "that great majority of the population which, being effectively subject to the seigneural ban, enjoyed neither noble nor clerical status, the un-free and the illiterate. Modern historians have no excuse for blurring a distinction which is quite plain, socially, legally, and conceptually, in their sources and in particular no excuse for using 'popular' as a synonym for 'lay.'" R. I. Moore, "Anti-Semitism and the Birth of Europe," in *Christianity and Judaism*, ed. Diana Wood (Oxford: Blackwell Publishers, 1992), 43f.

19. Chazan, *Medieval Stereotypes*, 5.

20. On this system see Lester K. Little, "The Jews in Christian Europe." In *Essential Papers on Judaism and Christianity in Conflict: From Late Antiquity to the Reformation*, ed. Jeremy Cohen (New York: New York University Press, 1991), 280, and James Parkes, *A History of the Jewish People* (Baltimore, Md.: Penguin Books, 1964), 73–77.

21. Roth, "Medieval Conception," 305f.

22. Roth, *Encyclopaedia Judaica*, vol. 8, 668, 673.

23. Solomon Grayzel, "The Papal Bull *Sicut Judeis,*" in *Essential Papers on Judaism and Christianity in Conflict: From Late Antiquity to the Reformation*, edited by Jeremy Cohen (New York: New York University Press, 1991), 242 and see whole article.

24. Roth, *Encyclopaedia Judaica*, 689, which refers to Solomon Grayzel, *Church and the Jews in the Thirteenth Century* (1933).

25. Abram Leon Sachar, *A History of the Jews* (New York: Alfred A Knopf, 1982), 197.

26. Cohen, "Scholarship and Intolerance."

27. Hood, *Aquinas and the Jews*.

28. This term, also spelled in English *marinos* or *maranos*, is "swine" in Spanish. It probably comes from Arabic *mahram* meaning something prohibited, derived from the fact that eating pork was outlawed by Muslim and Jew. See further Roth, *Encyclopaedia Judaica*, 11:1018.

29. The *minyan*, or quorum, was ten male adults over thirteen years of age. This was required for a public synagogue service and certain other religious ceremonies. Supposedly based on ten spies of Numbers 14:27, or various other appearances of the number ten in Scripture.

30. A Russian term designating an attack, accompanied by destruction, looting, murder, and rape of one section of population against another. From the words *po* (on, at, according to) and *grom* (thunder). Webster describes it as "an organized massacre and looting of helpless people with the connivance of officials." See Philip Bobcock Gove,. *Webster's Third New International Dictionary of the English Language Unabridged* (Springfield, Mass.: Merriam-Webster Inc., 1986) and also Roth, *Encyclopedia Judaica*, 13:694.

31. Sachar, *History of Jews*, 241.

32. Parkes, *History of Jewish People*, 95.

33. Trepp, *Judaism*, 74.

34. Roth, *Encyclopaedia Judaica*, vol. 3, 106. Martin Luther, "On the Jews and Their Lies, 1543," in *Luther's Works* (Philadelphia: Muhlenberg Press, 1962), 137–306, esp. 268–72. It is only fair to cite these words from Luther written twenty years earlier, in 1523: "Therefore, I would request and advise that one deal gently with them and instruct them from Scripture; then some of them may come along. Instead of this we are trying only to drive them by force, slandering them, accusing them of having Christian blood if they don't stink, and I know not what other foolishness. So long as we thus treat them like dogs, how can we expect to work any good among them? Again, when we forbid them to labor and do business and have any human fellowship with us, thereby forcing them into usury, how is that supposed to do them any good? If we really want to help them, we must be guided in our dealings with them not by papal law but by the law of Christian love. . . . If some of them should prove stiff-necked, what of it? After all, we ourselves are not all good Christians either." See also Martin Luther, "That Jesus Was Born a Jew, 1523," in *Luther's Works*, 229. For a brief discussion of Luther's attitude towards Jews see Martin H. Bertram's introduction to *Luther's Works*.

35. Roth, *Encyclopaedia Judaica*, vol. 8, 693.

12. Into the Modern World

1. Trepp, *Judaism*, 106. For a fuller discussion of Columbus and the Jewish question see Ivan G. Marcus, "Judaism in Northern and Eastern Europe to 1500" in *The Encyclopedia of Religion*, ed. Mircea Eliade (New York: Macmillan Publishing, 1987), 1:35-40. See also 3:1396f.

2. See Trepp, *Judaism*, 94. Johann Caspar Lavater (1741–1801), a Swiss clergyman, had challenged him to explain Judaism on the basis of reason or else become a Christian.

3. Howard M. Sacher, *A History of the Jews in America* (New York: Alfred A. Knopf, 1992), 270.

4. Sacher, *Jews in America*, 270.

5. Roth, *Encyclopaedia Judaica*, vol. 6, 702.

6. Roth , *Encyclopaedia Judaica*, vol. 7, 1433–1452, gives the rough dates for the movement as 1770s–1880s. I draw upon this essay for much of my discussion.

7. Isidore Epstein, *Judaism: A Historical Presentation* (Harmondsworth: Penguin Books Ltd., 1959), 291, suggests that David Friedländer (1756–1834) was the real originator of the movement. None dare, however, put his ideas into action until Israel Jacobson (1768–1828), beginning in 1808 in Berlin, and Eduard Kley (1789–1867), beginning in 1818 in Hamburg, are credited with these innovations. This was the beginning of Reform Judaism.

8. Phillip Sigal, *Judaism:The Evolution of a Faith* (Grand Rapids, Mich.: Eerdmans, 1988), 204.

9. Roth, *Encyclopaedia Judaica,* 14:25.

10. Roth, *Encyclopaedia Judaica,* 14:26. These were the words of Samuel Holdheim (1806–1860), whose ideas became the basis for Reform Judaism in America. Somewhat more moderate was the influential Abraham Geiger (1810–1874).

11. Geiger, for one, gave expression to this, summing up religion as vague religious feeling: "*Is not the Jewish people . . . endowed with . . . a genius, with a religious genius?* . . . An aboriginal power to understand more vividly, and feel more intensely the close relation between the spirit of man and the Supreme Spirit?" (Leo Trepp, *Judaism: Development and Life* (Belmont, Calif.: Wadsworth Publishing, 1982), 98, cited from Gunter Plaut, *The Rise of Reform Judaism* (New York: World Union for Progressive Judaism, 1963), 126f).

12. It may be of interest to note concerning Columbus that there is considerable circumstantial evidence to suggest that he was of Marrano extraction. In any case, he got his patronage from the Spanish ruler largely through the support of a group of "New Christians," or Marranos, around the Aragones court. It was to these he wrote his account of the successful trip. See Roth, *Encyclopaedia Judaica,* 5:756–757 for the details. On Torres, see Roth, *Encyclopaedia Judaica,* 15:1266.

13. Gerald Sorin, *Tradition Transformed:The Jewish Experience in America* (Baltimore, Md.: The John Hopkins University Press, 1997), 16.

14. Roth, *Encyclopaedia Judaica,* vol. 2, 810. I follow this discussion in the account above.

15. Trepp, *Judaism,* 108.

16. Sorin, *Tradition Transformed,* 34. In 1880 only 3 percent of the world's Jews lived in the United States; 6 million of the world's 7.7 million Jews lived in Eastern Europe, or 75 percent of the total. In 1881–1882 alone pogroms were carried out against Jews in 225 cities and towns in Russia, and in 1882 the May Laws were passed, forbidding Jews to live in villages in Russia. Five hundred thousand Jews were expelled from rural areas. See page 39 of Sorin.

17. Roth, *Encyclopaedia Judaica,* 2:812. One might note that in all of Latin America there were at this time some 750,000 Jews.

18. See Sorin, *Tradition Transformed*, 4f. The language used there is assimilationists or survivalists and the transformationists. The "assimilationists" here refers to those who see already too much assimilation and so bring this critique to bear on the Jewish community.

19. Sorin, *Tradition Transformed,* 130. See also page 129 for above statistics.

20. Among other things it said: "It will not do to offer our prayers in a tongue which only few scholars nowadays understand. We cannot afford any longer to pray for a return

to Jerusalem. It is a blasphemy and lie upon the lips of every American. . . . We accept as binding only its [the Scripture's] moral laws, but reject all such as are not adapted to the views and habits of modern civilization. . . . We hold that all such Mosaic and rabbinical laws as regulate diet, priestly purity and dress originated in ages and under the influences of ideas entirely foreign to our present mental and spiritual state. . . ."Trepp, *Judaism*, 114.

21. Sorin, *Tradition Transformed*, 171 and 204.

22. Reconstructionism grew out of Conservative Judaism. As Epstein describes it, it is "Conservatism minus its religious affirmations" (Epstein, *Historical Presentation*, 298). That is to say, it drops the concern with belief in a personal God and all that entails for understanding revelation, election, messiahship and the rest. Religion is understood to be a civilization or culture that characterizes a particular people.

23. Sorin, *Tradition Transformed*, 1. Many examples could be given. Here are some quotes about New York in 1937: ". . . By 1937 Jews owned two-thirds of the 34,000 factories and 104,000 wholesale and retail establishments in New York City. . . . By the mid-1930s, 50 percent of the applicants to medical school and an almost equally disproportionate number of applicants to law school were Jewish. . . . In 1937 in New York City, Jews, who constituted 25 percent of the population, made up 65 percent of the lawyers and judges, 64 percent of the dentists, and 55 percent of the doctors" (Sorin, *Tradition Transformed*, 162–163)

24. Comments of demographer Barry Kosmin, cited in Sorin, *Tradition Transformed*, xv and 254

25. Sorin, *Tradition Transformed*, 242.

26. Sorin, *Tradition Transformed*, 241.

27. Stephen J. Whitfield, *American Space, Jewish Time: Essays in Modern Culture and Politics* (Armonk, N.Y.: North Castle Books, 1996), 184.

28. Sorin, *Tradition Transformed*, 6.

29. Sorin, *Tradition Transformed*, 62.

30. Sorin, *Tradition Transformed*, 64. See also page 235f.

31. Whitfield, *American Space*, 6.

32. Whitfield, *American Space*, 7.

33. Sorin, *Tradition Transformed*, 41.

34. Sorin, *Tradition Transformed*, 113ff.

35. Sorin, *Tradition Transformed*, 173. Finnish Americans, it might be noted, formed 50 percent.

36. Sorin, *Tradition Transformed*, 149f., 176ff. Cf. also the chapter on "Liberalism" in Whitfield, *American Space*.

37. Whitfield, *American Space*, 112ff.

38. Whitfield, *American Space*, 93.

39. Sorin, *Tradition Transformed*, 14.

40. See, for instance, Sorin, *Tradition Transformed*, 181f. and Whitfield, *American Space*, 129ff.

41. Sorin, *Tradition Transformed*, 208ff.

42. Sorin, *Tradition Transformed*, 225ff.

43. Sorin, *Tradition Transformed*, 228f.

44. Important names in this early phase included Rabbi Judah Alkalai and Rabbi Zevi Hirsch Kalischer, both of whom moved from a more religious expectation to a more political activism, and Moses Hess, who as a secular socialist moved from a purely secular motivation to one that appreciated more the cultural, if not religious, tradition of the Jewish people. Our discussion in this section is largely shaped by Roth, "Zionism," *Encyclopaedia Judaica*, vol. 16.

45. Roth, "Zionism," 1035.

46. Roth, "Zionism," 1046.

13. The Continuing Conversation

1. See, for instance, Pawlikowski, *Christ in the Light*, 5–6, where he acknowledges this divergence. For a summary of divergent viewpoints generally see the rest of this book as well as Peter Ochs, "Judaism and Christian Theology," in *Modern Christian Theologians* (place: press, year), 607–625, John T. Pawlikowski, *Jesus and the Theology of Israel* (Wilmington, Del.: Michael Glazier, 1989).

2. In my reading the most sophisticated and nuanced presentation of this view is Pawlikoski. See, for instance, Pawlikowski, *Christ in the Light* and Pawlikowski, *Theology of Israel*.

3. Matthew 27:25.

4. 2 Corinthians 3:15.

5. 1 Peter 2:8-9. Cf., for instance, Exodus 19:6.

6. Revelation 2:9.

7. John 8:44. In John, it is often pointed out, the word *Jews* is a term of implacable antagonism and amounts to a rejection of all Jews. This of course is not the case. Most uses are in a polemical context that refers to the collectivity of those who are opposed, who in fact were Jews. But it is also used several times as a neutral term simply designating all Jews without any negative sense, and even used in a positive sense as well.

8. I refer to the passage in Matthew 23. This chapter is perhaps the most vitriolic denunciation of the Pharisees anywhere in the New Testament, unless one would give that honor to Stephen's speech in Acts 7.

9. Romans 9:2-3.

10. Matthew 5:38-48.

11. Luke 23:34.

12. Acts 7:60.

13. John 4:22.

14. 1 Timothy 1:15.

15. Romans 9:4-5.

16. Romans 1:16.

17. The fact of the controversy between Jesus and his people cannot be washed out of the Gospels. He must be held accountable for the beginnings of conflict. Later witnesses only build on that.

18. See the early paragraphs of Martin Luther, "The Freedom of a Christian" (1520). *Luther's Works* (Philadelphia: Muhlenbert Press, 1962), 333–337.

19. Jacob Neusner and Bruce D. Chilton, *Revelation: The Torah and the Bible* (Valley Forge, Pa.: Trinity Press International, 1995), vii.

20. Marty recognizes and applauds Jacob Neusner's forthrightness in his book *Telling Tales: Making Sense of Christian and Judaic Nonsense*. Neusner writes, for instance: "I see no basis for a forthright dialogue with Christianity when Christianity is represented as having come to an end the day Jesus died, and Jesus' never having risen from the dead. What I see is an adaptation of the figure of Jesus to a Christology acceptable to a Judaism, not Jesus Christ God, son of God, God incarnate. Why should Christianity conduct a dialogue that at the outset denies what makes Christianity Christian, which is Christ Jesus risen from the dead? I see no call at all." The reverse also holds, so that "Judaism . . . is, for instance, accused of being legalistic. But its latter-day apologists demonstrate that it really was not [so] legalistic, because its legalism formed an expression of the covenant with God, thus 'covenantal nomism.' Explaining legalism by explaining it away, the mainly Protestant

defense of Judaism validates the faith by claiming it conforms to Protestant norms. That may serve for Reform Judaism, but it hardly forms a profoundly appreciated defense of a Judaism that encompasses dietary laws, Sabbath and festival observance, and a way of life affecting many corners of human existence treated by Protestant Christianity as neutral. Why should any Judaism conduct a dialogue that at the outset denies the Torah's holiness, affirming only those aspects of the Torah that conform to someone else's notion of what God can talk about anyhow?" Martin Marty, foreword to *Telling Tales: Making Sense of Christian and Judaic Nonsense* by Jacob Neusner (Louisville, Ky.: Westminster/John Knox Press, 1993). See also page 8f.

21. In what follows we draw upon the ideas in Bruce Chilton's discussion of "The Bible as God's Word" in Neusner and Chilton, *Telling Tales*.

22. Luke 4:16-21.

23. Compare James 5:16, where we read that "the prayer of the righteous is powerful and effective." The text then refers to Elijah's prayer for first drought and then rain as an illustration.

24. Cited in Neusner and Chilton, *Telling Tales*, 82.

25. Hebrews 11:18.

26. Matthew 15:26-28.

27. Luke 7:44-47.

28. Luke 18:1-5.

29. James 5:16.

30. Mark 15:34.

31. Galatians 3:13.

32. 2 Corinthians 5:21.

33. Neusner and Chilton, *Telling Tales*, 99. See Abot 2:4.

34. John 3:16.

35. Abot 2:4. Cited in Emil L. Fackenheim, *What Is Judaism? An Interpretation for the Present Age* (New York: Simon and Schuster, 1987), 134.

36. Cf. Deuteronomy 5:24-27.

37. Psalm 19:8. For whole passage see Fackenheim, *What is Judaism*, 135.

38. Fackenheim, *What Is Judaism*, 135.

39. Fackenheim, *What Is Judaism*, 137.

40. Philippians 3:4-6.

41. Galatians 1:13.

42. Galatians 1:15-16.

43. For the story of Paul's encounter with the risen Christ, see Acts 9:1-9.

44. Galatians 3:13.

45. Philippians 2:5-11.

46. Galatians 3:13.

47. 2 Corinthians 5:21.

48. Romans 11:28, 32.

49. Romans 10:14-15, 17.

50. Romans 11:5.

51. Matthew 27:25.

52. In this section I draw upon Pawlikowski, *Theology of Israel*, 88–99.

14. God Is like This!

1. John 1:18.

2. Acts 17:23.

3 If I were to speak of a third kind of knowing, I would suggest a term such as *clairvoyant knowing*. By this I mean knowledge or purported knowledge that is not mediated through the senses. One might also speak of it as intuitive, mystical, or an immediate kind of knowing.

4. Genesis 2:19-20.

5. John Hick's position is a perfectly consistent example of this tendency. A typical example is Hick, *Christian Theology*, 67.

6. Exodus 3:13.

7. Exodus 3:14.

8. For a very brief discussion see Terrence E. Fretheim, "Exodus," in *Interpretation: A Bible Commentary for Teaching and Preaching* (Louisville, Ky.: John Knox Press, 1991), 63. For a more detailed discussion see B. S. Childs, *The Book of Exodus: A Critical, Theological Commentary* (Philadelphia: Westminster Press, 1974), 60–70.

9. Terrence Fretheim opts for this. See Fretheim, "Exodus," 63.

10. John 1:18.

11. John 3:16.

12. Mark 2:5.

13. Mark 2:11.

14. Matthew 5:21ff.

15. Matthew 12:28.

16. Matthew 11:27.

17. John 20:28.

18. Philippians 2:6-11.

19. 2 Corinthians 4:6.

20. Cf. Romans 11:33-36.

15. Should We Evangelize Everyone or Dialogue?

1. Galatians 3:27.

2. 1 Corinthians 12:28.

3. John B. Cobb, *Beyond Dialogue: Toward a Mutual Transformation of Christianity and Buddhism* (Philadelphia: Fortress Press, 1982).

4. The most common term for repentance is *metanoeo*. The term which the Latin Vulgate translates as *conversio* is *epistrepho*. Luke uses this much more than any other writer. Some verses in which these two words occur together are Luke 17:4; Acts 3:19; 26:20.

5. Clemmens M. Granskou, oral narrator, and Jane Baker Koons, interviewer. St. Paul: Midwest China Oral History and Archives Project, 1976), 99–100.

16. Who Will Be Saved?

1. *Ad majorem Dei gloriam*, the motto of the Society of Jesus (Jesuits).

2. These citations are taken from Kosuke Koyama, *Mount Fuji and Mount Sinai: A Critique of Idols* (Maryknoll: Oribis Books, 1984), 167–170. For the original (in English) see Henry James Coleridge, trans., *The Life and Letters of St. Francis Xavier* (London: Burns Oates, 1902) 2:95f, 227–229, 347.

3. This is the notion of *naiskarmya* of the Bhagavadgita in chapter 3.

4. This, of course, is the major thesis of Mark S. Heim, *Salvations: Truth and Difference in Religion* (Maryknoll, N.Y.: Orbis, 1995).

5. Deuteronomy 6:6-9 indicates the importance of telling about the event to the children as they grow up.

6. Mark 15:34.
7. 2 Corinthians 5:21.
8. Romans 5:7-8.
9. Mark 7:18-23.
10. Galatians 5:19ff.
11. Galatians 5:16-26.
12. Theodore G. Tappert, *The Book of Concord* (Philadelphia: Muhlenberg Press, 1959),365.
13. Hebrews 7.
14. Acts 10 and repeated in 11.
15. Acts 10:34f.
16. Acts 10:28.
17. Hebrews 11:13.
18. Acts 14:16.
19. Acts 17:30.
20. Barth on parables of faith??
21. Romans 3:19.
22. Matthew 25:31-46.
23. Luke 13:24.

17. Faith Responds

1. Romans 8:31
2. See chapters 1 and 5, pages 6 and 57f.
3. Thich Nhat Hanh, *Peace*, throughout.
4. James 4:14.
5. For instance, Psalm 90:5f. and many other places.
6. Genesis 3:19. Cf. Psalm 9:3.
7. Psalm 49:12
8. Luther, *Small Catechism,* 345.
9. *Analects* 7.7.
10. *Analects* 4.6.
11. *Mencius* 2A.6.
12. See Chou Tun-yi's "Diagram of the Supreme Ultimate" (see, for example, Fung Yu-lan, *A History of Chinese Philosophy*, vol. 2, *The Period of Classical Learning*, translated by Derk Bodde (Princeton: Princeton University Press, 1953)) as one of the more famous statements of this. This notion of a trinity or "ternion" of Heaven, Earth, and Humanity suggests the idea of a moral whole to which humanity brings completion. For further discussion see Martinson, *World Religions,* 232–286.
13. *Mencius* 5A.5.
14. Psalm 8:4, 5.
15. Psalm 8:6-9.
16. Tsung-san Mou, *Zhongguo Zhexue di tezhi* (The uniqueness of Chinese philosophy) (Taipei: Taiwan hsueh-sheng shu-chu, 1963), 47.
17. Genesis 1:27.
18. Hebrews 1:3.
19. Hebrews 2:14.
20. Hebrews 5:8.
21. Hebrews 2:10; 5:9.
22. Hebrews 5:7.

23. Matthew 11:30.
24. Mark 10:32.
25. Exodus 20:4-5.
26. Exodus 32:4.
27. Psalm 115:3-8.
28. Jeremiah 10:5.
29. 1 Kings 18:27.
30. Klostermaier, *Hinduism*, 298.
31. John 1:14.
32. Luke 1:35.
33. Matthew 1:22-23.
34. 1 Corinthians 10:20.
35. As one believer in Krsna writes: "Never think of the Deity as made of stone or wood. Every worshipper must remember that Krsna is personally present. He is simply kindly presenting Himself before us in a way so that we can handle Him." See Deadwyler, *Gods of Flesh Gods of Stone*, 83, quoting a letter of Prabhupada, the founder of ISKCON, to Jayatirtha dasa, dated November, 1975. See also the ISKCON handbook, *The Process of Deity Worship*.
36. Diana Eck describes the importance of the eyes and the seeing: "The prominence of the eyes on Hindu divine images also reminds us that it is not only the worshipper who sees the deity, but the deity sees the worshipper as well. The contact between devotee and deity is exchanged through the eyes. It is said in India that one of the ways in which the gods can be recognized when they move among people on this earth is by their unblinking eyes. . . . In the later Hindu tradition, when divine images began to be made, the eyes were the final part of the anthropomorphic image to be carved or set in place. Even after the breath of life (*prana*) was established in the image, came the ceremoney [*sic*] in which the eyes were ritually opened with a golden needle or with the final stroke of a paintbrush. This is still common practice in the consecration of images, and today shiny oversized enamel eyes may be set in the eye sockets of the image during this rite. . . . When Hindus stand on tiptoe and crane their necks to see, through the crowd, the image of Lord Krsna, they wish not only to 'see,' but to be seen. The gaze of the huge eyes of the image meets that of the worshipper, and that exchange of vision lies at the heart of Hindu worship." Eck, *Darsan*, 5f.
37. *Icon* comes from the Greek *eikon* meaning a form or appearance.
38. *Idol* comes from a Greek word, *eidolos*, meaning a visible form or shadow. It is connected with the word for "seeing."
39. Frethheim writes, "The use of interpersonal language is also related to the prohibition of concrete images in Israel's worship. Though the Old Testament does not clearly articulate the reasons for this prohibition, it points more in the direction of a concern to protect God's relatedness than anything else. God is not present in the world in the form of an image which cannot see or speak or act." Then he writes, "This interpretation is also continuous with the point where the Old Testament does talk about a legitimate concrete image. It is the human being with all of its capacities for interrelationships which is believed to be the appropriate image of God in the life of the world (Genesis 1:26-27)." Frethheim, "Color of God," 265. Cf. also Garrett Green, who writes: "[T]he reason for the prohibition is not the material or finite *nature* of the images per se but rather . . . [the] confusion of creature and Creator. . . . There can be no *graven* image of God, not because God has no image but because he has already established his own, *human* image of himself." *Imagining God: Theology and the Religious Imagination* (San Francisco: Harper and Row, 1989), 91f. For a fuller discussion see pages 91–97. So also John T. Pawlikowski, who refers to Monica Hellwig's discussion that prohibition of idols is rooted in "deep conviction that there exists only

one image of God that reveals anything of importance, namely, the human person," *Christ in the Light of the Christian-Jewish Dialogue* (New York: Paulist Press, 1982), 10. See Monica Hellwig, "Christian Theology and the Covenant of Israel," in *JES* 7, no. 1 (winter 1970):50. Hellwig also refers to fact that "Jesus who said 'Philip, he who sees me sees the Father' (John. 14:19), also insisted that Christians should see him in every man, even the most wretched, in a total and radical identification (Matthew 25:31-46)."

40. Luke 24:39; 2 John 1:1.

41. Hebrews 1:3. Cf. 2 Corinthians 4:4; Colossians 1:15. It is for this reason also that avatar, the Hindu notion of divine manifestation or incarnation, is not the biblical incarnation. The very fact that these avatar are many, whether human or animal, is similar to the problem of crafted images. These are forms that divinity clothes itself in. They can be exchanged as a garment. It agrees with the assumption of a soul-body dualism that is the essence of reincarnation.

42. We will leave aside here the question of weeping Madonnas and the like in Roman Catholicism. This would seem to be an effort to invest images with a life that is not theirs.

43. Hebrews 5:7

44. Philippians 2:6-11.

45. Matthew 18:32-33.

46. Luke 15:18-19.

47. 1 John 4:8.

48. Genesis 22:16; Hebrews 6:13f.

49. Hosea 11:8-9.

50. Philippians 2:6-8.

51. 1 Corinthians 15:24, 28.

52. Romans 8:32, 35, 38-39.

BIBLIOGRAPHY

'Ali, 'Abdullah Yusuf. *The Holy Qur'an: Text, Translation and Commentary*. Brentwood, Md.: Amana Corp., 1989.

Arberry, Arthur J. *The Koran Interpreted: A Translation*. New York: Collier Books, 1986.

Augustine, Saint, Bishop of Hippo. *Concerning the City of God against the Pagans. A New Translation by Henry Bettenson, with an Introduction by David Knowles*. Ed. and trans. Henry Bettenson. Harmondsworth: Penguin Books, 1972.

Bertram, Martin H. Introduction to *Luther's Works*, 123–36. Philadelphia: Muhlenberg Press, 1962.

Blumenkranz, B. "The Roman Church and the Jews." In *Essential Papers on Judaism and Christianity in Conflict: From Late Antiquity to the Reformation*, edited by Jeremy Cohen, 193–230. New York: New York University Press, 1991.

Buhler, G. *The Laws of Manu*. Oxford: Clarendon, 1886.

Chan, Wing-tsit. *A Source Book in Chinese Philosophy*. Princeton: Princeton University Press, 1963.

———. *The Way of Lao Tzu*. Indianapolis: Bobbs-Merrill, 1963.

Chazan, Robert. *Medieval Stereotypes and Modern Anti-Semitism*. Berkeley: University of California Press, 1997.

Childs, B. S. *The Book of Exodus: A Critical, Theological Commentary*. Philadelphia: Westminster Press, 1974.

Ching, Julia. *Chinese Religions*. Maryknoll: Orbis Books, 1993.

Cobb, John B., Jr. *Beyond Dialogue: Toward a Mutual Transformation of Christianity and Buddhsim*. Philadelphia: Fortress Press, 1982.

Cohen, Jeremy. "Scholarship and Intolerance in the Medieval Academy: The Study and Evaluation of Judaism in European Christendom." In *Essential Papers on Judaism and Christianity in Conflict: From Late Antiquity to the Reformation*. New York: New York University Press, 1991.

Creel, Herrlee G. *What is Taoism?* Chicago: University of Chicago Press, 1970.

Dinoia, J.A. *The Diversity of Religions: A Christian Perspective*. Wahsington, D.C.: The Catholic University of America Press, 1992.

Eck, Diana L. *Darsan: Seeing the Divine Image in India*. Chambersburg, Penn.: Anima, 1981.

Epstein, Isidore. *Judaism: A Historical Presentation*. Harmondsworth: Penguin Books, 1959.

Fackenheim, Emil L. *What Is Judaism? An Interpretation for the Present Age*. New York: Simon and Schuster, 1987.

Foucher, A. *The Life of the Buddha According to the Ancient Texts and Monuments of India*. Middletown, Conn.: Wesleyan University Press, 1963.

Fretheim, Terrence E. "The Color of God: Israel's God-Talk and Life Experience." In *Word and World* 6 (summer, 1986): 156–165.

———. "Exodus." In *Interpretation: A Bible Commentary for Teaching and Preaching*. Louisville, Ky.: John Knox Press, 1991.

Fung Yu-lan. *A History of Chinese Philosophy*, vol. 2, *The Period of Classical Learning*, translated by Derk Bodde. Princeton: Princeton University Press, 1953.

Gill, Sam. "Whirling Longs and Colored Sands." In *Native American Religious Action: A Performance Approach to Religion*, 47–57. Columbia, S.C.: University of South Carolina Press, 1987.

Girardot, N. J. *Myth and Meaning in Early Taoism: The Theme of Chaos (Hun-tun)*. Berkeley: University of California Press, 1983.

Glazer, Nahum N. *Hillel the Elder: The Emergence of Classical Judaism*. Washington, D.C.: Bnai Brith Hillel Foundations, 1959.

Gove, Philip Bobcock. *Webster's Third New International Dictionary of the English Language Unabridged*. Springfield, Mass.: Merriam-Webster Inc., 1986.

Graham, Angus C. *Unreason within Reason: Essays on the Outskirts of Rationality*. LaSalle, Ill.: Open Court, 1992.

Granskou, Clemens M., oral narrator, and Jane Baker Koons, interviewer. St. Paul: Midwest China Oral History and Archives Project, 1976.

Grayzel, Solomon. "The Papal Bull *Sicut Judeis*." In *Essential Papers on Judaism and Christianity in Conflict: From Late Antiquity to the Reformation*, edited by Jeremy Cohen, 231–59. New York: New York University Press, 1991.

Griffiths, Paul. "Concentration or Insight: The Problematic of Theravada Buddhist Meditation Theory." In *JAAR* 49 (1981): 606–24.

———. *On Being Buddha*. Albany, N.Y.: SUNY, 1994.

———. *On Being Mindless*. La Salle, Ill.: Open Court, 1986.

Heim, S. Mark. *Salvations: Truth and Difference in Religion*. Maryknoll, N.Y.: Orbis, 1995.

Hellwig, Monica. "Christian Theology and the Covenant of Israel." In *JES* 7, no. 1 (winter 1970): 37–51.

Hick, John. *A Christian Theology of Religions: The Rainbow of Faiths*. Louisville, Ky.: Westminster John Knox Press, 1995.

Hood, John Y. B. *Aquinas and the Jews*. Philadelphia: University of Pennsylvania Press, 1995.

Hume, Robert Ernest. *The Thirteen Principal Upanishads Translated From the Sanskrit*. London: Oxford University Press, 1877.

Humphreys, Christian. *Buddhism*. Harmondsworth: Penguin Books, 1951.

Ibn Hisham, 'Abd Al-Malik. *The Life of Muhammad: A Translation of Ishaq's Sirat Rasul Allah*. Translated and with introductory notes by A. Guillaume. London: Oxford University Press, 1955.

Johnston, William. *Christian Zen*. New York: Harper and Row, 1971.

———. *Silent Music: The Science of Meditation*. New York: Harper and Row, 1974.

Kaltenmark, Max. *Lao Tzu and Taoism*. Stanford: Stanford University Press, 1969.

Kalupahana, David J. *Buddhist Philosophy: A Historical Analysis*. Honolulu: The University Press of Hawaii, 1976.

Katz, Nathan. *Buddhist Images of Human Perfection*. Delhi: Motilal Barnarsidass, 1982.

King, Sallie B. "Thich Nhat Hanh and the Unified Buddhist Church." In *Engaged Buddhism: Buddhist Liberation Movements in Asia,* edited by Christopher S. Queen and Sallie B King, 321–63. Albany, N.Y.: SUNY, 1996.

King, Winston. *Theravada Meditation: The Buddhist Transformation of Yoga*. University Park, Penn.: Pennsylvania State University, 1980.

Klostermaier, Klaus K. *A Survey of Hinduism*. Albany, N.Y.: SUNY, 1989.

Koyama, Kosuke. *Mount Fuji and Mount Sinai: A Critique of Idols*. Maryknoll: Orbis Books, 1984.

Langmuir, Gavin I. "The Faith of Christians and Hostility to Jews," In *Christianity and Judaism*, edited by Diana Wood, 77–92. Oxford: Blackwell Publishers, 1992.

Lefebure, Leo D. *The Buddha and the Christ: Explorations in Buddhist and Christian Dialogue*. Maryknoll: Orbis, 1993.

Liebeschütz, H. "The Crusading Movement in Its Bearing on the Christian Attitude towards Jewry." In *Essential Papers on Judaism and Christianity in Conflict: From Late Antiquity to the Reformation*, ed. Jeremy Cohen, 260–275. New York: New York University Press, 1991.

Lindbeck, George A. *The Nature of Doctrine: Religion and Theology in a Postliberal Age*. Philadelphia: Westminster, 1984.

Little, Lester K. "The Jews in Christian Europe." In *Essential Papers on Judaism and Christianity in Conflict: From Late Antiquity to the Reformation*, edited by Jeremy Cohen, 276–97. New York: New York University Press, 1991.

Luther, Martin. "On the Jews and Their Lies, 1543." In *Luther's Works*, 137–306. Philadelphia: Muhlenberg Press, 1962.

———. "That Jesus Christ Was Born a Jew, 1523." In *Luther's Works*, 199–229. Philadelphia: Muhlenberg Press, 1962.

———. "The Freedom of a Christian" (1520). In *Luther's Works*, 333–77. Philadelphia: Muhlenberg Press, 1962.

———. *The Small Catechism*. In *The Book of Concord*, translated and edited by Theodore G. Tappert. Philadelphia: Muhlenberg Press, 1959.

Marcus, Ivan G. "Judaism in Northern and Eastern Europe to 1500." In *The Encyclopedia of Religion*, edited by Mircea Eliade, 180–86. New York: Macmillan Publishing Co., 1987.

Marcus, Jacob R. *The Colonial American Jew 1492–1776*. Detroit, Mich.: Wayne State University Press, 1970.

Martinson, Paul Varo. *A Theology of World Religions: Interpreting God, Self, and World in Semitic, Indian, and Chinese Thought*. Minneapolis: Augsburg Publishing House, 1987.

———. "Imaging the Human through Culture, Religions, Christ." *Word and World* 10, no. 4 (1990): 330–38.

———. "World Religions: The Problem of Imaging Christ." In *Imaging Christ: Politics, Art, Spirituality*, edited by Francis A.O.S.A Eigo, 105–48. Villanova, Penn.: Theology Institute Publications, 1991.

Martinson, Paul Varo, and Ida M. Martinson. "The Religious Response of the Chinese Family to Childhood Cancer." *American Asian Review* 6 (3) (Fall 1988): 59–92.

Marty, Martin. Foreword to *Telling Tales: Making Sense of Christian and Judaic Nonsense* by Jacob Neusner. Louisville, Ky.: Westminster/John Knox Press, 1993.

Meeks, Wayne A. and Robert L. Wilken. *Jews and Christians in Antioch in the First Four Centuries of the Common Era*. Missoula, Mont.: Scholars Press, 1978.

Miller, Roland E. *Muslim Friends: Their Faith and Feeling. An Introduction to Islam*. St. Louis, Mo.: Concordia Publishing House, 1995.

Moore, R. I. "Anti-Semitism and the Birth of Europe." In *Christianity and Judaism*, edited by Diana Wood, 33–57. Oxford: Blackwell Publishers, 1992.

Morgan, E. *Tao the Great Luminant: Essays from "Huai Nan Tzu," with Introductory Articles, Notes and Analyses*. Shanghai: Kelly and Walsh [1933?].

Mou Tsung-san. *Zhongguo Zhexue di tezhi* (The uniqueness of Chinese philosophy). Taipei: Taiwan hsueh-sheng shu-chu, 1963.

Needham, Joseph. *Science and Civilization in China*, vol. 2, *History of Scientific Thought*. Cambridge: At the University Press, 1962.

Neusner, Jacob. *A Short History of Judaism: Three Meals, Three Epochs*. Minneapolis: Fortress Press, 1992.

———. *An Introduction to Judaism: A Textbook and Reader*. Louisville, Ky.: Westminster/John Knox Press, 1991.

———. *The Way of Torah: An Introduction to Judaism*. Belmont, Calif.: Dickenson, 1970.

Neusner, Jacob, and Bruce D. Chilton. *Revelation: The Torah and the Bible*. Valley Forge, Pa.: Trinity Press International, 1995.

Nielsen, Niels C., Jr., et al. *Religions of the World*. New York: St. Martin's Press, 1988.

Nyanaponika. *The Heart of Buddhist Meditation*. London: Rider and Co., 1969.

Ochs, Peter. "Judaism and Christian Theology." I n *The Modern Theologians: An Introduction to Christian Theology in the Twentieth Century*, edited by David F. Ford, 607–25. Cambridge: Blackwell, 1997.

Overmyer, Daniel L. *Religions of China: The World as a Living System*. San Francisco: Harper and Row, 1986.

Parkes, James. *A History of the Jewish People*. Baltimore, Md.: Penguin Books, 1964.

Pawlikowski, John. *Christ in the Light of the Christian-Jewish Dialogue*. New York: Paulist Press, 1982.

Philippi, Donald L. *Kojiki*. Tokyo: University of Tokyo Press, 1968.

———. *Jesus and the Theology of Israel*. Wilmington, Del.: Michael Glazier, 1989.

Plaut, Gunter. *The Rise of Reform Judaism*. New York: Wrld Union for Progressive Judaism, 1963.

Queen, Christopher S. and Sallie B King. *Engaged Buddhism: Buddhist Liberation Movements in Asia*. Albany, N.Y.: SUNY, 1996.

Rahman, Fazlur. *Major Themes of the Qur'an*. Minneapolis: Bibliotheca Islamica, 1980.

Roth, Cecil. *Encyclopaedia Judaica*. 16 vols. Jerusalem: Keter Publishing House, 1971, 1972.

———. "The Medieval Conception of the Jew: A New Interpretation." In *Essential Papers on Judaism and Christianity in Conflict: From Late Antiquity to the Reformation*, edited by Jeremy Cohen, 298–309. New York: New York University Press, 1991.

Sachar, Abram Leon. *A History of the Jews*. New York: Alfred A. Knopf, 1982.

Sacher, Howard M. *A History of the Jews in America*. New York: Alfred A. Knopf, 1992.

Sigal, Phillip. *Judaism: The Evolution of a Faith*. Grand Rapids, Mich.: William B. Eerdmans, 1988.

Simon, Marcel. "Christian Anti-Semitism." In *Essential Papers on Judaism and Christianity in Conflict: From Late Antiquity to the Reformation*, edited by Jeremy Cohen, 131–173. New York: New York University Press, 1991.

Sorin, Gerald. *Tradition Transformed: The Jewish Experience in America*. Baltimore, Md.: John Hopkins University Press, 1997.

Tannisho. Ryukoku Translation Series, vol. 2, translated and annotated by R. Fujiwara, 22–23. Kyoto: Tsuohiyama Printing Company, 1962.

Tappert, Theodore G. *The Book of Concord*. Philadelphia: Muhlenberg Press, 1959.

Thich Nhat Hanh. *Peace Is Every Step: The Path of Mindfulness in Everyday Life*. Edited by Arnold Kotler. New York: Bantam Books, 1991.

Trepp, Leo. *Judaism: Development and Life*. 2d ed. Belmont, Calif.: Wadsworth Publishing Co., 1982.

Watson, Burton. *The Complete Works of Chuang-tzu*. New York: Columbia University Press, 1968.

Whitfield, Stephen J. *American Space, Jewish Time: Essays in Modern Culture and Politics*. Armonk, N.Y: North Castle Books, 1996.

Zaehner, R. C. *The Bhagavadgita: With a Commentary Based on the Original Sources*. Oxford: Clarendon Press, 1969.